MODERN WORLD
HiSTORY to

James Mason

Oxford University Press

Oxford University Press, Great Clarendon Street, Oxford OX2 6DP

Oxford New York
Athens Auckland Bangkok Bogota Bombay
Buenos Aires Calcutta Cape Town Dar es Salaam Delhi
Florence Hong Kong Istanbul Karachi
Kuala Lumpur Madras Madrid Melbourne
Mexico City Nairobi Paris Singapore
Taipei Tokyo Toronto Warsaw

and associated companies in
Berlin Ibadan

Oxford is a trademark of Oxford University Press

First published 1997

ISBN   0 19 917166 1 School edition
          0 19 917169 6 Bookshop edition

Printed in Spain

Acknowledgements

*The publishers would like to thank the following for permission to
reproduce photographs:*

Corbis/Bettmann: pps 17, 136; Corbis/Bettmann/UPI: pps 61, 88;
Corbis/Hulton Getty Picture Library: p 158; Mary Evans Picture Library:
pps 14/15; Mary Evans Picture Library/Fougasse: p 53; John
Frost/Historical Newspapers Loan Service: p 77; Hulton Getty Picture
Library: pps 39, 116; David King Collection: p 59 (right), 110; Peter
Newark's Pictures: p 128; Rex Features/Images: p 59 (left); Bilderdienst
Suddeuscher Verlag: pps 156, 160.

The illustrations are by: Stefan Chabluk, Jeff Edwards

Cover photograph: courtesy of Topham Picturepoint

Introduction

If you are working towards a GCSE exam in Modern World History, then this book is for you. It has been designed to provide you with all the historical knowledge you need for whichever syllabus you are following. It covers the core content required by all the different Examination Boards as well as three depth studies: The USSR, The USA, and Germany.

In the exam, some questions will ask you to

- give factual information
- explain historical terms or concepts
- describe events
- explain people's motives
- describe and explain causes, consequences, and changes

This book will help you to do all these things. It will also help you to answer questions involving sources. In your exam you will be asked to use your knowledge of a topic to help you to use, understand, interpret, or evaluate sources. This book provides you with that essential knowledge.

Modern World History to GCSE is arranged in four sections: first the core content, then the three depth studies. To help you find you way around, each section is colour-coded. Within each section topics are covered on clear, easy-to-use double-page spreads. Just occasionally you will come across a three-page spread.

Contents Use this to find the topics you want to study or revise.

Aims You will find these at the start of each spread. They tell you what you should be able to do once you have studied it.

Questions These help you to make sure you understand and can remember what you have studied on each spread.

Index Use this if there is a particular person, event, topic, or historical term which you need to look up.

Note to teachers

This book offers a fresh approach to preparation for Modern World History GCSE. It takes up the challenge of the increased emphasis on knowledge and understanding, and provides students with a comprehensive summary of key information and concepts. Its compact, visually attractive spreads make it ideal for use in the classroom

- to introduce topics
- for homework assignments
- to provide summaries
- for exam revision

Contents

Depth Study: Russia and the USSR 1900-1964

Depth study: USA 1919-1980

Depth study: Germany 1918-1945

The Road to War: Europe 1900-1914

By the end of this spread you should be able to explain why:
1 tension increased in Europe, 1900-1914
2 war broke out in 1914

Fig. 1 Tensions in Europe

Britain
1 was angered by German support of Boers during the Boer War (1899-1902)
2 feared German rivalry in
a industry and trade
b naval power
c empire
3 abandoned its policy of 'splendid isolation' and began to build 'ententes' (friendly agreements).

Germany
1 was a new nation (since 1871) anxious about its security
2 felt particularly threatened by France and Russia
3 wanted colonies as Kaiser Wilhelm II was jealous of Britain's empire
4 was building the Berlin-Baghdad Railway through the Balkans.

Russia
1 needed an outlet to the sea and therefore wanted a weak or friendly power in control of the Dardanelles
2 opposed Austrian or German influence in the Balkans
3 saw the Berlin-Baghdad Railway as a threat to its position in the Balkans
4 wished to protect other Slav peoples:
a hostile to Germany which ruled Polish Slavs
b supported Serbs and Bulgars.

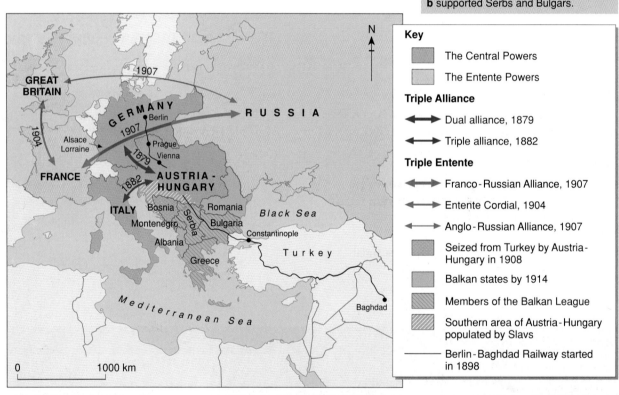

Key
- The Central Powers
- The Entente Powers

Triple Alliance
- ◄──► Dual alliance, 1879
- ◄──► Triple alliance, 1882

Triple Entente
- ◄──► Franco-Russian Alliance, 1907
- ◄──► Entente Cordial, 1904
- ◄──► Anglo-Russian Alliance, 1907
- Seized from Turkey by Austria-Hungary in 1908
- Balkan states by 1914
- Members of the Balkan League
- Southern area of Austria-Hungary populated by Slavs
- Berlin-Baghdad Railway started in 1898

France
1 was angered by the loss of Alsace-Lorraine to Germany after Franco-Prussian War (1870)
2 feared further German aggression
3 wanted to protect its empire, especially in North Africa.

Austria-Hungary
1 was an empire of many nationalities
2 was worried by national groups which might want to rule themselves, especially Slav peoples in the south who looked to Serbia for leadership.

Serbia
1 was a new nation formed in 1878 after breaking away from the Turkish Empire
2 nationalists planned to create Yugoslavia (Southern Slavia) by bringing into Serbia all Slavs living in the south of Austria-Hungary.

Tensions Increase

The alliance system and war plans

1 To protect their interests the European powers form a network of alliances (fig. 1). This reflects the tension rather than causes it.

2 All countries to draw up war plans.

Results:

• By 1914 a war between any two powers is likely to lead to the involvement of the rest.

• Germany's Schlieffen Plan (page 8) commits it to attack France.

The arms race

1 a Germany plans to double the size of its navy.

b To meet this threat to its naval supremacy, Britain builds superior Dreadnought-class battleships.

c Germany responds with its own version.

2 1900-1914, the main European powers more than double expenditure on their armies.

Results:

• increase in Anglo-German mistrust

• Europe divided into two armed camps

Bosnia, 1908-1909

Austria takes over Bosnia from Turkey.

Results:

• Austria earns hatred of Bosnian Serbs

• Serbia claims Bosnia for itself

• In attempt to weaken Austrian influence, Russia encourages formation of the Balkan League (fig. 1)

The Balkan Wars, 1912-1913

1 Balkan League drives Turkey out of the Balkans.

2 Members of League quarrel and fight.

Results:

• Serbia gains extra territory

• Bosnian desire to join Serbia grows

• Austrian fear of Serbia increases

Countdown to war

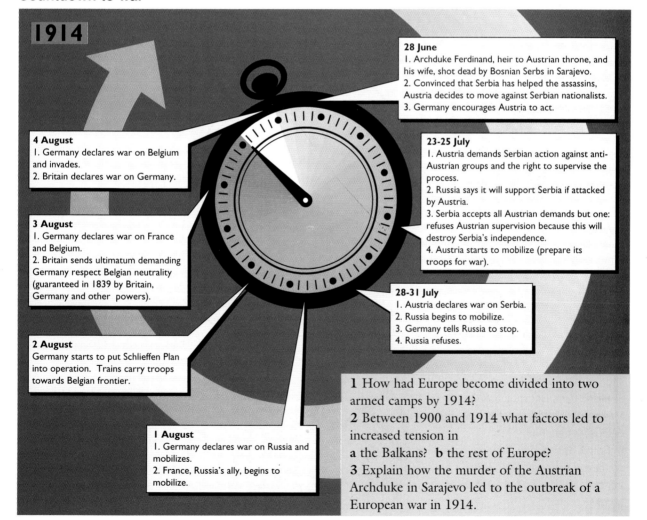

1914

28 June
1. Archduke Ferdinand, heir to Austrian throne, and his wife, shot dead by Bosnian Serbs in Sarajevo.
2. Convinced that Serbia has helped the assassins, Austria decides to move against Serbian nationalists.
3. Germany encourages Austria to act.

4 August
1. Germany declares war on Belgium and invades.
2. Britain declares war on Germany.

23-25 July
1. Austria demands Serbian action against anti-Austrian groups and the right to supervise the process.
2. Russia says it will support Serbia if attacked by Austria.
3. Serbia accepts all Austrian demands but one: refuses Austrian supervision because this will destroy Serbia's independence.
4. Austria starts to mobilize (prepare its troops for war).

3 August
1. Germany declares war on France and Belgium.
2. Britain sends ultimatum demanding Germany respect Belgian neutrality (guaranteed in 1839 by Britain, Germany and other powers).

28-31 July
1. Austria declares war on Serbia.
2. Russia begins to mobilize.
3. Germany tells Russia to stop.
4. Russia refuses.

2 August
Germany starts to put Schlieffen Plan into operation. Trains carry troops towards Belgian frontier.

1 August
1. Germany declares war on Russia and mobilizes.
2. France, Russia's ally, begins to mobilize.

1 How had Europe become divided into two armed camps by 1914?

2 Between 1900 and 1914 what factors led to increased tension in

a the Balkans? **b** the rest of Europe?

3 Explain how the murder of the Austrian Archduke in Sarajevo led to the outbreak of a European war in 1914.

The First World War 1: stalemate and trench warfare

By the end of this spread you should be able to:
1 explain how the war on the Western Front became deadlocked by 1915
2 describe a the nature and effects of trench warfare
b the impact of new weapons

The Schlieffen Plan

1 German war plan devised by General von Schlieffen in 1905.

2 Assumed

a war would be on two fronts against Russia and France

b Russia would be slow to mobilize its troops.

3 Based on use of railways to move troops.

4 Consisted of

a swift knock-out blow to France in the west through neutral Holland, Belgium and Luxembourg. Capture of Paris. Encirclement of French armies attacking Alsace-Lorraine.

b with France defeated in six weeks, transfer of German troops east to fight Russia.

The failure of the Schlieffen Plan

1 Plan fails to anticipate that Britain might enter the war to defend Belgium. The British Expeditionary Force (BEF) lands in France (**a**) and, taking huge casualties, holds up the German advance at Mons (**b**).

2 German forces in Belgium weakened when some withdrawn to fight the Russians, who had mobilized far more quickly than the Germans expected.

3 French plan to invade Alsace-Lorraine (**c**) fails. Armies then sent to deal with German invasion.

4 Germans, delayed by resistance (see **1**) and weakened by withdrawals (see **2**) make mistake of changing their plan. First Army diverted and sent on shorter route east of Paris instead of west (**d**).

5 French and British check Germans at the River Marne (**e**). Germans retreat 60 kms and then dig defensive trenches

6 Both sides race to Channel coast in attempt to outflank each other. Both fail and dig defensive trenches. By the end of 1914 these stretch to Swiss border.

Deadlock on the Western Front

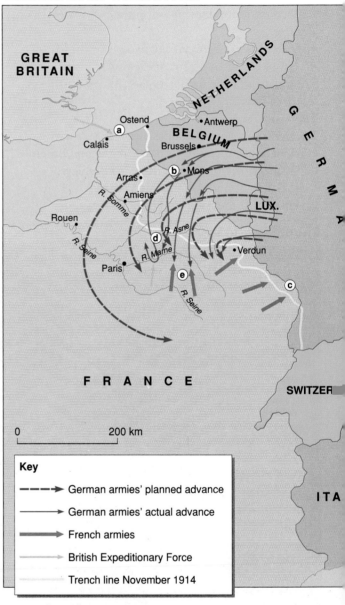

Key

- - - → German armies' planned advance
——→ German armies' actual advance
——▶ French armies
——→ British Expeditionary Force
—— Trench line November 1914

1 a What was the Schlieffen Plan?
b Why did it fail?
2 What were the features of trench warfare which made it so difficult for either side to achieve a break-through on the Western Front?
3 What was the impact of each of the new weapons used on the Western Front?

Trench Warfare

A front line of trenches was backed up by two more, the support and reserve lines. All three were linked by communications trenches. 'No-man's land' lay between the Allied and German front lines.

The front line trench

1 At least two metres deep and two wide. Dug in a zig-zag to reduce blast damage if shell exploded inside.

2 Sandbags at front and rear. Underground dug-outs at rear. Firestep at front so that soldiers could shoot over the parapet.

3 Often full of deep mud. Infested by rats.

The soldiers

1 Slept in their uniforms. Ate mainly tinned rations.

2 Many suffered from
a 'trench foot', a swelling caused by damp
b lice, caused by inability to wash or change clothes
c 'shell-shock', caused by noise of exploding shells.

Attack and defence

1 An attack began with a heavy artillery bombardment to kill and frighten the enemy and destroy barbed wire (but often simply entangled it more thoroughly).
2 The defenders sheltered from the bombardment in dug-outs or support trenches.
3 The attackers then left their trenches and moved towards the enemy lines across 'no-man's' land.
4 The defenders took up positions when the bombardment ended. Used machine-guns and rifle fire against attackers.

New weapons

While changing the face of warfare, these failed to create a breakthrough on the Western Front for either side.

Heavy artillery
1 New howitzers had a range of 13 kms. The war became, above all, an artillery war. The British alone fired 170 million shells during the war.
2 Shells killed and maimed, caused 'shell-shock', and destroyed the landscape, leaving vast craters.

Machine guns
1 Fired up to 600 rounds per minute.
2 Able to cut down lines of attackers. Caused huge casualties. Reduced the chances of success of a direct attack on the enemy trenches. 60,000 British troops killed on the first day of the Battle of the Somme, 1916.

Tanks
1 A British invention first used in 1916.
2 Slow-moving and, though able to cross trenches, hedges etc, often became bogged-down.
3 Most effectively used at Cambrai, 1917.

Poison Gas
1 Used by both sides after first use by the Germans at the Second Battle of Ypres, 1915.
2 Caused horrific injuries. Its effects could be avoided by wearing gas-masks, which were rapidly improved.

Aeroplanes
1 Single engined unarmed planes first used as 'spotters' to observe enemy movement. Later, planes were developed with the ability to fire machine-guns through the propeller. Also two and four engined bombers were developed.
2 The aircraft industry was boosted but planes did not play a major role in the war.

The First World War 2: from stalemate to Allied victory

By the end of this spread you should be able to explain:
1 the failure of Allied and German attempts to break the stalemate on the Western Front, 1915-1917
2 the reasons for Germany's eventual defeat

Failing to break the stalemate, 1915-1917

Gallipoli
When Turkey entered the war it closed the Dardanelles, cutting off a vital Allied supply route to Russia. Russia was short of supplies and under attack from the Central Powers. The Allied attack on Gallipoli aimed to:
1 defeat Turkey by the capture of its capital, Constantinople
2 reopen the supply route to Russia
3 lay the ground for an attack on Austria from the east, thus breaking the deadlock on the Western Front. After the failure of the Allied naval attack on the Dardenelles, British, Australian and New Zealand troops attempted an invasion of the peninsula. Poor planning led to heavy casualties and eventual withdrawal.

The Western Front
Generals on the Western Front, including the British commander, Sir Douglas Haig, believed they could break the deadlock by weight of numbers. But the trench system and the use of machine guns in defence proved them wrong. All Allied and German offensives led to heavy slaughter for little gain. At the Battle of the Somme, 1916, the British and French lost 620,000 men, the Germans, 450,000. The Allies advanced 15 kms at the furthest point.

The Battle of Jutland
Both British and German admirals were cautious, as defeat in a major sea battle would hand control of trade routes to the enemy and probably decide the outcome of the war. In 1916, however, the British Grand Fleet and German High Seas Fleet met at Jutland off the coast of Denmark. The British lost more ships and men; but the Germans returned to

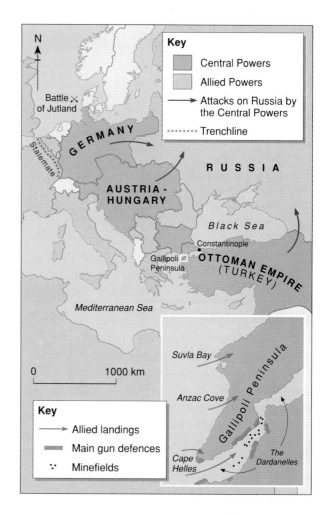

port and remained there for the rest of the war, unwilling to risk another battle.

Submarine warfare
After Jutland the German admirals relied on their U-boat (Unterseeboten) campaign, begun in 1915, to try to starve Britain into surrender by the sinking of merchant ships carrying food and supplies from the USA. This forced Britain to introduce rationing to combat severe food shortages (page 12). Britain survived because of the introduction, in mid-1917, of a convoy system, whereby merchant ships sailed in groups protected by the Royal Navy. As a result, shipping losses were greatly reduced. In 1917 German attacks on American ships brought the USA into the war.

The defeat of Germany

The USA

1 The USA supported the Allies with loans, weapons, and food supplies. U-boat attacks on American ships trading with the Allies, and the loss of 128 American lives on the British passenger liner *Lusitania* (1915), angered the Americans.
2 The resumption of German naval attacks after over a year's pause, caused the USA to declare war (April 1917).
3 Germany now faced the world's richest nation. She had to win before US troops reached Europe.

Collapse of Germany's allies

The allied defeat of Bulgaria (Sept 1918), Turkey (Oct) and Austria (Nov), left Germany without support.

Failure of Ludendorff offensive

1 The defeat of Russia (March 1918) allowed the Germans to transfer one million soldiers to the Western Front. The Germans now outnumbered the Allies but had only 6 months to win before American troops arrived.
2 General Ludendorff decided on a final all-out offensive. Rapid German advance (March).
3 The allied appointment of French General Foch as overall commander improved their ability to co-ordinate their armies. The Germans were stopped with American help (June).
4 Allied counter-attack drove Germans into retreat (July-Nov).

Failure of the U-boat campaign

1 A successful U-boat campaign against Britain might have tipped the balance of the war in Germany's favour. In 1917 Britain had only six weeks food supply.
2 The convoy system saved Britain.
3 The German attempt to step up the U-boat campaign back-fired, bringing the USA into the war.

British blockade of Germany

The successful British naval blockade of German ports caused serious food shortages in Germany. It weakened the German people's will to fight on and caused anger against the Kaiser.

Reasons for Germany's defeat

Attitude of Germany's leaders

The Germans had earlier rejected President Wilson's Fourteen Points (page 16) as a basis for peace. Although the Allied conditions for a cease-fire were now much harsher, the German generals recommended agreement to avoid
1 humiliation of their troops
2 blame for a defeat on German soil. The German Government wanted to avoid
1 further civilian suffering
2 the possibility of a Bolshevik revolution (page 110) in Germany.

Revolution in Germany

Anger with the Kaiser's government for its failure to deliver victories and food led to a mutiny by sailors in Germany's High Seas Fleet and the take-over of city governments by Socialists (Oct 1918). Politicians in Berlin
1 forced Kaiser Wilhelm to resign
2 proclaimed Germany a Republic
3 agreed to discuss peace with the Allies

---

1 By 1915 events on the Western Front had led to the war being in stalemate. Why was neither side able to break the stalemate between 1915 and 1917?

2 a Make a time-line to show the main events, 1917-1918, leading to the defeat of Germany.
b Explain the significance of each event.
c Which event was the most important? Explain your reasons.

The Home Front in Britain, 1914-1918: 1

By the end of the next two spreads you should be able to describe how the war affected:
1 everyday life in Britain

2 the role of the Government
3 the role and status of women in society and politics
4 social change and reform.

People and the Government

Recruitment
1 a 1914-1915: campaigns by Lord Kitchener, Secretary of State for War, recruit 2.25 million volunteers by October 1915.
b 1916: *Military Service Acts* introduce compulsory military service for all men aged between 18 and 41 (51 in 1918).
2 Conscientious objectors, who refused to fight because they thought it was wrong to kill, had to argue their case before special courts.
3 Women volunteers were recruited into the uniformed services (page 13).

Propaganda
1 Newspapers were censored.
2 Letters home from soldiers were censored to give a 'cheerful' impression of life at the front.
3 Untrue stories about the Germans were circulated to make people hate them, e.g. that they used the bodies of dead British soldiers to make fats and oils.
4 Poster campaigns were used to persuade people to eat less, buy less, join up, do voluntary work etc.

Food and rationing
1 Submarine warfare caused severe shortages (page 10).
2 1917: queues for food. Prices rose. The Government gave money to help keep down the prices of basic foods, e.g. bread and potatoes.
3 1918: food rationing, e.g. sugar, meat, margarine and butter, jam, and tea (coal for home use was already rationed).

The Government
The war demanded troops, weapons, ammunition and equipment on a scale never before experienced. To cope, the Government had to become more deeply involved in people's lives. In 1914 the *Defence of the Realm Act* (DORA) gave it, new, wide-ranging emergency powers.

Welfare
The Government became more involved in people's welfare (pages 14-15).

Work and industry
The Government
1 took over the running of food and munitions production, coal mines, railways, merchant shipping. Set up new ministries, headed by businessmen.
2 involved trade union leaders in making decisions about wages and working conditions in return for 'no strike' deals (all but the miners agreed).
3 encouraged women to take over the jobs of men leaving for the forces (page 13).
4 introduced British Summer Time to give more daylight during working hours.

Protecting civilians
1 Submarine warfare. See page 10 and 'Food and rationing'.
2 Bombing raids.
a First ever air-raids on Britain (first by Zeppelins, then by Gotha bomber aircraft) killed about 1400 people and injured about 3300. Caused widespread panic.
b Main defences were anti-aircraft guns and searchlights.

The rôle and status of women

	Before the War	During the War	After the War
Work	About 29% of women worked. Mainly in domestic service and textiles.	1 Despite union opposition, the Government encouraged women to take over jobs of conscripted men. 2 Women worked in many areas previously closed to them: munitions and aircraft factories, brickworks, steelworks, shipyards, Government departments. 3 Many volunteered for the uniformed services, e.g. Voluntary Aid Detachments (nurses), Women's Land Army (farmworkers), and the women's sections of the forces.	1 Women were expected to give way to men returning from the forces and to return to pre-war 'women's work'. 2 The assumption that 'a woman's place is in the home' returned. 3 The percentage of women at work returned to pre-war levels. 4 More women than before worked in offices.
Dress and behaviour	Women were expected 1 to run the home 2 to wear ankle-length skirts or dresses 3 not to go out alone 4 not to drink or smoke.	1 Clothes became more practical: shorter, looser, skirts; trousers for work. Hair worn shorter. 2 Behaviour became freer. Women began to go out alone, drink in pubs and smoke.	1 Shorter skirts and hair became fashionable. 2 Women went out with men without a chaperone. 3 Women smoked and wore make-up in public for the first time.
Political and social rights	Women not allowed 1 to vote in parliamentary elections 2 to work as lawyers or in the civil service.	1918: vote given to women over 30 who were householders or married to householders (out of 13 million women only six million qualified). Women allowed to stand for Parliament (but only eight women MPs by 1923).	1 1919: being female or married was no longer allowed to disqualify someone from holding a job in the professions or civil service. 2 1923: women given the same right as men to seek divorce on the grounds of adultery. 3 1923 and 1925: *Property Acts* allow married women to hold and dispose of property on the same terms as their husbands. 4 1925: widows and dependant children entitled to pension benefits. 5 1928: all women over 21 allowed to vote.

The Home Front in Britain, 1914-1918: 2

Social Change and reform

During the war	After the war
The number of 14 year olds or under at work increased fourfold. The *1918 Education Act*: **1** stressed the importance of educating the workforce **2** raised the school-leaving age to 14, and provided free full-time education for 5-14 year olds in elementary schools **3** increased the number of free places available in secondary schools (which were all fee-paying) for 11 year olds who passed an exam.	**1** A plan to provide part-time education for 14-18 year olds who had left school was abandoned because of lack of money. **2** Very few free secondary school places were taken up.

Attitudes

1 Conscription, the contribution of women, and the introduction of rationing for all began to break down social barriers.
2 People felt that working class families had made great sacrifices for their country and deserved to live in better conditions after the war.
3 People became used to the Government's greater involvement in their lives (page 12).
They expected it to introduce reforms.
4 Lloyd George's government started to introduce reforms, but most were not taken very far because of lack of money. Many people felt bitter about this.

National Insurance

During the war	After the war	
Unemployment **1** 1916: workers in the munitions industry allowed to join the unemployment benefit scheme set up in 1911 (previously open only to about three million workers). **2** 1918: every former member of the armed forces was entitled to 50 weeks unemployment benefit even if they had not paid contributions.	**Unemployment** **1** 1920: unemployment benefit system extended to nearly all workers **2** 1921: end of 15 week limit to unemployment payments. Further payment 'the dole' given for 32 weeks. Additional payments given for wives and children of unemployed men. **Pensions** **1** Pensions given to servicemen disabled by their wounds. **2** 1919: old age pension increased	to 10 shillings (50p) a week. **3** 1925: old age pension fund set up to which the Government and individuals contributed. Pensions also provided for widows and orphans. **Health** 1911 National Insurance scheme continued. Gave a wage-earner free medical attention and sick pay. The rest of the family still had to pay to see a doctor.

FOOD FOR THE GUNS.

Health and Housing

During the war	*After the war*
1 Despite shortages, officials noted some women and children were better fed than before the war. Partly because more women were working and earning higher wages. **2** Doctors and nurses were provided to look after workers in vital and dangerous jobs, e.g. making munitions. **3** *Maternity and Child Welfare Act* (1918) provided child welfare and ante-natal clinics **4** Pre-war shortage of decent housing for working class families continued. New building ceased.	**1** Ministry of Health set up to supervise public health, health insurance and housing. **2** *Housing Act* (1919) an important step forward despite slow start: **a** Local Councils had to survey housing needs in their area and submit plans to meet them. **b** Money provided to help Councils and private builders build new houses. Also to help Councils keep rents down.

Work

During the war	*After the war*
1 New ministries set up. Created many new jobs in the civil service. **2** Military demands boosted new industries (eg. canned foods, motor vehicles, aircraft, chemicals) and created new jobs. **3** Old industries (coal, iron, shipbuilding, textiles) also boosted.	**1** Increasing number of Government departments provide new administrative and secretarial jobs. **2** New industries turned to producing for peacetime. The number of new jobs increased. **3** Old industries went into decline creating massive unemployment.

1 What changes did the First World War bring to the everyday lives of men and women?
2 a In what ways did the Government become more involved in people's lives between 1914 and 1918?
b How far did it stay involved after 1918?

3 What changes did the First World War bring about in **a** social welfare **b** job opportunities for men and women?
4 In what ways did the First World War change the role of women in society **a** temporarily **b** permanently?

The Paris Peace Conference

By the end of this spread you should be able to:
1 describe the aims and motives of each of the Big Three at the Paris Peace Conference, 1919-1920
2 explain what they agreed and disagreed on
3 give some reasons why all the peacemakers did not achieve all their aims

1917	Dec	Cease-fire between Russia and Germany
1918	Jan	President Wilson's 'Fourteen Points' speech
	Nov	Cease-fire between Allied and Central Powe
1919	Jan	Start of Paris Peace Conference
	June	Treaty of Versailles (with Germany)
	Sept	Treaty of St Germain (with Austria)
	Nov	Treaty of Neuilly (with Bulgaria)
1920	Jan	First meeting of the Council of the League of Nations
	June	Treaty of Trianon (with Hungary)
	Aug	Treaty of Sèvres (with Turkey)

The Conference

Purpose

For the Allied Powers
1 to decide on the peace terms they would offer the Central Powers.
2 to sign peace treaties with them.

Countries present

The twenty-seven victorious Allied Powers

Countries excluded

1 Russia. Because
a although it had fought with the Allies, it had surrendered to Germany in 1917 (page 112).
b many Allied leaders distrusted its new Bolshevik government (page 111).
2 The Central Powers. They were not consulted about the terms of the Treaty.

The Big Three

Georges Clemenceau, Prime Minister of France, President Woodrow Wilson of the USA and David Lloyd George, Prime Minister of Great Britain, dominated the Conference and made the main decisions. They also met in secret, as the Council of Four, with the Prime Minister of Italy.

Although the Big Three agreed that their task was to make sure that such a terrible war could never happen again, each had very different ideas about what should be done.

Clemenceau was nicknamed 'The Tiger' because of his determination that France should not be defeated in the war. He had the strong backing of the French people. He wanted the peace treaties to protect France in the future and to compensate the French for their suffering. Most of the fighting had been on French soil. It had
1 killed 1.4 million French soldiers and wounded nearly twice as many
2 devastated thousands of square kilometres of farm land
3 destroyed factories and homes.

Wilson was a high-minded man. In 1918 he had proposed Fourteen Points as a basis for future world peace. He hoped that the countries at the Peace Conference would agree to these points.

Fourteen Points The main points were:
1 Countries should stop making secret treaties with one another. The peace should be negotiated in the open. After that there should be no more secret diplomacy.
2 They should reduce their weapons and armed forces.
3 People living under the rule of foreign countries should be allowed to form their own nations and choose their own type of government. Wilson called this the principle of national self-determination.
4 Countries should belong to a new organization to be set up to protect the independence of all states.

Lloyd George was a clever politician and negotiator but, above all, he was not prepared to ignore British public opinion. Britain had suffered 750,000 killed and 1.5 million wounded. The British public, which had just re-elected his government, wanted to 'Hang The Kaiser' and 'Make Germany Pay'.

The aims of the Big Three

Lloyd George

1 end the German threat to the British navy and Empire
2 make Germany a non-aggressive country, without colonies
3 prevent Germany becoming so weak that a revival of European industry and trade is hindered
4 prevent Germans becoming so poor that they turn to Communism
5 avoid humiliation of Germans so that they have no reason to seek revenge
6 help secure France against Germany, but prevent France becoming too powerful
7 Create a balance of power so that no one European country can threaten the others

Clemenceau

1 have revenge on Germany for French suffering
2 make Germany pay for the cost of the damage
3 punish Germany for the humiliation she had inflicted on France after defeating her in 1871 (page 6)
4 ensure that Germany would never be able to attack France again: take away German land; weaken her industries; reduce her armed forces

Wilson

1 prevent Germany from becoming aggressive again
2 punish Germany for her aggression, but avoid forcing her to pay very heavy damages
3 base the peace treaties on his Fourteen Points

Why did the peacemakers have to compromise?

Pressure of time Although the peacemakers in Paris faced complicated problems, they had to work very quickly because:
1 the Austro-Hungarian Empire had started to break up before the war ended and the new states were already quarrelling about their frontiers.
2 the Armistice was only a truce, and the Allies were continuing their blockade of Germany (page 11) until a formal peace was signed. As a result, thousands of German civilians were dying of starvation.
3 the Allied leaders feared that if a settlement was not agreed quickly, the Germans, and other peoples, might follow the Russians' example and choose Communist governments.

Conflict of interests
1 All twenty-seven countries at the Conference made their own demands.
2 Even the Big Three disagreed on many points.
3 The peacemakers had to do too much work in too short a time.
4 To achieve a settlement quickly, everyone had to compromise.

> 1 Look at the aims of the Big Three at the start of the Peace Conference in 1919. On which issues did they **a** agree **b** disagree.
> 2 **a** Why was Clemenceau so determined to be harsh on Germany?
> **b** The French believed they had suffered more than Britain or the USA in fighting Germany. Suggest two reasons for this.
> 3 Give two reasons why no country could achieve all its aims at the Conference.

The Paris Peace Settlement

By the end of this spread you should be able to:
*1 describe the main terms of the peace treaties, 1919-1920, as they affected **a** Germany **b** the other Central Powers*

2 explain how far the terms of the treaties satisfied each of the Big Three

Germany

The Treaty of Versailles (1919) began with the 'Covenant of the League of Nations'. This set up the new international organization proposed by Wilson and described how it was to work (see pages 24-25). The rest of the Treaty dealt with Germany.

It:

- said her troops had to keep out of the Rhineland

- made her give away land to other countries

- divided her into two

- put the Saar under the control of the League of Nations for 15 years (then its people would vote on whether to join France or Germany)

- forbade her to unite with Austria

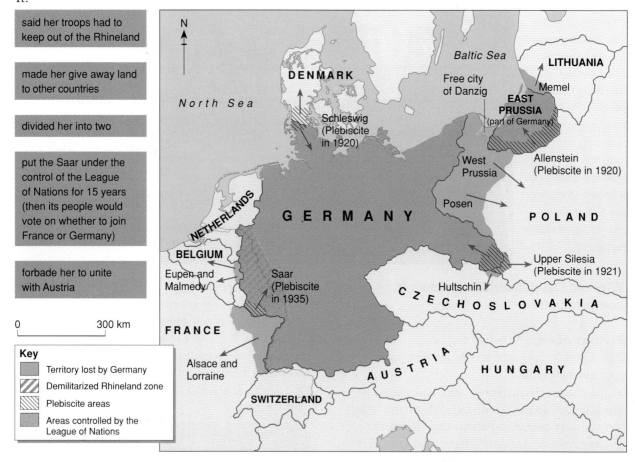

Key
- Territory lost by Germany
- Demilitarized Rhineland zone
- Plebiscite areas
- Areas controlled by the League of Nations

0 — 300 km

Colonies
German colonies given to other countries to govern as mandates on behalf of the League of Nations (page 24).

Military
German armed forces reduced: the army allowed 100,000 men. No tanks. The navy allowed six battleships. No submarines. No airforce allowed.

Financial
Clause 231, the so-called 'war guilt' clause, said that Germany and her allies were responsible for starting the war, and for causing all the damage suffered by the Allies. Germany had to pay reparations, or compensation, for the damage.

Central and Eastern Europe

Like the Treaty of Versailles all the other treaties signed as part of the Paris Peace Settlement began with the 'Covenant of the League of Nations'.

The Treaties of St Germain (1919) and Trianon (1920)
Austria-Hungary had begun to break up before the end of the war. These treaties:
1 recognized Austria and Hungary as separate and independent states
2 ordered them give up land, reduce their armed forces and pay reparations (though in the end they did not have to do so)
3 forbade Austria to unite with Germany
4 created new states: e.g. Poland, Czechoslovakia, Yugoslavia.

The Treaty of Neuilly (1919) made Bulgaria agree to:
1 give land to Yugoslavia and Greece
2 reduce her armed forces
3 pay reparations (though in the end she, too, did not have to do so).

Key
- former Austro-Hungarian Empire
- German land to Poland
- Russian losses
- Bulgarian losses

Russia
The peace settlement
1 gave back most, but not all, of the land conquered by Germany
2 made her Baltic provinces into independent states
3 made her give land to Poland and Romania.

Turkey

Allied motives in 1919 Several countries were interested in Turkey and her empire:
1 Britain wanted to control trade routes to India and protect her oil interests.
2 France and Italy wanted to extend their influence in the Middle East.
3 Many Greeks lived in Turkey. Greece wanted to rebuild its ancient empire there.

The Treaty of Sèvres, 1920
1 took away most of Turkey's land in Europe.
2 broke up her Empire giving much of it to France and Britain to govern as mandates on behalf of the League of Nations.
3 put the Turkish Straits under League of Nations control.
4 ordered British, French, Greek, and Italian forces to occupy Turkey itself.

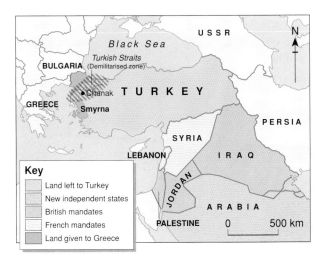

Key
- Land left to Turkey
- New independent states
- British mandates
- French mandates
- Land given to Greece

1 Make a chart on the Paris Peace Settlement to show
a countries that lost land and to whom
b countries that gained land and from whom
c new states created.
3 Use the information on pages 16-19.
a List Wilson's aims in 1919. For each aim write what the Settlement actually said.
b Repeat this for Clemenceau and Lloyd George
c How far did each of the Big Three have to compromise?

The impact of the Paris Peace Settlement 1: Germany

By the end of this spread you should be able to
1 describe the problems that arose as a result of the Treaty of Versailles

2 describe some of the opinions held about the Treaty at the time
3 explain who you think was right

Allied doubts

Even in 1919 some of the peacemakers had doubts about the way the Treaty of Versailles treated Germany. Their concerns were that:
1 the clauses about 'war guilt' and reparations had humiliated the Germans who might seek revenge.
2 Germany had been made to give up too much territory and would try to get it back in the future.

German Anger

In the 1920s the Germans called the Treaty of Versailles the 'Diktat', the 'dictated peace'.

They resented:
1 the loss of so much territory, especially the splitting of East Prussia from the rest of Germany.
2 the loss of resources. The Treaty took away 74% of their iron ore production and 26% of their coal.
3 foreign occupation of the Rhineland and Saar.
4 having to accept 'war guilt' and pay reparations. They argued that Germany alone was not responsible for the war.
5 the fact that while other peoples were given the right of self determination, Austrians and Germans were forbidden to unite.
6 the fact that Germany was the only country required to reduce its weapons and armed forces.

Reparations. Should the Allies make Germany pay?

Arguments for

Most, especially the Belgians and French:
1 wanted to keep Germany weak so that she would no longer be a danger to them.
2 pointed to the huge cost of the war to the Allies, much of it owed to the USA which insisted on repayment. They said it was right for Germany to contribute.

Arguments against

Some, like the British economist John Maynard Keynes, disagreed with reparations altogether. Others thought the payments were too high because:
1 many Germans would be forced to lead poor and miserable lives. Many would die. This was inhumane.
2 misery would fuel the Germans' desire for revenge and might drive them into the arms of the Communists.
3 the rest of Europe would suffer because of Germany's economic weakness.

Reparations: crises and modifications, 1921-1932

1921 The Germans are horrified when the Allies announce the amount they have to pay in reparations: £6,600 million, in 42 annual instalments.

1922 Germany pays a small amount, then asks for a two-year delay before the next instalment. The Allies refuse.

The invasion of the Ruhr, 1923

1 Germany fails to pay reparations.

7 The new Chancellor, Stresemann (page 157),
a calls off the Ruhr campaign
b says Germany will resume reparations payments
c introduces a new currency, the rentenmark, and has the worthless old notes burned.

6 Extra paper money causes serious inflation (prices going up and so causing the value of money to go down). In 1919 a loaf of bread had cost 0.63 marks; by November 1923 it cost 201,000 million. People's wages, savings, and pensions become worthless.

2 France and Belgium send troops into the Ruhr Valley, to seize coal, iron, and steel as payment in kind.

3 A furious German Government tells workers not to take orders from French and Belgian troops and refuses to pay further reparations.

4 In the Ruhr, German workers, either on strike or sacked by the French, need money to live.

5 The Government has no money so prints additional banknotes to give to the workers.

The Dawes Plan, 1924

1 *Background*
a Stresemann had proved he wanted to solve Germany's economic problems.
b The new French Prime Minister, Briand, was more sympathetic than his predecessor, Poincaré.
c Britain and the USA wanted to help Germany.
2 *Aims*
To ensure that
a reparations were paid to France in particular.
b payments were not so heavy that they held up Germany's economic recovery.
3 *Decisions*
a Germany to pay the proportion of its actual industrial output that it can afford.
b France to withdraw her troops from the Ruhr within twelve months.
c the USA to lend Germany money to rebuild her industry.

The Young Plan, 1929

Reparations total to be further reduced and paid over the next 60 years.

End of reparations, 1932

Germany stops paying as a result of
a the economic crisis caused by the great Depression (page 161).
b the rise to power of the Nazis (page 162).

1 a List the Allied arguments **i** for **ii** against a high level of German reparations.
b Make notes to say what the events involved in **i** the invasion of the Ruhr, **ii** the Dawes Plan, **iii** the Young Plan tell you about each of these arguments.
c Which side do you think was right, and why?
2 a Make a list of all the arguments put forward at the time **i** for **ii** against the way the Treaty of Versailles treated Germany.
b Which side do you think had the stronger case in 1919? Explain your reasons.

The impact of the Paris Peace Settlement 2: the other Central Powers

By the end of this spread you should be able to:
*1 describe the problems that arose as a result of the peace settlement in **a** Central and Eastern Europe*
***b** Turkey*
2 describe some of the criticisms of the treaties made at the time and say how reasonable you think they were

1919	Czechs occupy Teschen
1920	Poland and Russia at war
1921	Treaty of Riga (Poland and Russia)
1922	Turks drive Greeks from Turkey
1923	Yugoslavia gives Fiume to Italy
	Treaty of Lausanne

Central and Eastern Europe

1 *Geography* People of the same nationality did not always live within the same geographical area.

1 *Minorities* People living as a minority
a feared they might be badly treated by the majority
b resented not living in the state to which they felt they rightly belonged.

2 *Economic competition* Each of the new states formed from the Austro-Hungarian Empire set up its own customs barriers. Although they had been part of a free-trade area within the Empire, the Conference rejected the idea of organizing a new one. Therefore, they had to compete with each other.

National self-determination
The peacemakers tried to apply this principle (page 16) but found it very difficult to carry out in practice.
As a result, many states contained people of other nationalities living as minorities:
a Poland contained Germans, Russians, Hungarians and Ruthenes,
b Czechoslovakia contained Germans, Hungarians and Ruthenes, **c** Romania included more than 1.5 million Hungarians, previously her enemies.

Insecurity
The Peace Settlement left many states and peoples in the region feeling threatened and insecure. To try to increase their security:
a Poland and France agreed to defend each other if attacked by Germany (1921), **b** Czechoslovakia, Romania and Yugoslavia became allies to discourage Hungary from trying to take back lands given to them by the Settlement (1922), **c** Czechoslovakia and France became allies to protect each other from Germany (1924).

2 *Boundaries* They wanted to give each new state boundaries that could be defended such as mountains or rivers; but sometimes these separated people of the same nationality.

3 *Resources* They wanted each state to have sufficient resources such as coal; but sometimes these resources were on land occupied by people of a different nationality.

3 *Germany and Russia* Had been made to give away valuable lands, such as German coalfields to Poland and Russian oilfields to Romania. They were too weak to take action at once, but other countries feared that one day they would try to regain the land and people they had lost.

Disputes following the Paris Peace Conference

1 Poland wanted to extend her eastern boundary. In 1920 she occupied lands in Lithuania and Russia. She then won a war with Russia. In 1921, at the Treaty of Riga, Russia gave her most of the disputed land.

2 Czechoslovakia wanted the coalfields of Teschen, although the inhabitants were Polish. In 1919 the Czechs moved in and fought the Poles for control. The decision to award most of the area to Czechoslovakia infuriated Poland.

3 During the war the Allies had promised land from the Austro-Hungarian Empire to Italy. The Conference angered Italy by giving some of it to Yugoslavia, including Fiume with its mainly Italian population. In 1923 the Italian government used threats to persuade Yugoslavia to hand over Fiume.

Turkey

The Turks hated the Treaty of Sèvres and blamed their ruler, the Sultan, for signing it. In particular they resented:
a the occupation of Turkey by foreign troops
b the amount of land they had been made to hand over to the Greeks.
In 1921 the nationalist leader, Mustapha Kemal, deposed the Sultan. He then led his army against Greek forces based in the mainly Greek populated town of Smyrna. He drove them out of Turkey and then turned on British troops at Chanak (page 19). In 1922 the Allies agreed to renegotiate the peace settlement.

The Treaty of Lausanne, 1923, altered the Treaty of Sèvres. It:
a returned the lands that Turkey had had to give to Greece (page 19)
b gave Turkey control of the Turkish Straits again
c ordered all foreign troops to leave.

Criticisms of the Treaties

At the time there were many criticisms of the Treaties dealing with Central and Eastern Europe and Turkey. Some came from the peacemakers and some from the countries affected by the Treaties. For example:
a the principle of self-determination led to the creation of small states with insufficient economic resources, all in competition with one another
b too many states were created with dissatisfied minorities within them
c countries in Central and Eastern Europe were left feeling insecure
d the Treaty of Sèvres treated Turkey unfairly by favouring the ambitions of France, Britain, Italy, and Greece.

1 a What criticisms were made at the time of the peace treaties with the Central Powers other than Germany?
b What do you think are the arguments i for ii against each criticism?
2 a Make a list of the problems that arose in i Central and Eastern Europe ii Turkey as a result of the Peace Settlement.
b In each case say whether you think the problem was the fault of the peacemakers or of someone else.
c Which aspects of the Settlement in these regions do you think were i fair ii unfair? Give your reasons.

The origins and structure of the League of Nations

By the end of this spread you should be able to:
1 describe the origins and structure of the League of Nations
2 identify some of the strengths and weaknesses in its structure

The origins of the League of Nations

The impact of the First World War
1 Many people
a believed the war was being fought to protect small nations such as Serbia and Belgium from big nations
b were appalled by the horror and devastation of modern warfare.
2 Interest grew in the idea of a League of Nations to secure future world peace and confront aggressors. By 1915 many people belonged to League of Nations societies in France, Britain, and the USA.
3 Some statesmen began to argue for a League to be set up after the war.

President Wilson
1 included the idea of an association of countries to protect world peace in his Fourteen Points (page 16).
2 insisted that the formation of the League of Nations should become part of the peacemaking process at the Paris Peace Conference (page 16), rather than be left until later.
3 chaired the committee that planned the details.

The Covenant of the League of Nations
1 was an agreement about how the League of Nations would be organized and how members would behave towards one another.
2 formed the first part of every post-war treaty.

The League of Nations system

Membership
1 Open to any independent state except Germany, which was told to apply later, and the USSR, which was distrusted by Western powers.
2 Despite Wilson's enthusiasm, the USA chose not to join the League (page 126).

1914-1915	Formation of the first League of Nations societies
1918	President Wilson's 'Fourteen Points' speech
1919	Covenant for the League of Nations accepted by the Paris Peace Conference
first	Sir Eric Drummond appointed as the Secretary-General of the League
	League headquarters set up in Geneva
1920	First meeting of the Council of the League of Nations in Paris (without USA)
	US Senate finally rejected USA's membership of League
	Permanent Court of Justice set up in The Hague

Peacekeeping Every member promised
1 that if it quarrelled with another member it would go to the League and try to resolve the matter through talks before resorting to force
2 to help any member that was attacked in defiance of this agreement by
a imposing economic sanctions on the aggressor (ie, cutting off trade and financial relations)
b if necessary, joining forces with other members to take military action against the aggressor. This method of keeping the peace was called collective security.

The Mandate System
1 The Peace Treaties transferred all German and Turkish colonies to the rule of Allied powers to be governed on behalf of the League of Nations.
2 The League set up a Mandate Commission to supervise this. A mandate is a legal trust or responsibility given by a superior body.
3 The main mandatory powers (those given the task of government) were France, Britain, and British Dominions such as Australia and New Zealand.

The structure of the League of Nations

The Council

1 consisted of 4 permanent members, 5 after 1926 (Britain, France, Italy, Japan and Germany), and 4 non-permanent members (11 by 1936)
2 dealt with problems when Assembly not in session
3 could organize sanctions against an offending state
4 all decisions had to be unanimous

The Secretariat

1 consisted of permanent officials paid by the League
2 carried out all administrative functions
3 prepared reports for the Council and Assembly
4 was divided into sections, eg. finance, drugs, health, disarmament
5 its first Secretary-General, Sir Eric Drummond, aimed to develop a body of international civil servants loyal to the League rather than to individual states
6 based at the League's head-quarters in Geneva

The Assembly

1 was the League's debating chamber
2 met once a year
3 each member state had one vote
4 all decisions had to be unanimous
5 admitted new nations and controlled the budget
6 elected non-permanent members of the Council

Non-members could use these organizations

The Permanent Court of Justice

1 consisted of 15 judges, elected by Assembly, representing the world's different legal systems
2 gave decisions on cases referred to it by countries in dispute
3 advised the Assembly and Council if asked
4 based in The Hague, Holland

Agencies

Commissions and Special Committees were set up to carry out much of the League's work. Main ones were:

Disarmament (see page 27)

Mandates (see page 24)

Slavery

Refugees (see page 27)

Economics and finance

Protection of women and children

Drugs (see page 27)

Health

Military, naval and air

Communications and transit

Intellectual co-operation

The International Labour Organization (see page 27)

1 an association of all League members
2 aimed to improve working conditions worldwide
3 ruling body consisted of rep-resentatives of governments, employers and workers

1 a Draw a table with three columns. In the left-hand column list the main bodies of the League of Nations.
b In the next two columns make notes on each body's
i membership, ii function
2 a Explain how each of the following features of the League's structure contributed to its strength when it was set up: i the Council, ii the Secretariat, iii the Agencies, iv non-members could use some League organizations.

b What do you think was its greatest strength? Give your reasons.
c Explain why each of the following was likely to be a weakness in the League's structure: i the USA, Germany, and the USSR were not members, ii it had no army, iii it could act only when its members were unanimous.
d Which do you think was its greatest weakness? Give your reasons.

The League of Nations in the 1920s

By the end of this spread you should be able to:
1 describe the peacekeeping activities of the League of Nations in the 1920s
2 describe the work of some of its agencies
3 explain how successful you think the League of Nations was in the 1920s

Peacekeeping

In the 1920s the League of Nations dealt with ten international disputes and, in several cases, prevented war. However, the disputes mainly involved minor powers, and sometimes the League ended up handing the case over to the Conference of Ambassadors, an Allied committee empowered to decide post-war boundaries.

Some political disputes which the League of Nations tried to settle in the 1920s

The Dispute	The Problem	League Action	Result
The Aaland Islands, 1920	These islands belonged to Finland but were claimed by Sweden. Most islanders wanted to be ruled by Sweden.	The two countries referred their dispute to the League which decided that Finland should keep the islands, but that the islanders' Swedish way of life should be protected.	Both countries accepted the decision
Vilna, 1920	Both the new states of Poland and Lithuania claimed the ancient town of Vilna, the capital of Lithuania in the Middle Ages but now inhabited mainly by Poles. A Polish army seized Vilna.	The League asked the Poles to withdraw to allow the inhabitants to vote on their future. The Poles refused.	The Conference of Ambassadors awarded Vilna to Poland.
Corfu, 1923	The Italian members of a working party of the Conference of Ambassadors were ambushed and killed in Greece by unknown gunmen. Italy's leader, Mussolini, demanded an apology from the Greek government and a large fine in compensation. When the Greeks refused, the Italian navy bombarded the Greek island of Corfu and marines occupied it, thus breaking the League Covenant. The Greeks appealed to the League.	The League proposed Greece should pay money into a neutral account while an enquiry took place. Mussolini disagreed, said the League was interfering, and threatened to end Italy's membership. The League Council passed responsibility to the Conference of Ambassadors, of which Italy was a member.	The Conference ordered Greece to pay 50 million lira to Italy. The Italians left Corfu. Many people criticised the League for failing condemn aggression.
The Greek-Bulgarian War, 1925	Fighting broke out on the border between Greece and Bulgaria. The Greek army invaded Bulgaria which appealed to the League.	The League Council ordered both sides to stop fighting and withdraw, and threatened sanctions when the Greeks appeared reluctant to obey. A League enquiry later found Greece to be at fault and imposed a fine.	Both sides obeyed the League's orders and accepted the enquiry's findings.

The work of some League of Nations agencies

Agency	Aims	Work	Results
International Labour Organization	To improve working conditions in member states.	Discussed issues and produced 'conventions' which member states could adopt as part of their own law if they chose.	Produced some 70 conventions by 1939, eg. on wage rates, health and safety issues, employment of women and children.
Disarmament Commission	To persuade member states to reduce armed forces and weapon stocks.	Washington Naval Conference, 1921. Disarmament Conference 1926, 1930, 1932-34.	Naval powers agreed to reduce number of warships, 1921. No other agreements reached.
Refugee Committee	To repatriate prisoners-of-war after the First World War and to find homes for refugees.	Led by Norwegian explorer, Fridtjof Nansen, raised money, found transport, designed houses, provided medical aid.	April 1920-April 1922, helped over 425,000 prisoners to return home. Dealt with post-war refugee crisis and found homes for 600,000 Greeks fleeing from Turkey, 1919-23 (see page 23).
Drugs Committee	To stop the smuggling and misuse of dangerous drugs.	Persuaded states to tighten up customs and postal controls, and to educate people about the dangers of drugs. Investigated drugs trade and published findings. Tried to control poppy-growing.	Improved controls; but could not defeat determined drugs producers. Also some states reluctant to act, eg. against poor families relying on poppy-growing for income.

Steps towards World Peace

1920

League ations 48 members

1925

The Locarno Treaties
Germany signed these with Britain, France, Italy and Belgium. All agreed not to go to war over disputes. The Germans also agreed:
a to accept the western borders given to them in 1919
b that changes to their borders with Poland and Czechoslovakia should not take place by war, only by negotiation.

1926

Germany
joined the League. The Germans had disliked the League because they
a associated it with the hated Treaty of Versailles (page 18)
b were told they could not join until they showed they could fulfil its terms. Under Stresemann (see pages 156-157) their attitudes changed.

The USSR remained hostile but Soviet observers began to attend some League committee meetings, and Soviet doctors worked with the League's Health Organization.

1928

The Kellogg-Briand Pact
Forty-five nations, including Germany, agreed never to go to war again.

1929

The League of Nations
had 54 members

1 Which 1920s disputes suggested that, despite the League of Nations, aggression might pay? Give your reasons.
2 What were the main a successes b failures of the League's agencies?
3 By 1928, what evidence was there to suggest that the League a was succeeding in maintaining international peace and co-operation b suffered from significant limitations in carrying out these tasks?
4 How successful was the League in the 1920s? Give your reasons.

The collapse of international co-operation and order in the 1930s

By the end of this spread you should be able to:
1 describe the impact of the Great Depression on international affairs
2 identify the other main factors contributing to the collapse of international co-operation and order in the 1930s
3 explain their relationship to one another

The Great Depression

In 1929 the Wall Street Crash in the USA triggered the Great Depression worldwide (page 134). This was one of several factors which contributed to the collapse of international co-operation in the 1930s, to the rise of dictatorships and to major acts of aggression by Japan, Italy, and Germany.

Fig 1 The impact of the Great Depression

The Great Depression
a International trade collapsed.
b Banks, factories, and businesses closed down.
c About 25 million people worldwide lost their jobs.

Economic rivalry
Rivalry replaced co-operation as countries introduced new economic policies to try to protect their people from the worst effects of the Depression, e.g.
a the USA raised customs duties on foreign imports
b Britain imposed customs duties on foreign imports, except those from the British Empire
c Italy tried to do without any foreign imports at all.

Social distress
a Mass unemployment, e.g. over 5 million Germans without jobs in 1932.
b Mass poverty, e.g. the price of silk produced in Japan collapsed: peasant silk growers starved; factories closed; workers' wages fell.

Rise of dictators
a In many countries people blamed the Government for their poverty and lack of work. They gave their support to political parties offering to put things right. Many of these were led by dictators.
b About 25 countries became dictatorships after 1929.

Aggression
The leaders of Japan, Italy, and Germany tried to improve conditions at home by aggression towards other countries (see Fig 2). By taking over other lands they aimed to:
a gain land and resources
b increase national pride
c compete with the Empires of France and Britain.

1 How did the Great Depression make the work of the League of Nations more difficult after 1929?
2 a Use fig.2 to make a list of the main factors which contributed to the collapse of international order in the 1930s.
b For each one write short notes to explain its role. Use the information in fig.1 and the page references.
c Which factors do you think were the most important? Write notes to explain your decision.

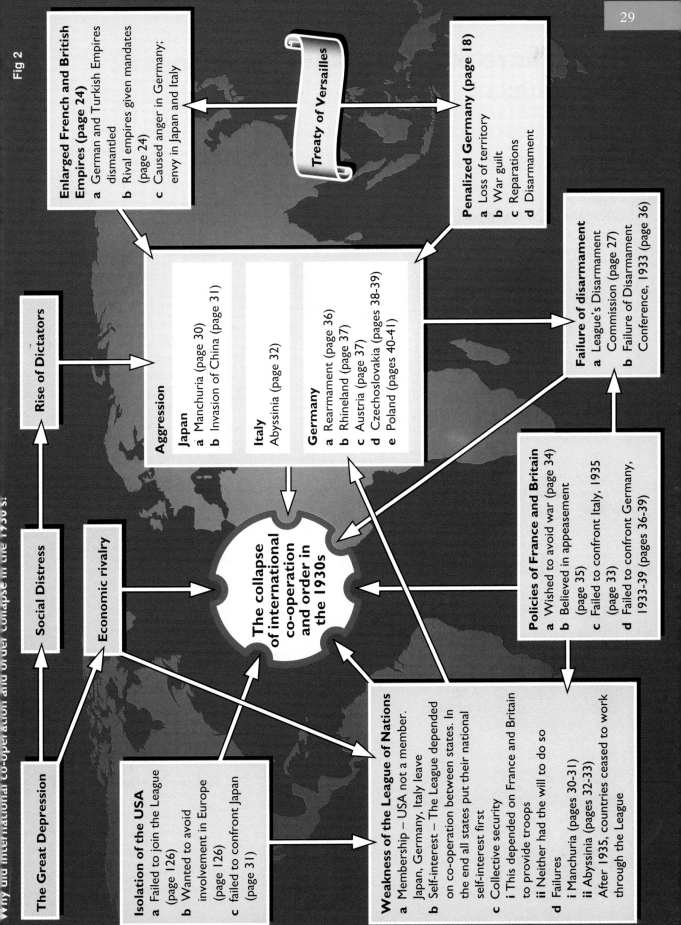

Fig 2

Why did international co-operation and order collapse in the 1930s?

Enlarged French and British Empires (page 24)
a German and Turkish Empires dismantled
b Rival empires given mandates (page 24)
c Caused anger in Germany; envy in Japan and Italy

Treaty of Versailles

Penalized Germany (page 18)
a Loss of territory
b War guilt
c Reparations
d Disarmament

The Great Depression

Social Distress

Rise of Dictators

Economic rivalry

Aggression

Japan
a Manchuria (page 30)
b Invasion of China (page 31)

Italy
Abyssinia (page 32)

Germany
a Rearmament (page 36)
b Rhineland (page 37)
c Austria (page 37)
d Czechoslovakia (pages 38–39)
e Poland (pages 40–41)

Failure of disarmament
a League's Disarmament Commission (page 27)
b Failure of Disarmament Conference, 1933 (page 36)

Isolation of the USA
a Failed to join the League (page 126)
b Wanted to avoid involvement in Europe (page 126)
c failed to confront Japan (page 31)

The collapse of international co-operation and order in the 1930s

Policies of France and Britain
a Wished to avoid war (page 34)
b Believed in appeasement (page 35)
c Failed to confront Italy, 1935 (page 33)
d Failed to confront Germany, 1933–39 (pages 36–39)

Weakness of the League of Nations
a Membership – USA not a member. Japan, Germany, Italy leave
b Self-interest – The League depended on co-operation between states. In the end all states put their national self-interest first
c Collective security
  i This depended on France and Britain to provide troops
  ii Neither had the will to do so
d Failures
  i Manchuria (pages 30–31)
  ii Abyssinia (pages 32–33)
  After 1935, countries ceased to work through the League

The failure of the League of Nations 1: Manchuria

By the end of this spread you should be able to:
1 describe how the League dealt with the crisis in Manchuria, 1931-1933

2 explain the reasons for, and describe the consequences of, its failures

Background and events

China's position
a Owned Manchuria.
b Needed its minerals.
c Resettled its surplus population there.

Manchuria
a Rich in minerals.
b Fertile soil.
c 94% of population was Chinese; about 1% Japanese.

Japan's position
a Silk exports had collapsed in Great Depression. Thousands of peasants needed new land.
b Saw Manchuria as buffer against Communist USSR.
c Claimed special rights in Manchuria: leased Liaotung Peninsula from China; kept its Kwantung Army based there; owned and operated South Manchurian Railway; ran parts of cities along its route.
d Army officers wanted to add Manchuria to Japanese Empire.

Fig. 1 The Manchuria crisis, 1931-33, and its consequences

1 *Sept 1931* Japanese Kwantung Army provokes an incident at Mukden. Then invades Manchuria. China appeals to League of Nations.

2 *Jan 1932* Japan attacks Shanghai.

3 *Feb 1932* Japanese complete occupation of Manchuria. Create semi-independent state of Manchukuo.

4 *1933* Japan occupies Jehol

5 *1933* Japan withdraws from Shanghai

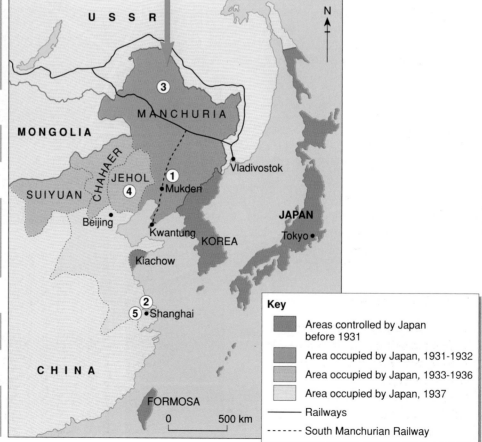

Key
- Areas controlled by Japan before 1931
- Area occupied by Japan, 1931-1932
- Area occupied by Japan, 1933-1936
- Area occupied by Japan, 1937
- Railways
- South Manchurian Railway

The League: actions and results

League action	Results
1 Ordered Japanese withdrawal (1931).	Japanese government agreed; army refused. No withdrawal.
2 Appointed Lytton Commission to investigate (1932).	Lytton Commission Report (1932): a Japanese forces guilty of forcibly seizing part of China's territory b no Chinese support for Manchukuo c Japan should withdraw and Manchuria become a semi-independent state.
3 a Accepted Lytton Report. b Instructed members not to recognise Manchukuo. c Invited Japan to hand Manchuria back to China.	Japan a kept Manchuria b left the League (1933) c withdrew from Shanghai d occupied Jehol (1933) e suffered international isolation until 1936.

Why did the League fail?

1 Members were unwilling to impose economic sanctions on Japan as the Depression had already damaged world trade and this would damage it further.

2 The Great Powers were unwilling to take military action. Britain, in particular, feared Japanese attacks on its colonies such as Singapore.

3 The USA was the most powerful country with interests in the Pacific region. It sent a representative to join the Lytton Commission, but it was not prepared to take any further action.

Long-term results

1 The world learnt that it paid to be aggressive.
2 Japan continued its aggression. It
a took over more north Chinese provinces (1933-36) (fig 1)
b formed the Anti-Comintern Pact (against USSR) with Germany (1936) and Italy (1937)
c invaded China (1937).

1929	The Wall Street Crash
1931	Japanese army invades Manchuria
1932	Japanese conquest of Manchuria League's Lytton Committee reports
1933	Japan withdraws from the League
1936	Japan forms Anti-Comintern Pact (against USSR) with Germany
1937	Japan invades China

1 Why did the League fail to use a economic b military sanctions against Japan in 1931-1932?
2 What did the crisis in Manchuria reveal about the weakness of the League of Nations?
3 What were the a short-term b long-term consequences of the League's failure in Manchuria?

The failure of the League of Nations 2: Abyssinia

By the end of this spread you should be able to
1 describe how the League dealt with the crisis
in Abyssinia, 1935-1936
2 explain the reasons for, and describe the
consequences of, its failures

1935	Italy invades Abyssinia
	League imposes sanctions on Italy
	Anglo-French Hoare-Laval Plan
1936	Italian conquest of Abyssinia
	Mussolini and Hitler form the Rome-Berlin Axis
	Hitler re-militarizes the Rhineland (March)
	League abandons sanctions against Italy (July)
1937	Italy leaves the League of Nations

Background and events

Abyssinia (now Ethiopia), ruled by Emperor Haile Selassie, was the only independent black African state. In 1896 its army had defeated an Italian invasion.

Mussolini, the Fascist dictator of Italy since 1922, had built up his armed forces and was determined to expand Italy's empire. His target was Abyssinia, sandwiched between two Italian colonies (see fig.1) where he could amass his forces.

Fig. 1 The crisis in Abyssinia, 1935-1936

1 *Dec 1934*
Italian troops provoke a clash with Abyssinians at Wal Wal as an excuse for a quarrel.

2 *Oct 1935*
Italy invades Abyssinia.

3 *Dec 1935*
Britain and France produce Hoare-Laval Plan. Large areas of Abyssinia to be given to Italy in return for troop withdrawal. Public outcry. Plan abandoned.

4 *May 1936*
Italy conquers Abyssinia. Unites it with Somaliland and Eritrea as Italian East Africa.

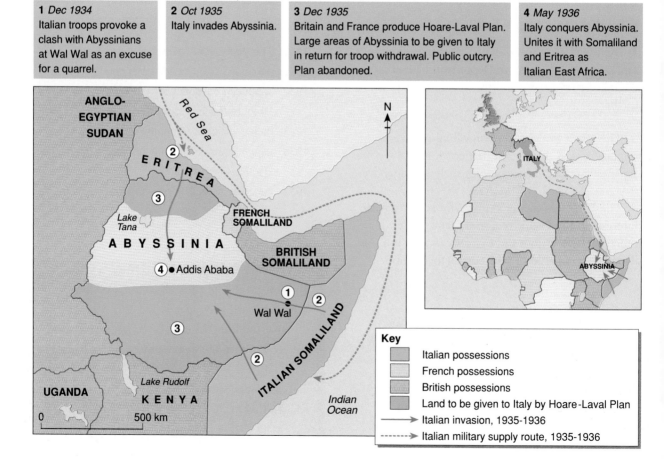

Key
- Italian possessions
- French possessions
- British possessions
- Land to be given to Italy by Hoare-Laval Plan
- → Italian invasion, 1935-1936
- ---→ Italian military supply route, 1935-1936

The League: actions and results

League action	Results
1 Dec 1934. Offer of arbitration.	Rejected by Italy.
2 Jan-Feb 1935. Debate in response to Abyssinian request for assistance.	No further action.
3 May-Sept 1935. Five-power commission on Abyssinia.	Abyssinia rejected proposals.
4 Oct 1935 **a** Condemned Italian invasion of Abyssinia. **b** Imposed economic sanctions.	Little impact. Sanctions did not include oil, iron, steel and coal. Non-League members eg, the USA and Germany, continued to trade with Italy.
5 March 1936. Threatened oil embargo on Italy.	No impact. Italians conquered Abyssinia. United it with Somaliland and Eritrea as Italian East Africa. Hitler **a** noted League weakness **b** re-militarized the Rhineland (March 1936) while attention was on Abyssinia.
6 June 1936. Haile Selassie addressed Assembly calling for League assistance against Italian aggression	No additional League action.
7 July 1936. Sanctions against Italy abandoned.	Italy **a** kept Abyssinia **b** turned to Germany **c** left the League (1937).

Why did the League fail?

1 Successful action against Italy depended on Britain and France; but they were unwilling to take strong measures because:
a they feared Mussolini might attack anyone who enforced economic sanctions and they were not ready for a war with Italy. They did not, therefore, cut off Mussolini's military lifeline by closing the Suez Canal to Italian oil supplies.
b they were frightened by the rise of Hitler's Germany (see pages 36-37). They wanted to keep Italy as ally against Germany and so were anxious not to offend Mussolini.
2 The attempt by Britain and France to find their own compromise solution to the crisis with the Hoare-Laval Plan (1935) disunited and weakened the League.

Long-term results

1 Countries lost faith in the League and its ideals.
2 Rather than put their trust in international co-operation, several countries including France and Britain begin to rearm.

1 Why did economic sanctions against Italy fail, 1935-36?
2 What did the crisis in Abyssinia reveal about the weakness of the League of Nations?
3 What were the **a** short-term **b** long-term consequences of the League's failure in Abyssinia?

Hitler's foreign policy aims; appeasement

By the end of this spread you should be able to describe and explain:
1 Hitler's foreign policy aims in the 1930s
2 The aims of other European countries
3 the British and French policy of appeasement

Fig.1 The foreign policy aims of Hitler and other European countries

Hitler:

Aim 1 Reverse the Treaty of Versailles
Restore German pride. Retrieve lands lost in 1919. Rearm.

Aim 2 Unite all German-speaking people in a 'Greater Germany'
Make Germany a single, united, homeland for all Germans. The Treaty of Versailles had allowed national self-determination for other races, but not for Germans, millions of whom now lived under foreign rule. In particular, it had forbidden *Anschluss*, the union of Austria and Germany.

Aim 3 Give Germans *lebensraum* or 'living space'
'Greater Germany' would have a population of 85 million people. Their lands would provide insufficient food and raw materials. To obtain these Germany would have to take over lands to the east in Poland and the USSR. The Poles and Russians were Slavs whom Hitler believed to be an inferior race to the Germans (page 170): the superior Germans were entitled to their lands.

France
1 Despite Locarno Treaties (page 27), distrusted Germany. Aimed to defend itself.
2 In 1929, started to build the Maginot Line of fortifications along joint border.
3 Closely linked its policy to Britain. In late 1930s supported appeasement.

Britain
1 Hoped to avoid involvement in Europe, but prepared to support France against direct German attack.
2 In mid-1930s adopted policy of appeasement.

Key
The Treaty of Versailles, 1919:
a Land taken from Germany
b De-militarized area
   German-speaking lands
.... Maginot Line

Italy
1 Mussolini shared Hitler's loathing of Socialists and Communists.
2 Wanted to expand Italian territory.
3 Hostile to union of Austria and Germany.
4 Friendly with Britain and France until mid-1930s

USSR
1 Stalin's Communist régime hostile to Hitler's Fascist Nazi régime.
2 Feared German expansion eastwards.

Appeasement

What was it?

1 A policy which aimed to prevent aggressors from starting wars by finding out what they really wanted and then agreeing to those demands which seemed reasonable.

2 Followed by Britain and France for most of the 1930s when neither was willing to risk another war with an aggressive power.

Britain and appeasement Most politicians thought it was in Britain's interests to avoid becoming entangled in Europe's affairs again. Most British people supported the policy of appeasement. Winston Churchill was one of the few politicians to speak out against it.

Appeasing Germany

Arguments for

1 The Empire was more important than Europe. The Japanese threatened to attack British colonies in the Far East. Britain could not afford also to fight Germany in the West.

2 British armed forces were not sufficiently large to fight another major war. Britain needed time to rearm.

3 To fight a successful war against Germany, Britain needed the support of the USA and of Dominions such as Australia. But they wanted to stay out of European affairs.

4 The horror of war lived on after 1918. Public opinion strongly supported disarmament.

5 The Government believed the next war would be fought in the air and that thousands of civilians would be killed by bombing raids. It wanted to avoid this.

6 Many British people

a felt guilty that the Treaty of Versailles had been too harsh.

b sympathised with the German desire to bring German-speaking peoples into one nation.

Arguments against

1 Aggressors have no 'final demands'. The more they are given the more they will try to take.

2 If Germany was allowed to become a powerful European state it would soon become a threat to the British Empire.

Landmarks of appeasement

1 Make a chart to show
a each of Hitler's foreign policy aims
b which countries were most likely to oppose each one, with a note to explain why.
2 Why did so many British people support a policy of appeasement in the 1930s?

Hitler's foreign policy and European reactions,

By the end of this spread you should be able to describe and explain:
1 Hitler's foreign policy, 1933-1938
2 European reactions to these events
3 How Germany, Italy and Japan had become allies by 1937

Event	What happened	European reaction	Result
Hitler withdraws Germany from Disarmament Conference and League of Nations, 1933	Hitler wants Germany to be allowed modest rearmament and major powers to reduce arms levels. French refuse to discuss.		League weakened.
Hitler orders rearmament, 1933	Army to be increased threefold to 300,000. New Air Ministry to train pilots and build 1000 aircraft.	Britain and France take no action.	Germany allowed to defy Treaty of Versailles.
Hitler thwarted in Austria, 1934	Murder of Austrian Chancellor, Dollfuss, by Austrian Nazis in attempt to take over government.	Mussolini moves army units to border to demonstrate his opposition to *Anschluss*.	Hitler retreats. Victory for firm response.
Saar plebiscite, 1935	Held in line with provisions of Treaty of Versailles. Over 90% Saarlanders vote to rejoin Germany.	None. The result was expected.	Hitler claims a triumph.
Hitler publicly announces German rearmament, 1935	Compulsory military service for all men. Army to be increased to 550,000.	1 Britain, France and Italy form the Stresa Front (1935). Condemn German rearmament and promise to uphold Locarno Treaties (page 27). 2 France and USSR form the Franco-Soviet Pact (1935). Promise to help each other if either attacked without provocation.	European powers 1 act independently of League of Nations 2 appear united against Germany.
Anglo-German Naval Treaty, 1935	Agreement that German fleet can be one third the size of Britain's and have same number of submarines.	1 Concern that agreement breaks disarmament clause of Treaty of Versailles. 2 Britain argues Hitler would build navy anyway: better to limit it by agreement.	1 Germany allowed to breach Treaty of Versailles 2 Unity of Stresa Front broken.
Abyssinian crisis, 1935	See pages 32-33	France and Britain 1 attempt to appease Mussolini 2 condemn him.	1 Economic sanctions shown to be useless. 2 League of Nations exposed as weak in the face of aggression. 3 Mussolini angered by refusal of

933-March 1938

Remilitarization of the Rhineland, 1936	Hitler orders troops to re-occupy the Rhineland. Prepared to withdraw if Allies make military response.	1 France and Britain protest; but there is some British sympathy for German action. 2 Britain refuses to support military response; France unwilling to fight alone.	Hitler successfully breaches Treaty of Versailles.
Spanish Civil War, 1936	Rebellion by army officers led by General Franco (the Nationalists) against the Socialist Government (the Republicans). Hitler wins Mussolini's friendship by joining him in sending troops to support Nationalists.	1 USSR sends troops to support Republicans. 2 Britain and France remain neutral.	Hitler 1 tests his armed forces 2 decides Britain and France are unwilling to intervene against aggression.
Rome-Berlin Axis, 1936	Alliance of Italy and Germany.		1 Hitler achieves aim of separating Italy from France and Britain. 2 In 1937 Mussolini says Italy will no longer defend Austria against German attack.
Anti-Comintern Pact, 1936-1937	Germany and Japan agree (1936) to work together against the Comintern, a Soviet agency set up to spread Communism worldwide.		1 Hitler gains powerful ally against the USSR. 2 Japan gains powerful ally against the USSR. 3 Italy joins in 1937.
Anschluss, March 1938	On Hitler's orders German troops invade Austria	1 Britain and France protest. 2 League of Nations protests.	1 Hitler successfully breaches Treaty of Versailles. 2 99% of Germans and Austrians vote in favour of Anschluss.

c Why did Britain, France and Italy fail to act together to stop Hitler's infringements of the Treaty of Versailles?
4 Germany was without allies in 1933.
a Which countries were its allies by 1938?
b How did this come about?

1 Make a list of the ways in which Hitler managed to break the Treaty of Versailles, 1933-1938. Write notes on each one.
2 Look at Hitler's foreign policy aims (page 34). How far had he achieved each one by March 1938?
3 a how did European countries react to each of Hitler's foreign policy actions between 1933 and March 1938?
b What were their reasons in each case?

The Sudetenland crisis, 1938

By the end of this spread you should be able to describe and explain:
1 the background to, and events of, the Sudetenland crisis

2 the role of Chamberlain
3 the Munich Agreement and its consequences

Fig. 1 Czechoslovakia in 1938

Germany
Hitler
1 thought the USSR might invade Germany through Czechoslovakia
2 hated the Czechs because they were Slavs (page 170)
3 wanted their wealth and resources
4 aimed to break-up their country. First step: support Sudetenland's claim to be part of 'Greater Germany'.

Czechoslovakia
1 Democratic government.
2 Rich in resources.
3 Strong industry, including armaments.
4 Powerful army.
5 Vulnerable to conflict between different nationalities.
6 Since 1919 Hungary and Poland had claimed Czech territory as rightfully theirs.

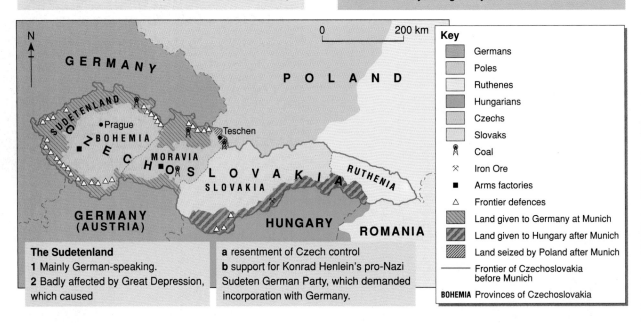

The Sudetenland
1 Mainly German-speaking.
2 Badly affected by Great Depression, which caused

a resentment of Czech control
b support for Konrad Henlein's pro-Nazi Sudeten German Party, which demanded incorporation with Germany.

The 1938 crisis

Hitler's actions
1 Tells Henlein
a to make impossible demands which Czech government will refuse
b to stage protest marches and riots
c the German army will then move in to 'restore order'.
2 Calls for right of Sudeten Germans to 'self-determination'.

3 Encourages a Sudeten German uprising which is crushed by the Czech government (Sept 12-13).

Chamberlain's beliefs The British Prime Minister, Neville Chamberlain, played an important part in attempting to resolve the crisis. He believed:
1 in the policy of appeasement (page 35)
2 the British people wanted peace at any price
3 Britain had to buy time: it could not threaten Hitler with force until it had increased its own military strength.

4 Hitler was a reasonable man who would honour an agreement. He accepted Hitler's assurance that the Sudetenland was 'his last territorial demand in Europe'.

Chamberlain's actions

1 Meets Hitler (Sept 15)
a Hitler says he will risk war to bring the Sudeten Germans into Germany. **b** Chamberlain accepts that areas in which more than half the population is German should be handed over.
2 With France persuades the Czechs to accept this compromise.
3 Meets Hitler again (Sept 22-23) to finalize details
a Hitler makes new demands:

i Germany to occupy entire Sudetenland by Sept 28
ii Czechs to hand over territory claimed by Hungary and Poland.
b Chamberlain rejects demands.
4 With Europe on the brink of war, Chamberlain asks Mussolini to persuade Hitler to agree to an international conference. Hitler agrees and postpones his planned invasion of the Sudetenland.

The Munich Conference, Sept 29-30

1 Countries present: France, Britain, Italy and Germany.
2 Czechoslovakia and USSR not invited.
3 Sudetenland transferred to Germany.
4 Britain and Germany agree not to go to war in future.

The results of the Munich agreement

Europe saved from war

This assumes Hitler would have fought for the Sudetenland.
BUT
Some historians argue it would have been worth risking a war in 1938 anyway, because Hitler would have
1 faced strong Czechoslovakian forces plus those of France, Britain, and, possibly, the USSR
2 had to fight on two fronts with a much smaller army than he had by 1939.

Buying time

Britain and France gained time to build up their armed forces BUT so did Germany.

Czechoslovakia

was deserted by its allies and fatally weakened by the loss of resources and military defences (fig 1).
1 Germany gained the Sudetenland
2 Poland seized Teschen and Hungary was given lands in Slovakia
3 Under pressure from Slovaks and Ruthenes, the Czech government granted self-government to their provinces.

Hitler

1 decided Britain and France were unlikely ever to oppose him by force.
2 gained popularity at home and became more determined to achieve lebensraum.
3 in 1939 was able to take over a weakened Bohemia-Moravia (page 40) and gain more important industrial and military resources (fig. 1).

Stalin

1 was offended by being excluded from the talks.
2 decided Britain and France would stand back if Hitler moved against Poland and the USSR.

---

1 Why did Hitler want to take over the Sudetenland?
2 a Make a timeline of the events of the Sudetenland crisis
b What part did Chamberlain play?
c What were his aims?

3 a Which results of the Munich agreement might Chamberlain have **i** foreseen
ii not foreseen?
b With hindsight, what criticisms can be made of his policy?
c Can his actions be justified?

The collapse of peace, 1939

By the end of this spread you should be able to explain why in 1939:
1 Britain and France a abandoned appeasement
b failed to ally with the USSR against Germany
2 Germany and the USSR signed the Nazi-Soviet Pact
3 war broke out

The end of appeasement

The destruction of Czechoslovakia
In March 1939 Hitler took over most of the remainder of Czechoslovakia, and Memel (fig. 1). Britain and France immediately ended their policy of appeasement because:
1 Hitler had proved that he could not be trusted to keep a promise.
2 Chamberlain was furious at Hitler's betrayal of his trust.
3 Hitler's argument that he was bringing Germans into Greater Germany (page 34) no longer held since he was now taking over the lands of non-Germans.

Guarantees France and Britain agreed they had to prevent further German conquests. In 1939 they
1 speeded up rearmament
2 guaranteed to defend the independence of:
a Poland which was obviously Hitler's next target
b Romania and Greece (fig. 1).

The threat to Poland

Hitler
1 demanded the return of Danzig and the Polish Corridor (taken from Germany in 1919).
2 ordered his generals to prepare an invasion.
3 to avoid fighting on two fronts, had to neutralize the USSR. He feared joint action by France, Britain and the USSR to defend Poland.
4 wanted Mussolini's support. He achieved this with the Pact of Steel (fig. 1).
5 did not believe France and Britain would fight for Poland on their own.

France and Britain were too far away to defend Poland directly. They, therefore, hoped to persuade the USSR to add its guarantee to theirs. The USSR could attack from the east, while they attacked Germany from the west.

Stalin
1 knew Hitler hated Communism and aimed to take over Soviet territory.
2 aimed to:
a protect the USSR against German aggression
b avoid a major war because of the USSR's political and economic weakness (pages 120-123)
c buy time to build up armies weakened by recent purges (pages 118-119).
3 had to choose between
a joining France and Britain against Germany
b making a deal with Hitler.

The Nazi-Soviet Pact, August 1939

The Pact
1 publicly agreed that the USSR would not object if Germany attacked Poland.
2 secretly agreed that, once Poland was overrun, the two powers would divide it between them. Thus the USSR would regain land lost to Poland in 1921 (page 23).

Why did talks fail between Britain, France and the USSR?
1 Stalin would not simply guarantee to defend Poland. He proposed a full military alliance with France and Britain so that they would fight together in time of war.
2 France and Britain were unwilling to agree because they
a disliked Communism and did not want to defend it
b suspected Stalin aimed eventually to control eastern Europe
c thought the Red Army was too weak to fight effectively.
3 Poland refused to allow Soviet troops on its soil.
4 Stalin mistrusted Britain and France because they had left him out of the Munich talks. He suspected they would be happy to see Hitler fight the USSR.

Why did negotiations between the USSR and Germany succeed?

1 Stalin

a realised that France and Britain were not serious about military talks

b could not face Germany alone

c could not manage to fight in Europe as well as against the Japanese on the Manchurian border

d wanted to take land in Poland.

2 Hitler needed a deal. The deadline for invading Poland was close.

Fig. 1 The road to war, 1939

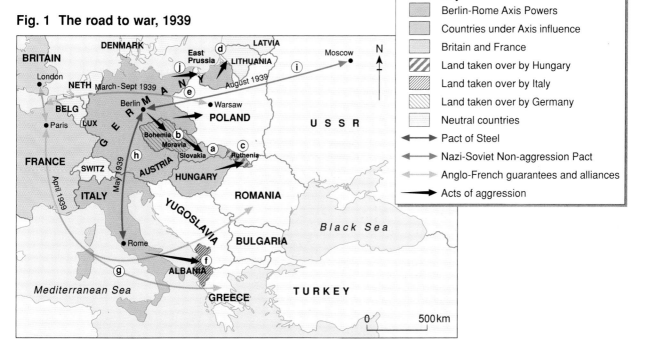

March 14-16, 1939

1 Encouraged by Hitler, Slovakia (**a**) declares itself independent.

2 Germany occupies Bohemia-Moravia (**b**).

3 Slovakia asks for German protection. German troops move in.

4 With Hitler's support, Hungary occupies Ruthenia (**c**).

March 23

Germany occupies Memel (**d**), a German-speaking area taken away from Germany in 1919 and awarded to Lithuania (page 18).

March 31

Britain and France guarantee to defend Poland against German attack (**e**).

April 3

Hitler secretly orders his generals to prepare to invade Poland on 1 September.

April 7

Italy invades Albania (**f**).

April 13 Britain and France guarantee to defend independence of Romania and Greece (**g**).

April 18

USSR proposes a defensive military alliance with Britain and France.

May 22

Germany and Italy sign the 'Pact of Steel', undertaking to help each other in time of war (**h**).

Aug 23

Germany and USSR sign Nazi-Soviet Pact (**i**).

Sept 1

1 German forces invade Poland and annex Danzig (**j**).

2 Britain and France demand their withdrawal.

Sept 3

Britain and France declare war on Germany.

1 Why did **a** Stalin **b** Hitler sign the Nazi-Soviet Pact?

2 What factors encouraged Hitler to invade Poland in September 1939 despite the Anglo-French guarantee?

Events in the 1930s: a summary

	1930	1931	1932	1933	1934	1935	1936	1937	1938	1939
Japan		Invades Manchuria	Conquers Manchuria; Expansion of armed forces	Occupies Jehol; Leaves League of Nations			Anti-Comintern Pact with Germany	Invades China	Conquers lands in east China	
Italy					Wal Wal incident in Abyssinia	Invades Abyssinia	Conquers Abyssinia; Helps Franco in Spanish Civil War; Rome-Berlin Axis	Leaves League of Nations; Joins Germany and Japan in Anti-Comintern Pact	Munich	
Germany	Evacuation of Rhineland by Allies			Hitler Chancellor; Leaves League of Nations; Rearmament begins in secret	Hitler Führer	Further expansion of armed forces announced; Saar Plebiscite	Remilitarization of Rhineland; Helps Franco in Spanish Civil War; Berlin-Rome Axis; Anti-Comintern Pact with Japan		Union with Austria; Occupies Sudetenland; Munich;	Nazi-Soviet Pact with USSR; Invades Czecho-slovakia; Invades Poland
League of Nations		Orders Japanese army to withdraw from Manchuria	Start of Geneva Disarmament Conference; Lytton Commission	Hitler walks out of Geneva Conference; Germany and Japan leave League	End of Geneva Disarmament Conference; USSR joins League; USA joins ILO	Condemns Italian aggression; Imposes sanctions on Italy	Abandons sanctions on Italy	Italy leaves the League		

France		Pact with USSR	Hoare-Laval Plan	Non-intervention in Spanish Civil War; Begins rearmament		Munich	
Britain			Hoare-Laval Plan	Non-intervention in Spanish Civil War; Begins rearmament		Munich	
USA	Representative joins League's Lytton Commission	Joins International Labour Organization	First Neutrality Act		Second Neutrality Act	Begins rearmament	
USSR		Pact with France; Joins League		Helps Republic in Spanish Civil War			Nazi-Soviet Pact with Germany

Key:

- Acts of aggression/withdrawal of co-operation
- Start of rearmament
- Alliances and pacts

- Non-intervention
- Use of sanctions against aggression
- Use of force against aggression
- Attempts to end aggression through negotiation

Blitzkrieg and Operation Barbarossa, 1940-1942

By the end of this spread you should be able to describe and explain:
1 German military successes in the West, 1939-1940

2 the fall of France and survival of Britain
3 Operation Barbarossa and events on the Eastern Front, 1941-1942

Blitzkrieg, 1939-40

1 Invasion of Poland. German blitzkrieg defeats Polish army within a month. Soviet Red Army invades according to Nazi- Soviet Pact.

2 Invasion of Denmark and Norway. Aims to secure North Sea route used for shipping Swedish iron ore when Baltic frozen. British relief expedition fails. Churchill replaces Chamberlain as British Prime Minister.

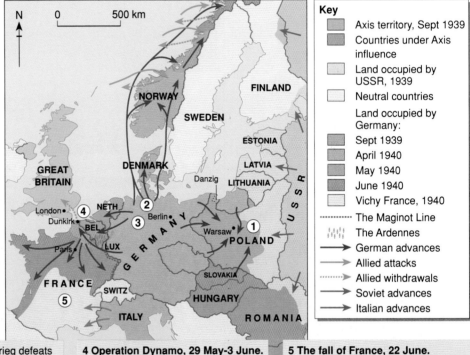

Key
- Axis territory, Sept 1939
- Countries under Axis influence
- Land occupied by USSR, 1939
- Neutral countries
- Land occupied by Germany:
  - Sept 1939
  - April 1940
  - May 1940
  - June 1940
  - Vichy France, 1940
- ·········· The Maginot Line
- The Ardennes
- → German advances
- → Allied attacks
- ·········· Allied withdrawals
- → Soviet advances
- → Italian advances

3 Invasion of France. Blitzkrieg defeats Netherlands and Belgium in three weeks. British and French driven back to Dunkirk. Paris occupied 14 June.

4 Operation Dynamo, 29 May-3 June. Over 200,000 British and 130,000 French soldiers rescued from the beaches of Dunkirk.

5 The fall of France, 22 June. Germans run occupied northern France. Marshal Pétain allowed to run unoccupied, but German-dominated, south from town of Vichy.

Reasons for German success

1 Blitzkrieg (page 50). French and British overcome by speed and weight of German attack.
2 Germans superior in armoured divisions: 10 to Allied 4.
3 German air superiority: 4000 aircraft to Allied 1400 (Churchill reserved 1000 for defence of Britain).

4 Germans attacked France through least expected and least defended place - the Ardennes Mountains. Outflanked Maginot Line.
5 Hitler free to fight on one front only. Able to leave only 10 divisions to hold Poland.

The Battle of Britain, 1940

1 Following Churchill's rejection of peace terms Hitler ordered the invasion of Britain (Operation Sealion).
2 The Royal Navy's control of the Channel meant Germans first had to win control in the air.

3 The Battle of Britain, July-Oct.
Stage 1, July: Luftwaffe attacks merchant shipping in the Channel.
Stage 2, August: airfields bombed to try to destroy RAF. Almost successful.

Stage 3, September: London bombed ('The Blitz') to try to destroy civilian morale. RAF gains upper hand.
4 Hitler postpones Operation Sealion. Later abandoned.

1 What were the consequences of Hitler's use of blitzkrieg, 1939-1940?
2 How did Britain manage to remain undefeated in 1940?
3 What factors help to explain
a Germany's initial success against the USSR
b the survival of the USSR?

Reasons for British success
1 Outstanding performance of Hurricane and Spitfire fighters and pilots.
2 Factories produced an additional 1836 fighters in 4 months.
3 Radar gave advance warning of enemy attacks.

4 Possession of 'Ultra', the key to the Germans' radio codes. It meant the British had advance warning of their plans.
5 Switch of German attack from airfields to cities relieved pressure on RAF at the critical moment.

Operation Barbarossa, 1941-42

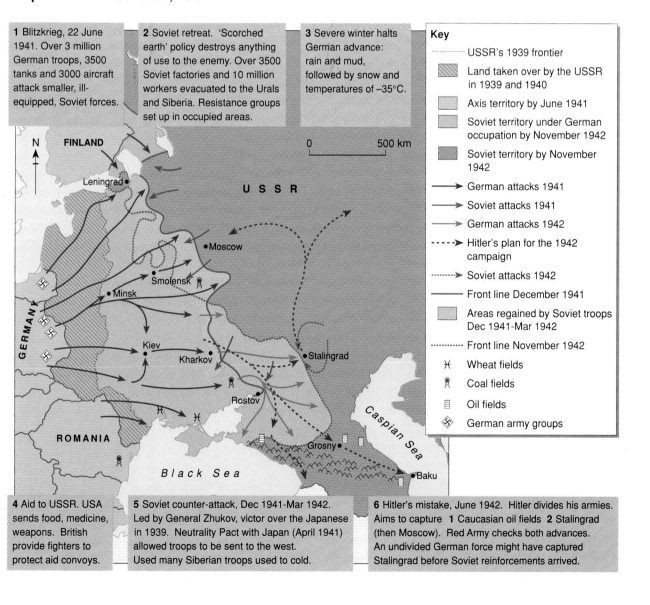

1 Blitzkrieg, 22 June 1941. Over 3 million German troops, 3500 tanks and 3000 aircraft attack smaller, ill-equipped, Soviet forces.

2 Soviet retreat. 'Scorched earth' policy destroys anything of use to the enemy. Over 3500 Soviet factories and 10 million workers evacuated to the Urals and Siberia. Resistance groups set up in occupied areas.

3 Severe winter halts German advance: rain and mud, followed by snow and temperatures of −35°C.

Key
- ⋯⋯⋯ USSR's 1939 frontier
- Land taken over by the USSR in 1939 and 1940
- Axis territory by June 1941
- Soviet territory under German occupation by November 1942
- Soviet territory by November 1942
- → German attacks 1941
- → Soviet attacks 1941
- → German attacks 1942
- ---→ Hitler's plan for the 1942 campaign
- ⋯⋯⋯→ Soviet attacks 1942
- — Front line December 1941
- Areas regained by Soviet troops Dec 1941-Mar 1942
- ⋯⋯⋯ Front line November 1942
- ⋇ Wheat fields
- ⚒ Coal fields
- ▤ Oil fields
- ⌖ German army groups

4 Aid to USSR. USA sends food, medicine, weapons. British provide fighters to protect aid convoys.

5 Soviet counter-attack, Dec 1941-Mar 1942. Led by General Zhukov, victor over the Japanese in 1939. Neutrality Pact with Japan (April 1941) allowed troops to be sent to the west. Used many Siberian troops used to cold.

6 Hitler's mistake, June 1942. Hitler divides his armies. Aims to capture **1** Caucasian oil fields **2** Stalingrad (then Moscow). Red Army checks both advances. An undivided German force might have captured Stalingrad before Soviet reinforcements arrived.

The defeat of Germany, 1942-1945

By the end of this spread you should be able to:
1 describe the events leading to the defeat of

Germany in 1945
2 explain the reasons for Germany's defeat

Reasons for Germany's defeat

The Allies

Strength of the USSR
The will of its people to resist, its vast army and its ability to manufacture weapons and equipment enabled the USSR to turn the tables on Germany.

Air and sea-power
Command of the air and sea gave the Allies the advantage in launching their counter-attacks. Allied bombers seriously damaged German industry.

Strength of the USA
The addition of its wealth, resources and fighting forces tipped the scales heavily in favour of the Allies.

Success in the Battle of the Atlantic, 1943 (pages 50–51)

Survival of Britain in 1940 (page 44)

Germany

Hitler's decisions
1 to attack the USSR (page 45). This committed him
a to a long and difficult war in the East
b to fight on two fronts.
2 to declare war on the USA (page 48). This brought the most powerful nation in the world into the war against Germany.

Overstretched resources
1 Germany had to fight on three fronts: East, West and Italy.
2 Its conquests in Europe and Russia gave Germany problems in supplying forces over long distances.
3 Large numbers of troops were needed to hold down conquered peoples as well as for fighting.
4 Occupying forces faced strong resistance movements in many countries.

Collapse of the economy
1 As more people were drafted into the forces Germany faced a labour shortage. By 1944 it depended on inefficient slave labour provided by foreign civilians and prisoners of war.
2 Allied bombing raids destroyed railways, factories and oil refineries.
3 As Soviet troops reconquered territory in the East they cut off the supply of oil and other raw materials on which German war production had come to depend. In the West, the Allied conquest of the Ruhr in 1945 took away Germany's major industrial area.

1 a Make a time-line of the events leading to the defeat of Germany.
b Explain the significance of each event.
2 a Take each of the factors which contributed to the defeat of Germany. Explain what each contributed.
b Which factors would you choose as being of *major* importance? Explain your reasons.

The road to victory: Allied advances, 1942-1945

1 Battle of Stalingrad, Nov 1942–Jan 1943.
Soviet victory: 150,000 Germans killed, 91,000 captured. Turning point of the war in Europe.

2 Battle of El Alamein, Oct-Nov 1942
Victory for British Eighth Army led by General Montgomery over Axis forces led by General Rommel. Turning point in North Africa.

3 Operation Torch, Nov 1942
Stalin wanted Allied invasion of Europe to open up a 'second front' and relieve pressure on Soviet forces in the East. But British and American troops not yet ready. Instead, Churchill and US President Roosevelt agree on joint attack on North Africa.

4 Casablanca Declaration, Jan 1943
Roosevelt and Churchill announce they will accept only unconditional surrender from Germany. Aim to reassure Stalin they will not make a separate peace with Hitler.

5 Battle of Kursk, July 1943
Largest tank battle of the war. Massive German attack checked. Soviet counter-attack shatters German forces. End of German ability to mount offensives in the East.

6 Invasion of Italy, Sept 1943
Allied invasion follows defeat of Axis forces in Tunisia in May and the invasion of Sicily in July. Fascists depose Mussolini. Italy surrenders but Hitler orders his troops to rescue Mussolini and disarm the Italian army. Start of long struggle to drive German army from Italy.

7 Battle of the Atlantic
May 1943 a turning point (pages 50 to 51).

8 Bomber offensive, 1943
Intensification of Allied 'area bombing' raids (page 50), begun in 1942. 50,000 killed by 'firestorms' in July raid on Hamburg. Raids continue to 1945.

9 Operation 'Overlord', D-Day 6 June 1944
Allied landings on Normandy coast under supreme command of American general, Eisenhower. Germans deceived into expecting invasion near Calais. One million Allied troops landed within 10 days.

10 Flying bombs, June 1944
Germans launch V-1 'flying bombs' against south-east England, followed, in September by V-2 rockets. 9000 civilians killed, 35,000 wounded, before final capture of launching sites in 1945.

11 Main Soviet offensive, June 1944
Timed to coincide with D-Day. Germans now outnumbered on both fronts. In August Soviets also advance in the south.

12 Battle of the Bulge, December 1944
Allied advance slows down and Hitler uses last reserves to launch counter-attack through Ardennes. In six week battle Allies halt Germans and inflict heavy losses. Hitler now incapable of further offensives.

13 German surrender, May 1945
Follows Allied offensives on all fronts and Hitler's suicide in April.

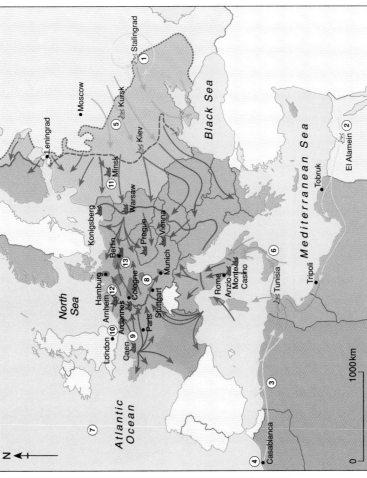

Key

Axis territory by June 1941

Vichy France

Area of USSR under German occupation by Nov 1942

Allied territory by Nov 1942

Allied advances   **Battles**
- 1942   1942
- 1943   1943
- 1944   1944
- 1945   1945

Front line
- ········· Nov 1942
- – – – Dec 1943
- ——— Dec 1944

Areas of Allied bombing 1942-1944

The war in the Pacific, 1941-1945

By the end of this spread you should be able to explain:

1 the causes of the outbreak of war in the Pacific
2 the reasons for the defeat of Japan

The outbreak of war in the Pacific

Japan
Had followed a policy of expansion since 1931 (page 30-31). Had third largest armed forces in the world.

USA
Had followed a policy of neutrality since 1920s (pages 28 and 126). After 1939 its policy changed to allow supply of war equipment to Britain and the USSR. Also feared Japanese expansion. Helped China by stopping the sale of goods such as aircraft and iron to Japan.

1 Japanese invasion of Indo-China, July 1941 USA responds by stopping sale of vital oil to Japan. Refuses to lift ban unless Japan agrees to negotiate peace with China. Japan refuses.

Key

	Area under Japanese control by 1939
	Area under Japanese control by December 1941
	Japanese ally
	Allied territory in December 1941
	Area under Japanese control by August 1942

Japanese:
→ advances   ┈┈▸ bombing raid
• offensive bases

Allied:
→ advances
offensive bases:
• American   • British

2 Pearl Harbor, December 1941
Needing a new source of oil, Japan plans to attack British and Dutch colonies in SE Asia. Since not strong enough to fight combined British and American forces in Pacific, Japanese begin with surprise attack on US Pacific Fleet (page 50). USA, Britain, Australia and 11 other countries immediately declare war on Japan. In support of their ally Japan, Germany and Italy declare war on USA.

3 Japanese expansion December 1941-August 1942
Rapid Japanese conquest of SE Asia. Surrender of thousands of British and American troops. Japanese now in control of oil and other vital supplies.

---

1 Use the information on pages 30-31 and 48-49.
a What were the main stages of Japanese expansion 1931-1942?
b Why did war break out in the Pacific in 1941?
2 a Make a timeline of the events leading to the defeat of Japan.

b Explain the significance of each event.
3 a Take each of the factors which contributed to the defeat of Japan. Explain what it contributed.
b Which factors would you choose as being of major importance? Explain your reasons.

Japan in retreat

1 Battle of Midway
The turning point in the Pacific war. US Pacific Fleet defeats Japanese attack. Sinks four enemy aircraft carriers and destroys 296 aircraft.

2 'Island hopping'
Allied forces attack strategic islands with harbours and airbases bypassing less important ones. Fierce Japanese resistance. Heavy casualties on both sides.

3 American bombing campaign, March–August 1945
Using captured airfields and new B29 Superfortress bombers, the USAAF destroy a quarter of all Japanese houses in firebomb attacks. Millions abandon the cities to seek food and shelter in the countryside, leaving factories without enough workers and reducing industrial output.

4 British and Imperial forces recapture Burma after Battle of Imphal and threaten Japanese in South east Asia.

Key

- Area under Japanese control by August 1942
- Allied territory, August 1942
- → Allied advances
- Areas regained by Allies by August 1945
- Area under Japanese control by August 1945
- ✗ Allied air bases
- Battles
- Atomic bomb attacks

5 Japanese peace initiative, summer 1945
Japanese leadership divided between 'war group' and 'peace group' led by Prime Minister Suzuki. Government makes secret approaches to USSR (still officially neutral) to act as go-between with USA. USSR does not pass on proposals but Americans learn of them via intelligence service.

8 Japanese surrender, 2 September 1945

7 Soviet attack, 8 August 1945
Stalin attacks the Japanese in Manchuria hoping to share victory with the USA. But Britain and the USA want to prevent build-up of Soviet influence in the Far East.

6 US atomic bomb attacks, 6 and 9 August, 1945
Hiroshima: 80,000 killed, rising to over 138,000 as a result of radiation sickness.
Nagasaki: 40,000 killed, rising to over 48,000.

Collapse of the economy

1 US submarines sank more than 75 per cent of Japan's merchant ships.
2 US bombing destroyed Japanese homes and factories.
3 In 1945 many people were starving and industrial production collapsed

Air and sea-power

At the the battles of Coral Sea, Midway, and Leyte Gulf the Americans gained command of the sea and air. This was essential for successful operations in the Pacific Islands.

Japan   • • • • • • • •   **Why was Japan defeated in 1945?**   • • • • • • • •   **USA**

The dropping of the atomic bombs

Although some military commanders wanted to fight to the last, this persuaded Emperor Hirohito to surrender. He did not know that the Americans had no more atomic bombs.

Resources over-stretched

Its rapid conquests meant that it had too large an area to control and defend. It had no allies

Superior resources

Able to produce more aircraft, aircraft carriers and weapons than Japan

Technology and warfare, 1939-45

By the end of this spread you should be able to:
1 describe the nature and impact of
a blitzkrieg in the West, b intensive

bombing campaigns, c Pearl Harbor,
d submarine warfare in the Atlantic
2 explain the significance of the use of nuclear weapons in 1945

Blitzkrieg

What was it? Blitzkrieg, or 'lightning war', described a new attacking method of mechanized warfare.
Based on the aeroplane and the tank it depended on surprise, speed, and weight of forces.
a Bombers attacked enemy airfields and communications centres.
b Parachutists dropped behind enemy lines to capture bridges and other important targets.
c Dive bombers moved ahead of the tanks attacking enemy strong points.
d Tanks broke through weak points in the enemy line and travelled fast across country.
e Motorized infantry followed to mop up resistance.

What was its impact? Blitzkrieg enabled Germany to deliver knock-out blows to weaker or unprepared forces in Poland, France, Belgium, Holland (page 44), and the USSR (page 45)

Intensive bombing campaigns

What were they? The use of bomber fleets to bomb wide areas of enemy cities. Precision bombing, to hit military targets only, proved a failure. Both sides turned to 'area bombing' to try to **a** destroy railways, docks, factories, etc **b** kill civilians in order to damage morale (pages 45, 47 and 49).

What was their impact?
1 For the first time large numbers of civilians were involved in direct military action and intentionally killed.
2 Disruption of civilian life, eg, air-raid precautions, etc (page 53).

3 Heavy civilian casualties: over 500,000 Germans and 60,000 British killed.
4 Widespread destruction of homes and buildings.
5 Many made homeless: 7.5 million in Germany. Thousands of refugees, e.g. from Hamburg (1943).
6 Civilian morale often badly affected at first, but never broken by either side

Pearl Harbor

What happened? On 7 December 1941, 360 Japanese dive-bombers and torpedo-bombers made a surprise attack on the US Pacific Fleet at anchor in Pearl Harbor (page 48). They were launched in two waves from six aircraft carriers sailing 400 kms away.

What was its impact?
1 US Pacific Fleet crippled. Eight battleships and ten other ships sunk or put out of action; 340 planes destroyed; 3581 Americans killed or wounded. But four American aircraft carriers and vital fuel storage tanks escaped harm.
2 In two hours Japan gained command of the Pacific Ocean at the cost of 29 aircraft. She was free to launch her Far Eastern offensive unopposed (page 48).
3 Demonstration of deadly potential of aircraft carriers.
4 USA brought into the war (page 48).

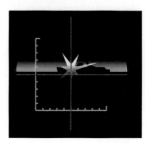

Submarine warfare

What happened?
1 German U-boats attacked British and (after 1941) American merchant ships carrying vital supplies from the USA to Britain.

2 Despite use of a convoy system with merchant ships protected by fast destroyers, the Allies suffered heavy losses in the Battle of the Atlantic.
3 From May 1943, using faster escort vessels, equipped with radar and asdic to locate submarines, and long-range aircraft, the Allies began to destroy U-boats at the rate of 40-50 per month.

What was its impact?
1 Severe shortages of food and raw materials in Britain (page 52).
2 By March 1943 Britain was almost prevented from fighting on.
3 From May 1943 Allied use of new weapons and technology, and better tactics, ensured Britain's survival.

The atomic bomb

Should the USA use the atomic bomb?

Arguments for
1 The 'war party' in Japan was still in control. It had rejected peace terms.
2 The cost of invading Japan.
a Many Japanese were prepared to fight to the death as a matter of honour. At Iwo Jima only 200 out of 22,000 Japanese defenders had been left alive.
b Japan still had 4 million troops and 4,800 kamikaze aircraft for suicide missions. Advisers told President Truman that the war might last until 1946 with one million American casualties.
c Americans wanted peace quickly with minimum casualties.
3 The USSR
a The USA and Britain feared Stalin intended to move into the Far East just as he had moved into Eastern Europe (page 57).
b The longer the war against Japan lasted, the more chance he would have. A swift ending would forestall him.
4 The cost of the project
The USA had spent millions of dollars developing the bomb. Now that it had been successfully tested (July 1945), it should be used.

Arguments against
1 The atomic bomb was too terrible a weapon to use. It would cause appalling civilian casualties both directly and through radiation sickness (page 49).
2 Japan had already been almost defeated using conventional weapons (page 49). The use of the atomic bomb would not make any difference.
3 The 'peace party' in the Japanese government was known to want to discuss peace terms.

The results of using the atomic bomb
1 Destruction of Hiroshima and Nagasaki. Massive casualties (page 49).
2 Unconditional surrender of Japan.
3 US occupation of Japan. USSR not involved.
4 Birth of the Nuclear Age (page 70).

1 a Using pages 8-10 and 50-51 make a chart to show what was similar and what was different about warfare in the First and Second World Wars.
b How did technological developments change the nature of warfare 1939-1945?
2 Take each of the points in favour of the USA using the atomic bomb. How might an opponent have argued against each one?

The Home Front in Britain, 1939-1945: 1

By the end of the next two spreads you should be able to describe how the war affected:
1 everyday life in Britain
2 the role of the Government
3 the role and status of women in society and politics
4 social change and reform.

People and Government

Recruitment

1 1939: all men aged between 19 (later 18) and 41 were called up to fight. 1940: those at home joined the Home Guard for defence against invasion.
2 1941: all unmarried women aged between 19 and 30 were conscripted. They could choose between Women's Land Army, women's sections of the armed forces (though not allowed to fight) and work in factories. Many other women joined voluntary groups, e.g. Women's Voluntary Service (WVS).

The Government

1939: *Emergency Powers Act* gave the Government almost limitless power over people's lives in order to run the war. Its involvement was deeper and more closely planned than in First World War.

Food and rationing

1 Submarine warfare (page 51) caused food shortages from the start.
2 1940: rationing of basic foods (sugar, butter, margarine, cheese, bacon, tea). Policy of equal shares of these for all (page 55). Other rationed foods (e.g. tinned food, meat, and sweets) available on a 'points' system. Long queues.
3 Ministry of Food ran 'Dig for Victory' campaign. Also gave advice on recipes and healthy eating.
4 Soap, shoes and clothes rationed. 'Make Do and Mend' campaign and 'utility' designs aim to conserve materials.

Work and industry

1 The Government took direct control of 75 per cent of British industry. By 1943 production was 8.5 times greater than in 1939.
2 Ernest Bevin, Minister of Labour, worked closely with the unions. Strike action before using arbitration was made illegal. Employers were made to improve working conditions, e.g. canteens.
3 Women were conscripted into essential industries to replace men in the forces.

Propaganda

1 The Censorship Bureau banned all press photographs showing wounded soldiers, dead air raid victims, or houses destroyed by bombs.
2 Many Government poster campaigns: 'Your Britain. Fight for it now', 'Careless Talk Costs Lives', 'Is Your Journey Really Necessary?' (See also 'Food and rationing').
3 Government ministers, especially Churchill, used radio broadcasts to encourage people to support the war effort and make them feel their contributions were valued.

Welfare

The Government became closely involved with people's welfare (page 55)

"'.... strictly between these four walls !'"

CARELESS TALK COSTS LIVES

Protecting civilians

Submarine warfare
See page 51 and 'Food and rationing'.

Bombing campaigns
1 Air raid precautions: civilian defence force set up, Air Raid Precautions (ARP); black out regulations; gas-masks issued against gas attacks (none came); shelters constructed ('Anderson' for the garden, 'Morrison' for indoors); buildings sand-bagged; barrage balloons placed to stop bombers flying low; search-light and anti-aircraft batteries installed.
2 Evacuation. Impact see Health

3 The raids:
1940-1941: 'Blitz' on London and other major cities.
1942-1943: intermittent raids
1944-1945: V1 'flying bomb' and V2 rocket attacks on London and the South East.
4 Impact of raids: over 60,000 civilians killed; 250,000 made homeless; some damage to factories and communications, but not vital; short-term drop in civilian morale, but little long-term effect. Civilian morale boosted by Churchill's radio speeches and visits to devastated areas giving a sense of unity between Government and people.

The Home Front in Britain, 1939-1945: 2

Social change and reform

Education

During the war

Education Act, 1944:
1 Abolished fee-paying grammar schools and provided free secondary education for all. Children who passed an exam at 11 went to grammar schools. The others were to go to technical and secondary modern schools. The three types were to have equal status.
2 Local Authorities to provide school meals, free milk, and regular medical inspections.
3 The Government to provide grants for students going on to higher education.

After the war

1 Very few technical schools built.
2 Girls education improved now that they had the same chances as boys in secondary schools.
3 Expansion of university places.
4 1950s: doubts expressed about selection at 11.

Housing

During the war
1 Despite the building programme 1919-1939, four million people still lived in unmodernized nineteenth-century 'slum' housing.
2 Bombing destroyed 3.5 million homes. New building ceased.

After the war
1 100,000 prefabricated houses ('prefabs') were built as a temporary measure.
2 One million council houses (with three bedrooms and inside bathroom) built by 1950. Many more needed. House building remained a priority in the 1950s.
3 *New Towns Act* (1946) provided for the development of new towns. Aimed at a balance of social classes and self-contained employment and leisure facilities. Twelve begun by 1950.

Changing attitudes

1 As the war went on many people became determined that:
a divisions in pre-war British society between the better off and the very poor should be ended
b it was the Government's task to do this.
2 Reasons for this change were
a the involvement of civilians in 'total war': the evacuation, and the shared experience of bombing and rationing, began to break down social barriers
b Government intervention, e.g. the policy of 'fair shares for all', proved that its actions could be effective
c thinkers such as JB Priestley, who broadcast regularly on the radio, talked about building a 'new Britain' after the war.

The Beveridge Report

The Government itself began to plan for a better future. It asked Sir William Beveridge to produce a plan for social welfare. His report, *Social Insurance and Allied Services* (1942) sold 635,000 copies and became a best-seller. It said the Government should:
1 spend more on education
2 use its spending power to keep full employment
3 create a National Health Service
4 increase the number of council houses
5 set up one simple insurance scheme to tackle the problem of poverty.

Health

During the war

1 Improvement in average diet as a result of:

a 'fair shares for all' rationing scheme aimed at 'levelling-up' of living standards of the poor

b new types of food from the USA, e.g. dehydrated milk, eggs, vegetables

c free orange juice and cod-liver oil for babies and free milk for babies and school children

d extension of school meals service

e works canteens providing cheap well-balanced meals

f higher wages

g Ministry of Food information.

2 Inoculation programmes to prevent epidemics as a result of the 'blitz' wiped out 'killer' diseases such as diptheria.

3 To cope with war casualties, the Government took control of most hospitals through the Emergency Hospital Scheme.

4 The poor health of many evacuees brought home to middle-class people the need to improve diet and healthcare for the poorest families.

After the war

National Health Service Act (1946) set up a free health service for all:

1 free treatment available from doctors, dentists and opticians (small charges for some services from 1951)

2 surgeries opened in all areas

3 the Government paid doctors and took over the running of hospitals

4 Local Authorities to provide free services: ambulances, midwives, immunization, and vaccination.

Work

During the war

1 The demands of war created full employment.

2 'New' industries were boosted, e.g, aircraft, electronics.

3 Women took over the jobs of conscripted men. Some union opposition but less than in First World War. Women involved more widely. Held nearly half the jobs in the Civil Service. Fall of numbers in domestic service from 1.2 million to 0.5 million

After the war

1 Job opportunities in 'new' industries

2 Government used its spending power (e.g. on roads, houses) to maintain full employment

3 More women stayed in work than in 1919: more determined; faced less opposition; more jobs available. But not paid equally to men.

National Insurance

During the war

Extension of pensions to war widows and orphans. Payments made to victims of the 'blitz'.

After the war

Creation of the 'Welfare State'.

1 *Family Allowances Act* (1945): all families given a weekly allowance for each child after the first while at school.

2 *National Insurance Act* (1946): in return for weekly contributions (also paid by the employer and the Government) every worker became entitled to sickness and unemployment benefits, retirement and widow's pensions, maternity benefits and help with funeral costs.

3 *National Assistance Act* (1946): those not in paid work could apply for help to the new National Assistance Board.

1 How did the role of the Government change between 1939 and 1945?

2 What changes did the Second World War bring to the everyday lives of civilians?

3 a What changes took place in the role and status of women during the Second World War in the areas of work, welfare, and education?

b Which were temporary and which were permanent?

4 What was the impact of the Second World War on social change and reform?

The Western Allies and the USSR, 1945-1946

*By the end of the next three pages you should be able to explain why
the wartime alliance between the Western Allies and the USSR broke down*

The background

The West: Capitalism and democracy
1 Free elections. Many political parties.
2 Most industry and agriculture was owned by private individuals.
3 Limits on Government interference in people's lives.
4 Freedom to speak and write freely.

Conflicting systems
The societies of the USSR and the West were organized on very different principles.

The USSR: Communism and dictatorship
1 Led by a dictator, Joseph Stalin. Only the Communist Party was allowed to exist.
2 Industry and agriculture was owned by the State. People were encouraged to work for the common good.
3 The Government controlled most aspects of people's lives.
4 Restrictions on what could be said or written.

Western mistrust of the USSR
1 Communism threatened the Western values and way of life.
2 Dislike of Stalin's dictatorship which had led to many deaths and the 'purges' of 1935-1938 (page 118-119).
3 Stalin had signed the Nazi-Soviet Pact, 1939 and divided Poland with Hitler (page 40).

Mutual mistrust
This had built up since 1918.

Soviet mistrust of the West
1 Communists believed
a the Capitalist system was evil since the rich prospered at the expense of the poor
b it would collapse and be replaced by Communism, which was a superior system.
2 In 1918-1919 Western states had briefly intervened against the Communist government in the Russian Civil War, using troops originally sent to help to fight Germany.

3 In 1919 the Paris Peace Settlement gave Russian lands to other countries including Poland (page 19).
4 In 1938-1939 Stalin suspected that France and Britain did not want to protect the USSR against Hitler (page 40).
5 In 1942 Stalin was angry that Britain and the USA refused to invade Europe quickly and thus open up a second front to take pressure off the USSR (page 47).

Western Allies
1 Support democracy. Hold free elections in all states.
2 Keep Poland's western boundary as it was.
3 Help Germany to produce its own goods and food again and to take part in world trade.

Conflicting aims in Central and Eastern Europe, 1945
During the fighting the USSR had suffered by far the greatest loss of lives and property. It was determined to protect itself in the future.

USSR
1 Create a 'buffer' of friendly states between Germany and the USSR. Ensure all new governments support the USSR.
2 Re-draw Poland's western boundary.
3 Keep Germany weak.

From friendship to suspicion

Key

▓	USSR, 1939
░	Areas taken over by USSR, 1945
▨	Poland, 1921-1939
▧	Areas taken over by Poland, 1945
- - - - -	Polish frontier, 1945
– – – – –	Germany, 1937
░	Germany and Austria, 1945
⟶	German refugees
────	Boundary of Soviet- occupied areas, 1945-1946

The Yalta Conference, February 1945

Present	Decisions	Tensions
Stalin (USSR). Roosevelt (USA). Churchill (Britain).	1 *Germany*: a to be defeated, then disarmed b to be split into four zones of occupation (the Big Three plus France). c to pay reparations. 2 *Eastern Europe*. Countries to be allowed to hold free elections to choose how they would be governed. 3 *Poland*: a Free elections to be held. b Eastern frontier to return to pre-1921 position (page 23) **(A)** 4 *USSR* to join the war against Japan three months after Germany's defeat. 5 *United Nations Organization* to be set up (page 92).	1 Western Allies concerned because USSR wanted a Poland's western frontier moved into Germany b the German population removed. 2 Despite disagreements both Western and Soviet politicians thought the conference successful and were hopeful for the future.

The Potsdam Conference, July 1945

Present	Decisions	Tensions
Stalin (USSR), Truman (USA), Churchill (Britain) 17-25 July, Attlee (Britain) 25 July-1 Aug	1 *Germany* a Details of occupation zones finalized. b The Nazi Party to be banned and its leaders tried as war criminals 2 *Reparations* Each power to collect industrial equipment from its own zone. Since its zone was mainly agricultural, the USSR to receive additional reparations from the other zones. 3 *Poland* Western boundary to be along a line created by the Oder and Neisse rivers. **(B)** 4 *Repatriation* Germans living in Poland, Hungary and Czechoslovakia to return to Germany. **(C)**	1 Western suspicions about Soviet intentions in Eastern Europe increased: a In March Stalin had invited non-Communist Polish leaders to Moscow and then imprisoned them. Communists now held key positions in the Polish government. b Far more Germans were to be expelled from Eastern Europe than the Western Allies had expected. **(C)** 2 Truman did not tell Stalin that the USA intended to drop an atomic bomb on Japan.

Post-war tensions, July 1945-1946

The atomic bomb

1 Stalin was angry that Truman had not told him before using the bomb against Japan.

2 Suspicious of the USSR, the USA and Britain then refused to share the secret of how to make an atomic bomb.

3 This infuriated Stalin who feared the USA would use the threat of the atomic bomb to win worldwide power. He ordered his scientists to develop a Soviet bomb.

4 The USA, in turn, saw this as a possible threat.

The 'Iron Curtain' speech, March 1946

Churchill described the frontier of Soviet-occupied Europe as an 'iron curtain'. He said:

1 the countries behind it were **a** subject to Soviet domination **b** losing their democratic freedoms.

2 the USSR aimed to spread Communism world-wide.

Stalin replied a few days later. He

1 accused Churchill of stirring up a war against the USSR

2 said the USSR had to have loyal governments in Eastern Europe to ensure its future safety.

Eastern Europe

Rather than allowing free elections, the USSR began to impose Communist rule on the countries it had occupied (pages 62-63).

Points of tension

Germany

Disputes arose over

1 *Reparations*

a The Western Allies accused the USSR of breaking agreements about what could be taken from Germany as reparations.

b In 1946 they stopped the arrangement, agreed at Potsdam, whereby they gave the USSR reparations from their zones.

2 *Reconstruction*

a The Western Allies wanted to help Germany recover as quickly as possible.

b The USSR wanted a weak Germany.

3 *Democracy*

a The Western Allies wanted elections to be held throughout Germany.

b The USSR blocked moves to do this.

1 What factors made the wartime alliance between the USSR and the Western Allies an uneasy one?

2 On what issues could the USSR and the Western Allies not agree at the Yalta and Potsdam conferences in 1945?

3 What were the main points of disagreement between the USSR and the Western Allies between July 1945 and 1946?

4 a List the ways in which **i** the USSR **ii** the Western Allies were to blame for the breakdown of their alliance.

b Which side was most to blame? Give your reasons.

The Truman Doctrine and the Marshall Plan, 1947-1948

By the end of the next three pages you should be able to describe
a the motives behind b the nature of and c the impact of:
1 the Truman Doctrine
2 the Marshall Plan

The superpowers

With France and Britain economically exhausted by the Second World War, the USA and the USSR emerged as the world's two superpowers. By 1947 Truman and Stalin were beginning to see their countries as rivals.

President Truman believed the USSR

1 stood for a way of life that denied individual freedoms

2 was destroying the possibility of democracy in Eastern Europe

3 aimed **a** to undermine the West **b** to spread Communism worldwide

4 was using its veto in the UN Security Council (page 93) to wreck the UN and chances of world peace.

Stalin believed

1 Capitalism was evil (page 56)

2 the worldwide expansion of American business and trade after the War was an attempt to spread Capitalism and undermine Communism

3 the USA would use the threat of the atomic bomb to enforce its will worldwide.

What did it say?
The USA should support free peoples who were resisting attempts to overwhelm them by armed minorities or by outside forces.

The Truman Doctrine
The name given to the policy announced by President Truman in a speech to Congress, March 1947.

Why did Truman make this policy?
1 In February 1947 Britain said it could no longer afford to support Greece and Turkey (page 60). Both appealed to the USA for money.
2 Truman decided the USA should help. He believed
a if one country fell to Communism, those nearby would be at risk. This became known as the 'domino theory'.
b the USA should adopt a policy of containment. This meant supporting nations in danger of Communist take-over with economic and military aid.

What were its consequences?
1 Greece defeated the Communists and Turkey successfully resisted Soviet pressure.
2 The rivalry between the USA and the USSR increased:
a Truman had publicly stated that the world was divided between two ways of life: the free (non-Communist) and unfree (Communist).
b The USA became committed to 'containment'.
c Stalin set up the Communist Information Bureau (COMINFORM) to link Communist Parties in Eastern Europe, and worldwide, in common action (1947).

Europe in 1947

The USA
1 had withdrawn most troops
2 had contributed money to the United Nations Refugee and Relief Agency to help Europe recover from the War
3 did not plan further European involvement.

Western Europe
All countries were
1 exhausted by the war
2 had very little money
3 had to repair damage done to houses, factories, and communications.

Eastern Europe
All countries
1 faced the same problems as those in Western Europe
2 were dominated by the USSR
3 were being taken over by Communists (page 62).

The USSR
1 wanted to ensure its security
2 intended to keep control of Eastern Europe
3 needed to rebuild houses, factories, roads, and railways destroyed in the War.

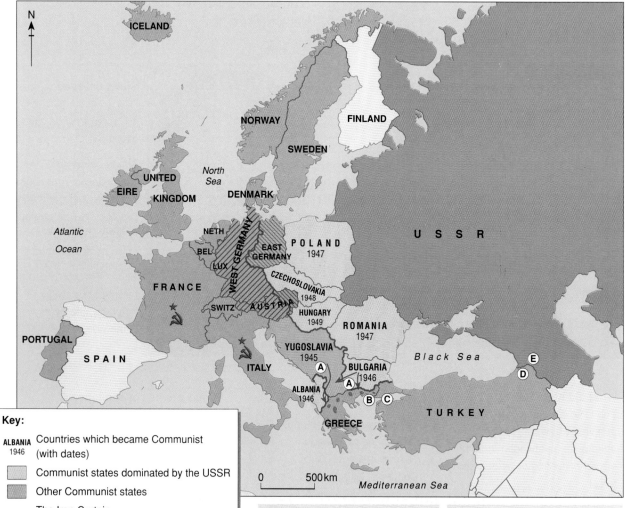

Key:

ALBANIA 1946 — Countries which became Communist (with dates)

Communist states dominated by the USSR

Other Communist states

—— The Iron Curtain

Areas of Germany and Austria under Western control

Areas of Germany and Austria under Soviet control

Communist-held areas in Greece

→ Main supply routes to Greek Communists

★ Western European states with strong Communist parties

Countries which joined the Organization for European Economic Co-operation (OEEC)

Greece
1 Although rejected in elections, Greek Communists were fighting a guerrilla war against the Royalist Government.
2 Britain was supporting the Royalists with money and 40,000 troops.
3 Yugoslavia and Bulgaria were supporting the Communists (**A**).
4 Stalin demanded a naval and military base at Alexandroupolis (**B**).

Turkey
Was under pressure from the USSR.
1 Stalin demanded
a a naval base in the Turkish Straits (**C**)
b the return of land seized by Turkey in 1918 (**D**)
2 Soviet troops threatened the Turkish border (**E**)
3 Britain was supporting Turkey with money

What was it?

A programme of aid to help war-torn Europe to re-equip its factories, and revive agriculture and trade.

1 The USA offered money, equipment and goods to states willing to work together to create economic recovery.

2 In return, they would agree to buy American goods and allow American companies to invest capital in their industries.

3 Marshall invited European states to meet together and decide how to use American aid.

What did the USA aim to achieve?

A strong and properous Europe to bring:

1 economic benefits **a** to the Europeans themselves **b** to the USA through the revival of trade.

2 political benefits. The Americans believed that unless living conditions in Western Europe improved quickly, people might vote for Communist Parties. Prosperous countries would resist the spread of Communism.

The Marshall Plan

Announced, June 1947, by US Secretary of State, General George Marshall.

What were its consequences?

1 Sixteen Western European states set up the Organization for European Economic Co-operation (OEEC) to put the Plan into action.

2 By 1953 the USA had provided 17 billion dollars to help them rebuild their economies and raise their standards of living.

3 Europe became even more firmly divided between East and West. Stalin

a withdrew the USSR from discussions because he **i** mistrusted the motives of the USA **ii** did not wish to show how weak the USSR really was

b prevented interested Eastern European countries, such as Czechoslovakia and Poland, from becoming involved.

c accused the USA of using the Plan to **i** dominate Europe **ii** create a strong West German state hostile to the USSR (page 64).

1 a Why did Truman see the USSR as a threat to American interests in 1947?
b Explain how far you think his fears were justified.
2 Why did the USA put forward the Marshall Plan in 1947?
3 What immediate impact did **a** the Truman Doctrine **b** the Marshall Plan have on superpower relations?

Soviet expansion in Eastern Europe, 1945-1949

By the end of this spread you should be able to:
1 describe Soviet expansion in Eastern Europe,
1945-1949
2 explain how it was achieved

The Iron Curtain
The frontier between Soviet-dominated Europe and the West. During 1947-1948 it was closed on Stalin's orders, ending all tourist and trade contacts between them.

Fig. 1 Soviet domination of Eastern Europe, 1945-1949

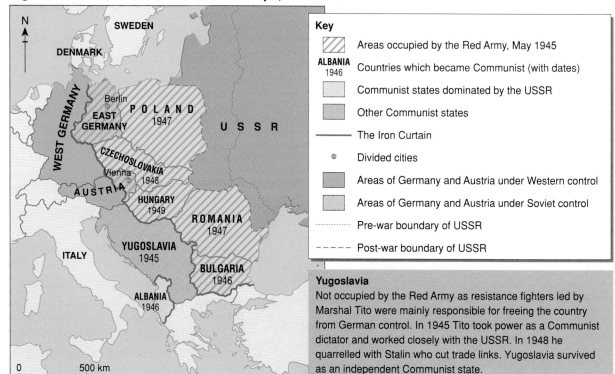

Key

(hatched)	Areas occupied by the Red Army, May 1945
ALBANIA 1946	Countries which became Communist (with dates)
(shaded)	Communist states dominated by the USSR
(shaded)	Other Communist states
——	The Iron Curtain
●	Divided cities
(shaded)	Areas of Germany and Austria under Western control
(shaded)	Areas of Germany and Austria under Soviet control
··········	Pre-war boundary of USSR
– – – –	Post-war boundary of USSR

Yugoslavia
Not occupied by the Red Army as resistance fighters led by Marshal Tito were mainly responsible for freeing the country from German control. In 1945 Tito took power as a Communist dictator and worked closely with the USSR. In 1948 he quarrelled with Stalin who cut trade links. Yugoslavia survived as an independent Communist state.

Case study: Poland

1939 Poland's pre-war leaders set up the Free Polish Government in exile in London.
Polish resistance fighters set up Home Army loyal to Free Polish Government.
1940 In the Katyn Forest, the Red Army massacres 4500 captured Polish army officers likely to lead post-war opposition to Communist rule.
1941 Germans drive Red Army from Poland.
Stalin sends agents to help resistance by Polish Communists loyal to Moscow.
1944 The Red Army enters Poland again.
In Warsaw the nationalist Home Army rises against the Germans.
The Red Army waits for the Germans to destroy the

nationalists before taking Warsaw (Jan 1945).
Soviet agents set up a Communist Provisional Government.
1945 At Yalta (page 57) Stalin agrees that members of the Free Polish Government will join the Provisional Government.
Stalin invites 16 Home Army leaders to Moscow and imprisons them (page 57).
The Provisional Government of National Unity set up. Non-Communist members include Free Poles.
1947 Many members of popular non-Communist parties are imprisoned.
Despite their unpopularity, the Communists win an election.
Communist leader, Bierut (trained in the USSR) becomes head of a one-party Communist state.

Fig. 2 How did the USSR manage to dominate Eastern Europe, 1945-1949?

The events and timing were different in different countries but there was a common pattern:

Step 1 1939-1945. Many Eastern European Communist Parties, though small in numbers (and politically weak), take a lead in resisting German occupation.

Step 2 1944-1945. The Red Army drives German forces west and occupies Eastern Europe. By May 1945, Soviet troops controlled all states but Yugoslavia, Albania, and Greece (fig. 1).

Step 3 1944-1945. Communist Parties welcome the Red Army and receive its support. Pro-German groups were executed or debarred from power. Despite being a minority, Communists exercise strong influence.

Step 4 1944-1945. The emergence of Communist leaders prepared to take orders from Moscow. Many return home after spending part of the War in the USSR.

Step 5 1945. Coalition governments are set up. They include Communists and non-Communists. Since Eastern Europe was mainly agricultural with land worked by peasants, most non-Communists came from the popular political parties representing peasants and small farmers.

Step 6 1946-1949. Backed by Moscow and the Red Army, the Communists gradually force non-Communists out of power. Methods include intimidation, vote rigging, show trials, imprisonment, and executions. By 1949 all countries behind the Iron Curtain are one-party Communist states taking orders from the USSR.

Case study: Czechoslovakia

Until 1938 Czechoslovakia had held free elections and enjoyed a free press. In 1945 the Czechs expected these freedoms to be restored. In 1948 it was a shock to the West when the only pre-war democracy in Eastern Europe, finally turned Communist.

1945 Czech President Benes wants Soviet help in rebuilding the country. In return, he agrees to appoint Communists to run important ministries in charge of the police, communications, and the armed forces.

1946 'National Front' coalition government set up of non-Communists and Communists. Divisions among non-Communists give Communist minority additional influence.

1947 Stalin forbids the Czechs to take part in the USA's Marshall Plan (page 61)

1948 Communist Interior Minister dismisses senior police officers, replacing them with pro-Communists. Non-Communist ministers resign in protest hoping to bring down the Government.

Armed Communists take over the offices of radio, newspapers, and political parties. Police crush student protests.

Leading non-Communist minister, Jan Masaryk, is found dead. Unclear whether it's suicide or murder. Communists win general election after take-over or suppression of all other parties.

Purge of non-Communists in civil service, education, armed forces.

Benes resigns and is replaced by a Communist.

1 Make a timeline to show when the various states of Eastern Europe fell under Communist control.
2 a Use the experience of Poland to illustrate the six steps to Soviet control (fig. 2).
b What other factors were significant in Poland's case?
3 a In what respects was Czechoslovakia different from other Eastern European states?
b Why was the USSR eventually able to take control there?

The Berlin blockade, 1948-1949

By the end of this spread you should be able to:
1 explain the reasons for a the breakdown of
co-operation in Germany between the Western
Allies and the USSR b the Soviet blockade of Berlin
2 describe the Western response to the blockade

Democracy

The USSR

1 gave political authority in its zone to the minority Communists.
2 tried to force the Socialist majority elected to run Berlin city council to merge with the Communists. Socialists refused with Western support.
3 blocked Western attempts to create democracy throughout Germany.

Reconstruction

1 The war left Germany devastated. Food and fuel were scarce. Thousands were homeless.
2 The USA and Britain wanted to help Germany recover its prosperity as quickly as possible.
3 The USSR
a objected because it wanted a weak Germany
b refused to allow its zone to trade with the other three.

From co-operation to conflict

Allied agreements, 1945

1 Divide Germany into four zones of occupation (fig. 1). Run it through a Joint Allied Control Commission.
2 Divide Berlin into four zones. Run it jointly (although it was in the Soviet zone. Fig. 1).
3 Keep Germany as one country:
a remove the Nazis
b hold free elections
c sign a peace treaty with the new government.

Points of conflict, 1945-1947

Reparations

In 1946 the Western Allies stopped giving the USSR reparations from their zones (page 57).

Berlin

1 Within the Soviet zone (fig.1). Soviet troops able to control all access.
2 Western Allies allowed access to their sectors by road, rail, canal, and air 'corridors'.
3 The USSR believed the Western Allies had no right to be in Berlin. It saw their presence as a threat because
a they had a base inside the Soviet zone
b the Capitalist way of life was on show there.
4 Western Allies wanted to be there
a to prevent the USSR controlling the capital
b to observe Soviet activity behind the Iron Curtain.

1 Between 1945 and 1947, what factors contributed to the rise in tension in Germany between the Western Allies and the USSR?
2 Look at the actions taken by the Western Allies and the USSR between January and 24 June 1948. In each case
a Why would one side have objected?
b How would the other have justified its action?
3 Why did Berlin become the focus of the dispute between the USSR and the Western Allies in 1948?

Fig. 1 Germany, 1945-49

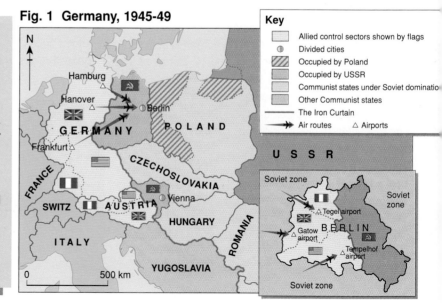

Key
- Allied control sectors shown by flags
- Divided cities
- Occupied by Poland
- Occupied by USSR
- Communist states under Soviet domination
- Other Communist states
- The Iron Curtain
- Air routes   △ Airports

Towards a crisis, 1948

Western Allies

Attitudes

1 Frustrated by the Soviet refusal to co-operate towards

a economic revival, including a much-needed new currency

b setting up of democracy.

2 Decide to develop these in their own zones.

Actions

January Merge US and British zones into one economic unit (the Bizone)

April 1 include Western zones in OEEC and Marshall Plan (page 61)

June 1 Announce plans (with France) to create a West German state

June 18 Introduce new currency into Western zones

June 23 Introduce new currency into Western sectors of Berlin

USSR

Attitudes

Fears that

1 a strong, democratic, united Germany will be hostile

2 any new 'Western' currency will spread into the Soviet zone and undermine Soviet control of economic life.

Actions

March Representative walks out of the Allied Control Commission complaining that Western attitudes make it unworkable

April Troops begin to hold up and search road and rail traffic entering Berlin from the Western zones.

June 23 Introduces its own new currency into Soviet zone including Berlin

June 24 Accuses West of interference in its zone. Cuts off all road, rail, and canal traffic into Western sectors of Berlin.

Blockade and airlift, 1948-1949

Soviet aims

To force the Western Allies

1 to pull out of their sectors by starving West Berlin into surrender

2 to abandon their plans for the separate development of their German zones.

Western options

1 Abandon Berlin. The Americans and British agreed they could not do this because it meant:

a handing two million West Berliners over to Communist rule

b losing their only base behind the Iron Curtain

c opening the way for Soviet domination of Western Germany.

2 Send troops to force the routes open again. This might mean war with the USSR.

3 try to supply West Berlin by air. The USSR could stop this only if it shot down the planes.

The airlift

1 The Americans and British organized a round-the-clock airlift of essential supplies such as food, fuel, medicines.

2 In 11 months a total of 275,000 flights delivered an average of 4000 tonnes of supplies per day.

3 As a warning to the USSR, the USA stationed B-29 aircraft capable of carrying atomic bombs in Britain.

4 Despite shortages and hardship, West Berliners supported the Western Allies and rejected Soviet pressure to become part of one city under a Communist council.

5 On 12 May 1949 the USSR reopened the land routes to Berlin.

The Cold War, 1948-1956

By the end of this spread you should be able to describe and explain:
1 the results of the Berlin blockade
2 the formation of NATO and the

Warsaw Pact
3 superpower involvement in the Korean War
4 the impact of Khrushchev

The results of the Berlin blockade

Two Germanys
Joint control of Germany ended.
In 1949
1 the three Western zones became the Federal Republic of Germany, an anti-Communist state firmly allied to the West.
2 the Soviet zone became the German Democratic Republic, a one-party Communist state under Soviet control.

The Berlin blockade led to

NATO
In 1949 the Western Allies decided to set up the North Atlantic Treaty Organization (NATO) a defensive alliance against the USSR.

Worldwide awareness of the Cold War
It made it clear that
1 Europe was now divided between the superpowers
2 a state of permanent hostility existed between them. This became known as the 'Cold War' because the hostility fell short of actual fighting.

Armed camps

NATO
Background
1 The Western European states feared Soviet aggression but even jointly could not match the USSR's power. They needed the support of the USA.
2 The USA was reluctant to be involved in a European military alliance but was persuaded by **a** Communist take-over of Czechoslovakia **b** Berlin blockade.
Aims A defensive alliance: NATO would fight only if attacked. An attack on one member was to be regarded as an attack on all.

The Warsaw Pact
Background
1 The USSR called NATO an 'aggressive' alliance, although it already had a network of alliances with East European states, giving it virtual control of their armies.
2 The Pact was a counter move to the admission of West Germany to NATO.
Aims Members were to support each other if attacked. Joint command structure set up with Soviet Supreme Commander.

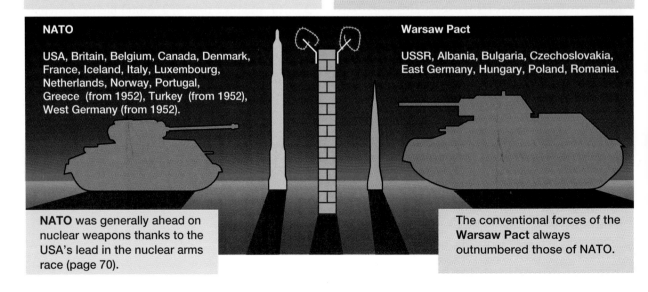

NATO

USA, Britain, Belgium, Canada, Denmark, France, Iceland, Italy, Luxembourg, Netherlands, Norway, Portugal, Greece (from 1952), Turkey (from 1952), West Germany (from 1952).

Warsaw Pact

USSR, Albania, Bulgaria, Czechoslovakia, East Germany, Hungary, Poland, Romania.

NATO was generally ahead on nuclear weapons thanks to the USA's lead in the nuclear arms race (page 70).

The conventional forces of the **Warsaw Pact** always outnumbered those of NATO.

The Korean War

The international background

1 China

a October 1949. Following the defeat of the Nationalists, Chinese Communists, led by Mao Zedong, set up the People's Republic of China.
b The USA
i supported the Nationalists who fled to Taiwan and set up the Republic of China
ii blocked Communist attempts to attack Taiwan
iii used its veto to prevent the People's Republic taking the Nationalists' seat in the UN.
c February 1950. China and the USSR signed a treaty of friendship.

2 US policy

a Events in Eastern Europe and China convinced Truman that Communism was succeeding worldwide.
b Early in 1950 he decided that the USA should
i remain committed to the policy of 'containment' (page 59) **ii** increase its armed forces in order to be able to carry it out.

The superpowers in Korea
See pages 94-95

The outbreak and course of the war
See pages 94-95

The impact of the war
1 In Europe and the USA fear of Communist aggression increased.
2 Congress voted money to increase American forces.
3 Fearing West Germany would be the USSR's next target for attack, the Western powers agreed to allow it to rearm.

The impact of Khrushchev

Nikita Khrushchev
In 1953 the death of Stalin gave the new leaders of the USSR an opportunity to reassess his policies both at home and abroad. From 1955, Khrushchev was largely responsible for changes in Soviet policy. From 1958 he was the USSR's undisputed leader.

Speech at the Twentieth Party Congress, 1956
Khrushchev attacked Stalin for his persecutions, purges and dictatorial rule. Results:
1 A process of 'De-Stalinization' began in the USSR and Eastern Europe.
2 In Poland and Hungary (pages 68-69) this led to violent protest against Soviet rule.
3 Western states were encouraged that Soviet leaders acknowledged the evil of Stalin's regime.
4 Albania and China objected to the speech and to Khrushchev's suggestion that there could be 'different roads to Socialism'. From 1956 the Communist bloc appeared less united.

Peaceful co-existence

1 The idea
Khrushchev changed Communist doctrine by arguing that there need not be a war with the Western powers:
a the Communist system would eventually triumph over the Capitalist system because it was superior
b meanwhile the two systems could exist peacefully side by side
c the USSR would continue to compete with the USA.

2 Results
a Some improvement in East-West relations:
i 1955, the wartime Allies signed a peace treaty with Austria and withdrew their occupying forces
ii it became easier for Western tourists to travel behind the Iron Curtain
iii the 1959 summit conference between Western leaders and Khrushchev.
b East-West suspicions did not die, e.g. in 1955, the Warsaw Pact was formed.
c Serious crises continued to flare up, e.g. Berlin (page 73) and Cuba (pages 74-77).

---

1 a Why was
i NATO set up
ii the Warsaw Pact set up?
b What were their aims?
2 Why did the USA think it was so important to defend South Korea in 1950?
3 What changes did Khrushchev bring about in superpower relationships in the 1950s?

The Hungarian uprising, 1956

By the end of this spread you should be able to describe and explain:
1 a the causes b the events c the consequences of the Hungarian uprising
2 Western reactions to it

Patriotism Hungarians were proud and patriotic, aware of their traditions and long history.

Censorship There was no freedom of expression. The Government controlled the press, theatre, art, and music.

Education Soviet control of education meant that children were taught a Communist version of history that ignored Hungary's close links with Western Europe.

Why Hungarians opposed Soviet control

Secret police The hated State Protection Group (AVO) used terror and torture to suppress criticism of the Government, Communism, or the USSR.

Religion Hungarians were strongly Christian but Communists discouraged religious belief and penalized the Catholic Church. Its leader, Cardinal Minszenty, was imprisoned.

Soviet troops Hungarians objected to the continued presence of Soviet troops, a reminder of Soviet control.

Standard of living There were food shortages which many blamed on the new collective farming. Industrial workers were poorly paid and saw many goods shipped off to the USSR.

Revolt and repression, 1956

October 23
1 Popular demonstrations in Budapest lead to fighting with AVO.
2 Demonstrators want the reforming politician, Imre Nagy, to become Prime Minister.

October 24
1 Nagy named as Prime Minister.
2 Soviet tanks and troops enter Budapest. Fought by freedom fighters and most of Hungarian Army.

October 27
1 Nagy announces new government which includes members of non-Communist parties.
2 Cardinal Minszenty freed from prison.

October 29-31 Soviet forces withdraw from Budapest.

October 29-November 1
Nagy announces
1 the end of one-party rule
2 the complete evacuation of Soviet troops from Hungary
3 Hungary's withdrawal from the Warsaw Pact.

November 4
1 Red Army invades Budapest killing 27,000 Hungarians.
2 Janos Kadar becomes the new Prime Minister.

Why did Khrushchev take such harsh action against Hungary?

1 Although Nagy intended Hungary to remain Communist and friendly with the USSR, on October 29-November 1 he went too far for Soviet leaders. If they were to allow Hungary to become more independent, other Eastern European countries might want to do the same.
2 China strongly advised Khrushchev to deal firmly with Hungary.
3 The Western powers were distracted by the Suez crisis (page 97). They were unlikely to oppose Soviet action.
4 Khrushchev's own position in the Soviet leadership was uncertain. He could not afford to show any weakness.

The Western response

1 Public opinion supported the Hungarians and was horrified by Soviet actions in Budapest.
2 Western Governments were distracted by the Suez crisis and could only protest at Soviet actions.
3 The UN had no impact on events:
a Members of the Security Council wanted to call for a withdrawal of Soviet troops but the USSR used its veto (page 92) to block the resolution.
b The General Assembly set up a Committee of Investigation but the USSR refused to co-operate with it. It also refused to allow the UN Secretary-General, Dag Hammarskjöld, to visit Budapest.

Hungary

1 About 200,000 refugees fled to the West.
2 Nagy was tricked into leaving his refuge in the Yugoslav embassy. In 1958 he was hanged in Moscow.
3 Kadar ruled until 1988. He was loyal to Moscow but eventually allowed some freedom of discussion.

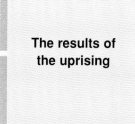

The results of the uprising

East-West relations

1 For a time these were very bitter. The USSR accused the West of supporting Nagy.
2 The Western powers realized that
a despite Stalin's death Soviet leaders were
i determined to keep control of Eastern Europe
ii prepared to be very brutal
b they were powerless to influence Soviet actions behind the Iron Curtain
3 They became more determined to resist any Soviet expansion in Europe.

Eastern Europe

Governments realized that the USSR would not allow them
1 any independence even if they stayed Communist
2 the freedom to follow policies different to Moscow's own.

1 a Why did Hungarians oppose Soviet rule?
2 What factors caused Khrushchev to deal with the 1956 uprising so harshly?
3 What lessons could
a Eastern European countries
b The West
learn about the USSR from its reaction to the Hungarian uprising?

The nuclear arms race, 1945-1963

By the end of this spread you should be able to describe:
1 the nuclear arms race, 1945-1963
2 civilian attitudes and responses to the nuclear threat

Why was there a nuclear arms race?

Strategic superiority Each side wanted a weapons system that would give it an advantage over the other one. This meant
1 developing new and more powerful weapons
2 trying to build up more of each type of weapon than the other side possessed. For example, when the 'Sputnik' was launched, American experts calculated (wrongly) that the USSR would soon have many more missiles than the USA. The USA would then suffer from a 'missile gap'. It, therefore, poured money into rocket research.

Costs
1 Both Khrushchev and the new American President, Eisenhower, needed to cut defence expenditure.
2 Given the huge destruction they could cause, nuclear weapons were cheaper to produce than conventional weapons.
3 It was more cost-effective for both sides to build up nuclear weapons than to pay for large armies with conventional weapons.

Deterrence
1 The aim of each side was not to launch a nuclear attack but to deter, or prevent, the other side from doing so.
2 Each realized that in a nuclear war they would both suffer appalling destruction. Once ICBMs were invented, it was certain that both could retaliate in the event of an attack.
3 The idea was to have so many nuclear weapons that they could not all be destroyed if the other side were to strike first: the enemy would not dare to strike first for fear of retaliation.

Landmarks in the nuclear arms race, 1945-1960

1945 USA tests and drops the first atomic (A) bombs
1949 USSR tests an A bomb.
1952 USA tests its first hydrogen (H) bomb.
1953 USSR tests its first H bomb.
1957 USSR
  1 tests an Intercontinental Ballistic Missile (ICBM) capable of carrying an H bomb from the USSR to the USA
  2 puts the space satellite 'Sputnik' into orbit.
1958 USA
  1 places Intermediate Range Ballistic Missiles (IRBMs) targeted on USSR in NATO countries. Both sides now capable of direct attacks on each other's cities.
  2 launches its own satellite.
1960 USA launches first nuclear-powered submarine capable of firing Polaris missile with atomic warhead from underwater.

1 Explain the meaning of the terms
a 'deterrence'
b 'missile gap'
c 'strategic superiority'.
2 What did the superpowers hope to achieve by conducting a nuclear arms race?
3 Describe the different ways in which civilians reacted to the nuclear arms race.

Prestige Many civilians on both sides saw the arms race, and the space race which became associated with it, as a test of the relative strengths of Capitalism and Communism. For example, when the USSR launched first 'Sputnik' then the first manned space flight (1961)
1 Khrushchev boasted about Soviet superiority.
2 Americans believed that
a they had fallen behind in the arms race and were vulnerable to Soviet attack
b their country had lost prestige.

Protection
1 In the West, governments gave civilians instructions about what to do in the event of a nuclear attack.
2 Some people, mainly in the USA, had specially designed fall-out shelters built in their gardens.

How did civilians react to the nuclear threat?

Protest Most civilians feared the consequences of a nuclear attack and hated nuclear weapons. In some, but not all, countries this led to protests.
1 In the USA there was little protest in the 1950s because in the McCarthy era (page 145) people feared doing anything which might lead them to be accused of Communist sympathies.
2 In the USSR there was no protest because it was not allowed.
3 In Europe, in the late 1950s, anti-nuclear groups grew up such as Germany's Campaign against Nuclear Death and Britain's Campaign for Nuclear Disarmament (CND).

The search for disarmament

Hopes dashed, 1955
1 Since 1946 proposals made by both sides had collapsed. In 1955 hopes for disarmament were high because
a East-West relations had improved
b both Eisenhower and Khrushchev wanted to achieve arms reduction.
2 The USSR proposed
a reduction of armed forces
b eventual abolition of atomic weapons
c an international inspection system to supervise this.
3 The USA wanted a stronger inspection system. It offered to allow Soviet planes to use aerial photography over the USA to check on weapons reductions, if the USSR would allow it to do the same.
4 The USSR could not agree to this 'open skies' proposal. The USA rejected Soviet alternatives as inadequate.

Failure again, 1960 The Paris Summit, arranged during Khrushchev's successful visit to the USA in 1959, was to deal with arms reduction. It collapsed because of the U-2 incident (page 72).

The Test Ban Treaty, 1963
1 The USSR, USA, and Britain agreed to carry out no further nuclear tests unless they were underground. Tests in the atmosphere, underwater, or in space were banned.

CND said that:
1 nuclear weapons were immoral because they caused **a** horrific injuries such as radiation sickness **b** destruction, death, and injury on such a vast scale.
2 the testing of nuclear weapons created radioactive fall-out harmful to both people and the environment.
3 Britain should give a lead to the world by abandoning nuclear weapons, even if other countries refused to do so. This was called unilateral nuclear disarmament.

2 France and China refused to sign and conducted further tests.

Why was the Test Ban Treaty signed?
1 It raised fewer difficulties because it dealt with one small part of the nuclear issue, not the whole disarmament problem.
2 Both the Soviet and Western governments wanted to respond to public opinion which had been concerned about the environmental effects of nuclear tests since 1954 when the crew of the Japanese fishing boat Lucky Dragon had been badly affected by fall-out after a test in the Pacific.
3 US President Kennedy and Khrushchev were anxious to build on improved East-West relations following the 1962 Cuban missile crisis (page 74-77)

The U-2 incident, 1960, and the building of the Berlin Wall, 1961

By the end of this spread you should be able to describe:
a the reasons for b the results of
1 the U-2 incident
2 the building of the Berlin Wall

The U-2 incident, 1960

Background

The U-2 spy-plane
1 A Lockheed aircraft developed for the USA's Central Intelligence Agency (CIA). First used in 1956.
2 Able to fly
a at very high altitudes (over 20 kilometres) out of range of Soviet fighters
b for very long distances (over 6000 kms).
3 Equipped with powerful cameras and radio receivers it could detect Soviet long-range bomber bases and missile sites.
4 Flights over the USSR were made between US air-bases in Pakistan and Norway.

The Paris Summit
1 To be held in May 1960 between the leaders of the USSR, USA, France, and Britain.
2 Planned to be a major step forward in East-West relations following Khrushchev's successful visit to the USA in 1959.
3 The main items for discussion were
a the future of Germany
b nuclear arms reduction.
4 Despite a desire for better East-West relations, the Summit faced problems:
a the Western powers and the USSR were unlikely to agree about a possible reunification of Germany
b Khrushchev was under severe criticism from
i the Chinese and ii some of his own generals for holding discussions with the West.

Consequences of U-2 incident

1 Paris Summit abandoned.
2 East-West tensions increased.

1960	Events
May 1	1 A U-2 plane flown by Gary Powers is brought down over the Ural Mountains by a Soviet missile.
	2 Powers is captured. Films and tapes are recovered from the plane.
May 5	1 The USSR announces the shooting down of the U-2.
	2 President Eisenhower denies it was spying.
May 7	Khrushchev announces Powers will be put on trial for spying.
May 11	Eisenhower forced to admit U-2 was spying.
May 14	1 The delegations arrive in Paris for the Summit.
	2 Khrushchev refuses to attend Summit unless
	a all U-2 flights are cancelled
	b Eisenhower apologises.
May 16	1 Eisenhower cancels the U-2 flights but refuses to apologise.
	2 Khrushchev walks out of the Summit.

3 Khrushchev showed Communist world, especially China, that he could be tough with the West. It is possible that he played up the U-2 incident in order to do this.

1 What does the U-2 incident tell you about the nature of superpower relations in 1960? Make a list of points and write a sentence or two about each one.
2 a What were Khrushchev's aims in Berlin in the late 1950s?
b Describe his attempts to achieve these aims.
c Why did he consent to the building of the Berlin Wall in 1961?

The Berlin Wall, 1961

Background

Berlin

1 East Berlin

a not prosperous

b under strict Communist rule.

2 West Berlin

a prosperous with the help of US aid

b its cinemas, shops, etc attract visitors from East Berlin. The USSR saw it as a Capitalist infection in the heart of East Germany.

c provides an easy escape route from East to West Germany for some 250,000 refugees each year.

Western aims

1 Prevent the USSR from gaining permanent control of East Germany.

2 The wartime Allies to sign a peace treaty with a united democratic Germany.

Soviet aims

1 Maintain control over East Germany.

2 Make the Western powers recognize it as an independent state.

3 Stem the flood of refugees from East to West Germany by gaining control of the access routes from West Berlin to West Germany. This was becoming urgent. The refugees were mainly skilled and professional who were badly needed in East Germany.

Soviet demands, 1958

1 Khrushchev

a demanded that the three Western occupying powers should **i** recognize the German Democratic Republic (GDR) **ii** withdraw their troops from West Berlin **iii** hand their access routes over to the GDR.

b said that unless they did this within six months he would **i** sign a separate peace treaty with the GDR **ii** hand East Berlin over to it.

2 The Western powers refused. Khrushchev backed down.

The Berlin Crisis, 1961

June Vienna Summit.

1 Khrushchev attempts to put pressure on the young and inexperienced new US President, John Kennedy. Again demands withdrawal of Western powers' occupying forces from West Berlin within six months.

2 Kennedy replies that the USA will protect the freedom of West Berlin.

July 17 The Western powers reject Khrushchev's Vienna demands.

July 23 The flow of refugees from East Germany to the West has reached 1000 a day. The East German government attempts to stem it by introducing travel restrictions.

July 25 Kennedy

1 repeats the USA's support for West Berlin

2 announces an increase in arms spending.

August 13-22 On the orders of Khrushchev and the East German government, a barbed wire barrier is put up across Berlin, followed by a wall of concrete blocks.

▶ *Consequences*

1 Berlin

a Is physically divided.

b Free access from East to West is ended.

c Many families are split.

2 Refugees

The flow almost ceased.

3 Kennedy

a accepted the Soviet action, although it broke the four-power agreement on Berlin

b refused proposals for US troops to tear down the Wall, fearing this was likely to provoke armed conflict

c had to accept that this made him look weak.

4 Khrushchev

a lost face by failing to remove the Western powers from Berlin

b believed that Kennedy's response showed that he was weak.

5 East-West relations

Tensions increased. Both sides started to test more powerful nuclear weapons.

The Cuban missile crisis 1

By the end of the next two spreads you should be able to describe and explain:
1 the events of the Cuban Revolution and American reactions to it

2 a the causes b the events c the consequences of the Cuban missile crisis
3 the roles of Kennedy and Khrushchev in it

The USA and Cuba

The Cuban revolution, 1959

1 Fidel Castro seizes power from the American-backed dictator, Batista, who has run a corrupt and unpopular regime.
2 Castro and his followers aim to
a improve Cuban prosperity, especially of peasants working on the land and in the sugar mills of American-owned companies
b end corruption and terror in Cuban politics
c help oppressed people in other countries in the region.
3 Castro
a appoints Communists to the Government
b signs a trade agreement with the USSR. In return for Cuban sugar, the USSR will provide oil, machinery and economic aid (1959)
c nationalizes all American companies (July 1961).

The American response

1 The USA was hostile to Castro because
a as the dominant power in the region it i expected to control governments in the Caribbean and South America ii feared Castro's ideas might spread
b although Castro himself was not yet a Communist, he had Communist supporters
c he was receiving Soviet support
d his policies threatened American companies.
2 The USA decided to
a refuse to buy Cuban sugar (July 1960)
b end all trade with Cuba (Oct 1960)
c cut off diplomatic relations (Jan 1961)
d support Cuban exiles in an attempt to dislodge Castro.

1 In Florida, the CIA forms a group of exiled Cuban politicians into a committee to take over from Castro.

The Bay of Pigs operation, April 1961

A force of Cuban exiles, backed by the US Central Intelligence Agency (CIA), failed in an attempt to invade Cuba and depose Castro. Although the Americans denied involvement in the operation, which had been set up under President Eisenhower and then approved by Kennedy, it was a humiliation for the new President.

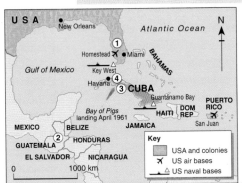

2 In Guatemala, the CIA trains a force of Cuban exiles.

3 1,400 exiles land, supported by US bombers flown by Cubans.

4 Castro's forces easily defeat the invaders, capturing over 1,200.

Communist Cuba

1 Castro
a declares himself a Communist (Dec 1961)
b asks the USSR to provide arms in order to defend Cuba against a possible American attack following the Bays of Pigs failure.
2 Khrushchev
a agrees to provide arms
b announces this publicly (Sept 1961)
c secretly decides to turn Cuba into a Soviet nuclear missile base.

The American response

1 Increased fear in the USA at
a having a Soviet-backed Communist state on its doorstep
b the spread of Communism in its own region.
2 Kennedy
a says the USA will isolate Cuba
b warns the USSR not to put nuclear missiles in Cuba.

Superpower tension

By 1962 this was high as a result of:
1 Kennedy's commitment of the USA to fresh efforts in the defence of freedom (Jan 1961).
2 The Berlin crisis and the building of the Wall (page 73).
3 The acceleration of the arms race which followed.

Why did Khrushchev send missiles to Cuba?

1 No one is certain. He ran a high risk that the USA would discover the missiles but probably
a hoped they would be in place before this happened
b calculated Kennedy would make a weak response.
2 Possible motives were to
a defend Cuba following the Bay of Pigs operation
b bargain for the removal of US missiles in Turkey
c bargain for the Western powers to leave Berlin
d catch up with the USA in the arms race by placing missiles where they could hit their targets more accurately
e score points off Kennedy by placing missiles on the USA's 'doorstep'.

1962

August	US spy-planes observe Soviet weapons in Cuba.
September	Khrushchev secretly starts to send nuclear missiles to Cuba.
September 4	Kennedy warns the USSR not to put nuclear missiles in Cuba.
September 11	Soviet government assures the USA it will not base nuclear missiles outside the USSR.
October 14	American U-2 spy-plane photographs nuclear missile launch sites.
October 16	Kennedy sets up a special committee to decide what to do.
October 22	Kennedy announces a naval blockade of Cuba.

What was Kennedy's reaction?

The problem
1 Kennedy wanted to remove all the missiles from Cuba.
2 His advisers told him he had ten days before the missiles were ready for use.

The choices
There were three possible courses of action:
1 A nuclear strike on the sites. But the USSR would almost certainly strike back.
2 A conventional bombing raid followed by an invasion. This would almost certainly lead to fighting with Soviet troops already on Cuba and start a war.
3 A naval blockade to stop the USSR from transporting more missiles to Cuba and to force them to remove those already there. This carried the least risk of war.

The decision
1 A naval blockade. All ships carrying weapons to Cuba to be turned back.
2 Armed forces placed on alert.
3 The USSR was told that the USA would retaliate to any missile launched from Cuba against a Western nation.

The Cuban missile crisis 2

The crisis unfolds

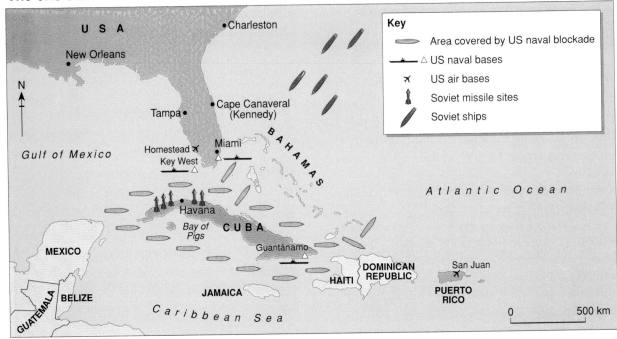

The Cuban missile crisis, 1962

October 22
On American television Kennedy
1 announces naval blockade of Cuba
2 says he cannot accept Communist missiles in an area known to have a special relationship with the USA
3 calls Soviet actions 'provocative'.

October 23
Soviet government says
1 the USSR is simply helping Cuba to defend itself
2 the USA is
a interfering with Cuba's affairs
b engaging in piracy by stopping ships
c pushing the world towards nuclear war.

October 24
Soviet vessels reach US blockade and stop. One oil tanker is allowed through unsearched. The rest turn back.

October 26
Khrushchev sends a letter to Kennedy saying that the USSR could remove the missiles if the USA
1 lifts its blockade
2 guarantees not to invade Cuba.

October 27
1 Khrushchev sends a second letter adding as a third condition that the USA should remove its missiles from Turkey. Kennedy cannot accept this.
2 An American U-2 is shot down over Cuba. Kennedy is urged to take military action, but resists.
3 Another U-2 flies into Soviet airspace. Kennedy apologises publicly.
4 Kennedy
a decides to agree to the terms of Khrushchev's first letter and to ignore the second one.
b secretly sends message to Moscow that he will withdraw US missiles from Turkey.

October 28
Khrushchev agrees to remove missiles from Cuba.

Khrushchev

1 claimed he had achieved his aim of preventing an American invasion of Cuba

2 was attacked by China for backing down in the face of American threats

3 lost face at home because of his misjudgement. The episode probably contributed to his downfall two years later.

Kennedy increased his reputation at home and worldwide by
1 managing to avoid a war
2 forcing Khrushchev to back down.

The consequences of the crisis

Superpower relations

1 Realising how close to war they had come, and the difficulty of communicating quickly in a crisis, Kennedy and Khrushchev agreed to set up a hotline between the Kremlin and the White House.
2 Both leaders attempted to improve relations. The Nuclear Test Ban Treaty (page 71) was one result.

Cuba

1 Although the USSR had been forced to remove its missiles, it continued to try to influence countries in the Caribbean and South America.
2 Cuba remained a Communist country dependent on Soviet aid and protection.

1 What were the USA's aims in dealing with Cuba after 1959?
2 Why did Kennedy believe he had to make the USSR remove its missiles from Cuba?
3 a List those actions taken during the missile crisis by **i** the USA **ii** the USSR which appeared to make the crisis more serious.
b In each case explain why this was so.
4 a List those actions taken during the missile crisis by **i** Kennedy **ii** Khrushchev which helped to resolve the crisis.
b In each case explain how it did this.

The war in Vietnam 1

By the end of the next two spreads you should be able to describe:
1 the background to the conflict in Vietnam
2 the reasons for American involvement
3 the nature of the War
4 its impact on a Vietnam b the USA
5 a the causes b the consequences of American defeat

Vietnam in 1963

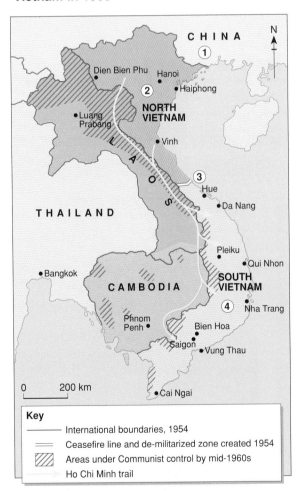

Key
— International boundaries, 1954
═ Ceasefire line and de-militarized zone created 1954
▨ Areas under Communist control by mid-1960s
→ Ho Chi Minh trail

The USA
a until 1954 supported the French against the Vietminh with money and equipment.
b 1954-1960, sent aid, equipment and military advisers to South Vietnam.
c 1960-1963, Kennedy steadily increased the amount of aid and number of 'military advisers', which rose from 900 to 11,000.

The **USSR** gave aid to North Vietnam.

1 China sent aid to the Vietcong via North Vietnam.

2 North Vietnam Was ruled by the Communist Vietminh leader, Ho Chi Minh, who
a aimed to unite Vietnam under his rule
b supplied the Vietcong along the Ho Chi Minh trail through Laos.

3 The Geneva Settlement, 1954
a gave independence to Vietnam, Laos, and Cambodia, all previously ruled by France.
b ended the war in Vietnam between the French and the Communist Vietminh.
c temporarily divided Vietnam into two countries, North and South, with the border along the 17th parallel.
d recognized the Vietminh as the government of the North and a French and American-backed régime as the government of the South.

4 South Vietnam
a Ruled by the unpopular Ngo Diem.
b Diem was opposed in a civil war by the National Liberation Front (NLF) and the Vietcong, its Communist guerrilla force.
c In 1963 Diem was deposed and replaced by a series of military rulers all hostile to the Communist North.

Why was the USA involved in Vietnam in 1963?
1 To 'contain' the spread of Communism.
2 To prevent what Eisenhower called the 'domino theory' coming true. He believed that if Vietnam became Communist, neighbouring countries would each fall in turn.

Steps to greater US involvement, 1964-1965

Step 1 In 1963 the Vietcong managed to take over about 40% of the rural areas of South Vietnam. Johnson decided to increase American support but still without sending combat troops. As a result
1 the Vietcong lost ground again
2 Ho Chi Minh sent units of the North Vietnamese Army to help them.

Step 2 In August 1964 North Vietnamese torpedo boats attacked US destroyers in the Gulf of Tonkin. This
1 gave Johnson the excuse to attack North Vietnamese naval bases
2 enabled him to persuade Congress to give him a free hand in Vietnam.

Step 3 In 1965 Johnson
1 started to bomb North Vietnam to try to end its support for the Vietcong.
2 ordered American combat troops into action for the first time because
a the army of South Vietnam was poorly led and weak
b he believed that the full commitment of American troops would be a quick and certain way of defeating the Vietcong.

The war in Vietnam, 1965-1973

— International boundaries
= Ceasefire line and demilitarized zone created 1954
Areas under Communist control by mid-1960s
Areas under Communist control by 1973
Ho Chi Minh trail
Towns attacked by Vietcong in Tet offensive, 1968
Major US bases
US air raids from 1965

Bombing

1 In March 1965 the US launched 'Operation Rolling Thunder', a bombing offensive against North Vietnam. The aims were
a to end North Vietnamese support for the Vietcong by destroying ports, bases, and supply lines.
b to do this without committing American troops to the war on the ground.
2 Although 'Rolling Thunder' failed, the USA continued to bomb the North heavily.
3 Bombing was also used extensively against the Vietcong in the South.
4 By 1970 the USA had dropped more bombs on Vietnam than on all previous targets throughout the twentieth century.

Weapons and tactics

1 The USA
a fought a 'high-tech' war relying on the latest technology, including **i** B-52 strategic bombers **ii** helicopters **iii** napalm to burn houses and forests in order to flush out the enemy **iv** defoliants, such as 'Agent Orange', to destroy forests which the enemy might use as cover.
b attempted to defeat an elusive enemy using 'search and destroy' operations.
2 The Vietcong
a fought a mainly 'low-tech' war using very successful guerrilla tactics.
b fought some set piece battles using modern equipment such as rockets, tanks and fighters, supplied by the USSR and China.

The 'Tet Offensive', 1968

1 During the Tet religious festival, the Vietcong made a surprise guerrilla attack on major South Vietnamese towns and American bases.
2 The attack
a showed the Vietcong could strike in the heart of American-held territory
b caused loss of American military morale
c suggested to the American public that the War was unwinnable and fuelled criticism of the USA's involvement.

The war in Vietnam 2

The impact of the War

Social

1 In the South 3000 people a month were killed by American and Vietcong action. In the North thousands more were killed and injured by American bombing. Altogether, two million Vietnamese were killed.

2 Civilians suffered brutal treatment including torture, rape and murder. In 1967, at My Lai, American troops massacred 300 civilians.

3 Villages and communities were destroyed by the fighting.

Political

In rural areas support for the Vietcong steadily increased in response to
1 the Vietcong ability to place its agents in villages to help villagers and win them over
2 fear of Vietcong attacks and punishments
3 dislike of the South Vietnamese government and army.

Economic

1 A poor country was made poorer by the widespread destruction of fields, animals, crops, and forests.

2 The Vietnamese were soon unable to grow enough to feed the population.

On Vietnam

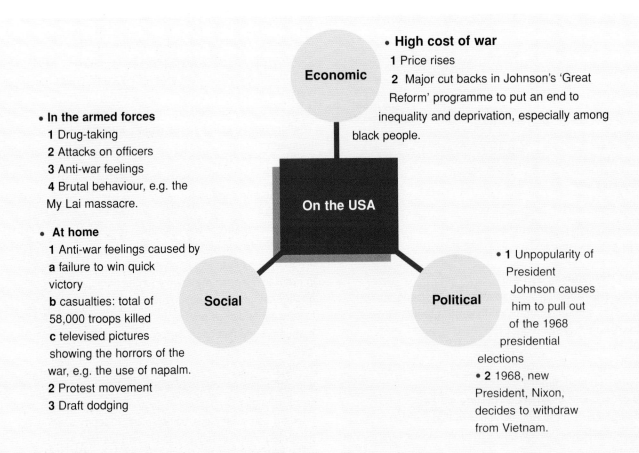

Economic

- **High cost of war**
  1 Price rises
  2 Major cut backs in Johnson's 'Great Reform' programme to put an end to inequality and deprivation, especially among black people.

- **In the armed forces**
  1 Drug-taking
  2 Attacks on officers
  3 Anti-war feelings
  4 Brutal behaviour, e.g. the My Lai massacre.

- **At home**
  1 Anti-war feelings caused by
  a failure to win quick victory
  b casualties: total of 58,000 troops killed
  c televised pictures showing the horrors of the war, e.g. the use of napalm.
  2 Protest movement
  3 Draft dodging

On the USA

Social

Political

- **1** Unpopularity of President Johnson causes him to pull out of the 1968 presidential elections
- **2** 1968, new President, Nixon, decides to withdraw from Vietnam.

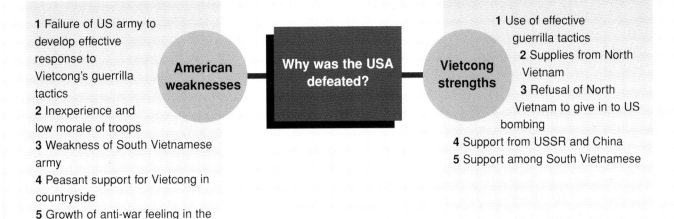

American weaknesses

1 Failure of US army to develop effective response to Vietcong's guerrilla tactics
2 Inexperience and low morale of troops
3 Weakness of South Vietnamese army
4 Peasant support for Vietcong in countryside
5 Growth of anti-war feeling in the USA

Why was the USA defeated?

Vietcong strengths

1 Use of effective guerrilla tactics
2 Supplies from North Vietnam
3 Refusal of North Vietnam to give in to US bombing
4 Support from USSR and China
5 Support among South Vietnamese

1968	Johnson decides to **1** end bombing of North Vietnam **2** open peace negotiations with the North
1969	Nixon decides to **1** start to withdraw US troops from Vietnam **2** hand over the fighting to the South Vietnamese army **3** continue to support the South while US troops are withdrawn
1970	US invades Cambodia to try to destroy North Vietnamese bases there
1971	Failure of South Vietnamese Army's attempt to cut Ho Chi Minh trail in Laos
1972	**1** North attacks South. Nixon orders bombing of the North to check the advance. **2** Break-through in peace negotiations
1973	**1** Cease-fire agreed by the USA, the two Vietnams and the Vietcong **2** Withdrawal of last US troops
1974	War continues in Vietnam despite ceasefire
1975	Communist troops victorious in South Vietnam, Laos and Cambodia
1976	Vietnam united in a single Socialist Republic

What were the consequences of the USA's failure?

1 The fall of South Vietnam.
2 The reunification of Vietnam as a Communist state.
3 Communist take-overs in Cambodia and Laos but not Thailand which remained a US ally.
4 Nixon announced the end of the Truman Doctrine (page 59). Americans lost confidence in their ability to 'contain' Communism and became hostile to military involvement abroad.
5 Some 700,000 veterans suffered psychological effects from fighting in the war.

1 Explain why
a the USA was involved in Vietnam before 1965.
b President Johnson decided i to send combat forces ii to attack North Vietnam.
2 a List the methods and weapons used by American forces to fight the war in Vietnam.
b What was the impact of these on Vietnam itself?
3 Why was the USA unable to win the war in Vietnam?
a Make a list of reasons.
b Write a few sentences to explain each one.
4 What effect did the Vietnam War have on the life and attitudes of Americans
a at the time
b afterwards?

Czechoslovakia, 1968

By the end of this spread you should be able to describe and explain:
1 the causes of Czech dissatisfaction in 1968
2 the policies of Alexander Dubcek
3 a the causes b the consequences of Soviet reactions to events in Czechoslovakia.

Worker democracy
Many workers wanted to have more say in the way their factories were run.

Secret police
People wanted an end to their powers to suppress criticism and to rule their lives by terror.

Freedom of expression
People wanted to be free to discuss ideas openly and to express their opinions in the press and on the radio.

Why did the Czechs oppose Soviet control?

1 Since 1948 Czechoslovakia had been run as a Communist police state loyal to Moscow.
2 Although little opposition ever showed itself, many Czechs wanted changes.

Political parties
People wanted the freedom to set up political parties and to vote freely in elections.

The economy
The USSR forced Czech industry to produce materials such as steel which it needed. Its policies prevented factories from producing consumer goods for sale at home and abroad. As a result
1 the Czechs had a low standard of living
2 many people, including some members of the Government, wanted to change the way industry was run.

The 'Prague Spring', 1968

Alexander Dubcek

New leaders
1 In 1968 the Czechoslovak Communist Party decided reforms were needed. It removed President Novotny who had ruled for over ten years.
2 a Alexander Dubcek became Party Secretary
b General Jan Svoboda became President of the Republic.

Aims Dubcek wanted to
1 make changes inside Czechoslovakia which would
a improve people's standard of living
b give them more freedom.
2 keep the country
a Communist
b closely allied to the USSR
c within the Warsaw Pact.

Reforms
Dubcek's government
1 removed some State controls over industry
2 allowed public meetings and discussion
3 relaxed press censorship
4 also proposed to
a allow political parties to be formed
b revive parliament
c abolish press censorship.

The Soviet response

1968

June	Soviet tanks remain in Czechoslovakia after Warsaw Pact military exercises
July	The 'Group of Five' Warsaw Pact members (USSR, Poland, Hungary, East Germany, Bulgaria) warn Dubcek that his planned reforms will remove power from the Communist Party.
August	1 Group of Five invade Czechoslovakia (August 20) and take control. 2 Dubcek arrested and taken to Moscow. 3 Svoboda goes to Moscow. Refuses to negotiate without Dubcek
September -October	Dubcek and Svoboda agree 1 to reverse most of their reforms 2 to allow Soviet troops to be stationed in Czechoslovakia
1969	1 USSR works with hardliners in the Czechoslovak Communist Party to remove Dubcek and his supporters from power. 2 New government installed under Gustav Husak (April).

East-West relations

1 Western powers protested at the Soviet actions.
2 Moves towards détente between the USA and the USSR (page 88) continued after only a slight break.

The Brezhnev Doctrine

1 The Soviet leader, Brezhnev, announced that if forces 'hostile to Socialism' tried to turn a Communist country towards Capitalism it was the duty of other Communist countries to intervene.
2 This idea caused a split in the Communist world. It angered
a countries such as Yugoslavia, Romania, and China
b Communist parties in the West

Why did the USSR decide to invade?

Soviet leaders believed Dubcek's reforms threatened their control of Eastern Europe in two ways:

1 Individual freedoms They thought
a Dubcek would be unable to control demands for even more freedom of expression and political freedom.
b if these were granted in Czechoslovakia, people in other Eastern European states would demand them too.
c if granted, these freedoms would eventually destroy the authority of Communist parties in these countries.

2 New alliances
a Yugoslavia was already an independent Communist state (page 62). Romania was refusing to attend Warsaw Pact meetings. Both countries were offering support to Dubcek.
b If Czechoslovakia formed an alliance with Yugoslavia and Romania the unity of the Communist bloc behind the Iron Curtain would be broken.

Czechoslovakia
1 The country returned to strict Communist rule.
2 Many people continued to believe in the changes Dubcek had tried to introduce.

Eastern Europe
People in Eastern European countries were
1 reminded that the USSR would allow no variation from strict Communist rule
2 concerned that the Warsaw Pact forces could be used against one of its own members
3 disliked the Brezhnev Doctrine.

> **What were the results of Soviet intervention?**

1 What were the reasons for Czech opposition to Soviet control in 1968?
2 What were Dubcek's aims?
3 Explain why the USSR decided to invade Czechoslovakia.
4 What do the events in Czechoslovakia in 1968 tell you about the nature of Soviet control there?

'Solidarity' in Poland, 1980-1990

By the end of this spread you should be able to:
1 explain the background to Polish discontent in 1980
2 describe Solidarity's ***a*** *aims* ***b*** *achievements in 1980*
3 describe the part played by Solidarity in the collapse of Communist rule in Poland

The background

Polish attitudes

1 *National feeling* was strong. Poles wanted their country to be free to make its own policies even if it was closely allied with the USSR.
2 *The Catholic Church*. Despite Soviet disapproval, this was strong in Poland. The Church wanted the freedom to
a preach as it wished
b run its own schools.
3 *Living standards*. Poles wanted an end to shortages of food and other goods.
4 *Freedom of expression.* Poles, backed by the Church, wanted a free press and the right to discuss issues openly.

The rule of Gierek, 1971-1978 Gierek became Party leader after widespread riots against price rises.
1 He aimed to introduce some reforms while keeping firm control.
2 Economic reforms led to some improvements in living standards; but Poland went further into debt and food shortages continued.
3 In 1976 police angered Poles by causing deaths and injuries while putting down strikes against proposed prices rises.

Pope John Paul II In 1978 the Polish Cardinal Wajtyla was elected Pope.
1 This caused a surge in Polish nationalist, and anti-Government, feeling.
2 The Church became an even stronger focus of opposition to the Government.

Solidarity Shipyard workers, led by Lech Walesa in Gdansk (pre-war Danzig), formed a movement called 'Solidarity'. It campaigned for
1 workers to have the right to form trade unions independent of the State

2 the Government to
a grant Poles more freedom
b improve standards of living and working.

Solidarity, 1980

Strikes
1 In 1980 there were more food shortages and price rises as the Government failed to improve Poland's economy.
2 In protest, workers in the shipyards along the Baltic coast went on strike.
3 The Government decided to negotiate. It feared the use of force would inflame the whole population.

The agreement
1 The workers agreed to accept
a the leading role of the Communist Party in Poland
b the Socialist economic system
c Poland's links with the USSR and the other East European Communist countries.
2 The Government agreed to
a the right to strike
b the right to form independent trade unions
c more open discussion of Government policy
d a relaxation of censorship
e improved wages and working conditions.

What was the significance of Solidarity's achievement?
1 An authoritarian Communist régime which did not allow opposition had been forced to make concessions by
a the action of industrial workers backed by popular opinion
b the use of non-violent methods.
2 The Communist government
a was incapable of solving Poland's economic difficulties
b had lost the confidence of the people
c did not dare to use force against the strikers.
3 The USSR with Gorbachev as leader (page 87),
a still wanted one-party Communist rule in Poland
b was unwilling to use force to maintain control.

The road to democracy, 1980-1989

Away from democracy ⬅ ➡ **Towards democracy**

Solidarity set up as an independent trade union with Walesa as its leader. Millions of workers join.

1981

Solidarity threatens its agreement with the Government by demanding free elections.

The USSR
1 decides that Polish military rule is the only way to maintain a one-party system,
2 backs the appointment of General Jaruzelski as the new Polish leader.

Jaruzelski
1 imposes martial law,
2 arrests Walesa and other union leaders.

Jaruzelski
1 bans Solidarity,
2 releases Walesa.

1982

Jaruzelski
1 ends martial law,
2 refuses to legalize Solidarity again.

1983

POLAND

1 The Church and Solidarity provide the focus of opposition to the Government.
2 The Government struggles to improve Poland's economy.

1984-1987

Severe economic crisis and workers strikes.

1988

1 Explain how the Poles' discontent with their Communist government built up in the 1970s.
2 **a** Describe the part played by Solidarity in bringing about change in Poland
i in 1980
ii 1981-1988
iii 1989-1990
b How did its role change between 1980 and 1990?
3 **a** How did the Communist government try to keep control in Poland between 1980 and 1989?
b Why did it fail?

1 Solidarity triumphs in elections. Communists do badly.
2 Leaders of Solidarity refuse to join the Communist government.
3 Jaruzelski forced to appoint a non-Communist Prime Minister.

In return for Solidarity's help in solving the country's problems, Jaruzelski agrees to
1 legalize Solidarity,
2 increase press freedom,
3 hold elections while reserving a majority of seats for Communists.

1989

Walesa elected President of Poland in free national elections.

1990

The collapse of the Soviet Empire in Eastern Europe

By the end of this spread you should be able to:
1 explain the reasons for East European discontent with Soviet control in the 1980s
2 describe **a** *Gorbachev's policies*
b *their impact in Eastern Europe*
3 describe the collapse of the Soviet Empire in Eastern Europe

Discontent with Soviet control

By the 1980s there was widespread discontent in Eastern Europe. Although the exact circumstances of each state varied, the main sources of dissatisfaction were common to them all:

Life under Soviet control	What people wanted instead
Communist Party rule No other political parties allowed.	Political parties and free elections. Open discussion about politics.
Police state Secret police suppressed criticism of the Government using torture and terror.	Abolition of secret police forces. Freedom to criticise the Government.
State controlled economy Inefficient. Unable to produce enough food or the kind of goods people really wanted.	More freedom to own and run businesses without State interference. Farms and factories to produce sufficient food and responsive to the demand of consumers.
Low standard of living In the 1980s prices and unemployment rose and there were shortages of food and consumer goods.	Improved living standards.
Censorship Press, radio and TV were all State controlled. There was no freedom of expression.	Freedom of the press. Freedom of expression.
Religious belief This was discouraged. Members of Churches were penalized.	Freedom of religious belief.
Communist loyalty People were expected to forget their national identity and to be loyal to the Communist ideal.	The right and opportunity to express their national identity. A nation state free from outside control which would act in the interests of its citizens.

The impact of détente

The improvement in East-West relations (pages 88-91) led to
1 An interest in Capitalist methods because of
a increased trade with the West
b Western companies investing in Eastern Europe.
2 Higher awareness of the much better standards of living in Western Europe.
3 A reduced military threat. East Europeans began to question the value of Soviet military protection.

1 What were the pressures for change in Eastern Europe before Gorbachev came to power in the USSR?
2 a How did Gorbachev's policies make change more likely?
b What particular actions did Gorbachev take in 1989 which affected events in individual countries?

Mikhail Gorbachev

In 1985 Gorbachev became Secretary-General of the Soviet Communist Party. At 54 he was a relatively young Soviet leader committed to carrying out reforms.

His impact on Eastern Europe
1 A flood of popular demands for similar changes.
2 A changed relationship between the USSR and Eastern Europe:
a Gorbachev wanted a more equal relationship between them
b the USSR was no longer prepared to use armed force to get its own way.
3 Difficulties for Communist leaders who
a had to adjust to Gorbachev's declarations that
i Marxism had proved a failure ii the Party was not always right
b were likely to lose control because i of the hostility to them ii they could no longer rely on Soviet support.

How the Soviet Empire in Eastern Europe collapsed

Poland
1988
Severe economic crisis. Strikes and revival of Solidarity.
1989
1 Jaruzelski agrees to
a legalize Solidarity
b increase press freedom
c hold elections while reserving a majority of seats for Communists.
2 Solidarity triumphs in elections. Communists do badly.
3 Jaruzelski appoints non-Communist Prime Minister.

East Germany
1989
1 Gorbachev criticises Party Secretary Honecker.
2 Demonstrations against Honecker. He resigns.
3 Free elections announced.
4 Demonstrators demolish the Berlin Wall.
1990
1 Communists defeated in elections.
2 East and West Germany reunified.

His inheritance
1 The Soviet standard of living was even lower than in most Eastern European states.
2 The USSR's wealth was not sufficient to bear the weight of the Government's military expenditure.
3 The USSR suffered severe food shortages and had to import grain from the USA and other Western countries.
4 Standards of health and housing were poor and declining.

His plan
1 Restructure the Soviet economy (*perestroika*).
2 Listen to public opinion and be more open about Government policy (*glasnost*).
3 Continue to keep real power in the hands of the Communist Party but allow some elections.
4 Reduce Party control of the economy.
5 Reduce military expenditure.
6 Encourage Western firms to invest in the USSR.

Hungary
1988
Kadar replaced by more 'liberal' Communist leader.
1989
1 Gorbachev agrees to withdraw Soviet troops.
2 Free travel allowed to Austria and the West.
3 Free elections, free press, freedom of belief allowed.
1990
Non-Communist government elected.

Czechoslovakia
1989
1 Demonstrators call for economic and political reform. Government uses force against them.
2 News of changes in Poland and East Germany encourages demonstrators to continue.
3 Gorbachev urges Party to respond to the people's demands.
4 Non-Communists join new government. Free elections organized.
5 Opposition leader, the author Vaclos Havel, elected President.

Bulgaria and Romania
1989
Hardline régimes overturned.
1990
Communists win free elections.

Detente, 1971-1979

By the end of this spread you should be able to describe:
1 the reasons for detente, 1971-1979
2 its achievements
*3 attempts to deal with **a** arms control **b** human rights issues*

What was detente?

1 Detente is a French term (détente) meaning relaxation. It is used to describe periods of 'thaw' in the Cold War when tensions between the Superpowers lessened and relations improved.
2 It is particularly applied to the years between 1971 when the first Nixon-Brezhnev Summit Conference was planned and 1979 when the USSR invaded Afghanistan causing a 'Second Cold War' (page 90).
3 Detente was restored after Gorbachev became Soviet leader in 1985 (page 91).

Particular Soviet reasons

1 A breakdown of relations with China meant it was important to reduce tension with the USSR's other potential enemy, the USA.
2 Now that the USSR had caught up in the arms race it felt more confident.
3 In 1969 West Germany had agreed with East Germany not to acquire nuclear weapons. This removed a potential threat.
4 The need to increase trade with the West.

Reasons in common
Try to reduce
1 the risk of nuclear war
2 the high cost of the arms race.

Why did the Superpowers want detente in the 1970s?

Particular American reasons

1 Failure in Vietnam. Nixon changed the direction of American foreign policy and set out to improve US relations with both China and the USSR.
2 Public pressure to reduce the risks of war.
3 The USSR had caught up in the arms race.

Superpower contacts

Summit Conferences

1 Five were held between 1972 and 1979, the first three between Nixon and Brezhnev (1972-1974).
2 They led to
a agreements about procedures to reduce the risk of confrontation and nuclear war
b a joint space mission (1975)
c increased trade links
d cultural exchanges.

The European Security Conference, 1973-1975

Delegates from Canada, the USA and thirty-three European countries met in Helsinki. In 1975 they signed the Helsinki Accords:

1 *Security*
a They recognized
i the frontiers of Eastern Europe
ii Soviet control over the region.
b West Germany recognized East Germany.

2 *Co-operation* They agreed to co-operate through
a trade links
b cultural exchanges
c exchanges of technological information.

3 *Human rights* They agreed
a to respect human rights
b to allow people to travel freely across Europe.

Human rights

1 Many in the West believed the Helsinki Accords marked a break-through in persuading the USSR to allow human rights, such as the freedoms of belief and expression, both at home and in Eastern Europe.
2 The USSR made little effort to improve human rights:
a It continued to suppress critics such as Andrei Sakharov.
b In Czechoslovakia members of the Charter 77 group were suppressed.
c When the West criticized the USSR's human rights record, Brezhnev said it was interfering in its internal affairs.
d When a US Congressman tried to have a trade agreement linked to the improved treatment of Soviet Jews, Brezhnev cancelled the deal.

Arms control

1 *Nuclear weapons* In 1969 talks began about a Strategic Arms Limitation Treaty (SALT). The Superpowers signed two treaties:
a In SALT I (1972) they agreed i to reduce their anti-ballistic missile systems ii limits on the numbers of their offensive missiles and bombers (see photo).
b In SALT II (1979) they agreed further limits on missiles but the talks were less successful than hoped. In 1980 US President Carter refused to ratify the treaty because of Soviet aggression in Afghanistan (page 90).

2 *Conventional forces* Talks to reduce these made very little progress. The USSR
a refused to reveal the size of Warsaw Pact forces
b made it clear it intended to maintain its superiority over NATO in this area.

Attitudes to detente

1 Brezhnev made it clear that detente did not mean an end to the struggle between Communism and Capitalism.
2 Western critics of detente said that
a the USSR was interested only in the benefits of detente to itself such as trade links and reduced arms expenditure.
b it was not interested in the improvement of human rights.
c the West had, therefore, made a mistake at Helsinki in accepting Soviet control of Eastern Europe.
3 Western supporters hoped that increased contact with the West would change attitudes in the East.
4 Despite detente, Superpower rivalry continued in the Arab-Israeli War (1973) and Angola (1974-1975).

1 What did a the USSR b the USA hope to gain from detente?
2 What did detente achieve between 1971 and 1979?
3 In what respects was detente a failure?

The end of the Cold War, 1979-1991

By the end of this spread you should be able to describe and explain:
1 the breakdown of detente in 1979
2 a its re-emergence in 1985
b the roles of Gorbachev and Reagan
3 the results of detente, 1985-1991
4 the end of Soviet control

Fig. 1 The war in Afghanistan

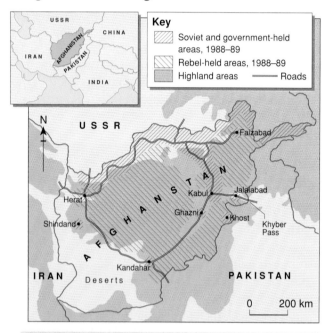

Key
Soviet and government-held areas, 1988–89
Rebel-held areas, 1988–89
Highland areas ——— Roads

The war
1 Villages and towns devastated by superior Soviet firepower.
2 Over 1 million people killed, mostly Afghan civilians. Over 5.5 million Afghan refugees fled to Iran and Pakistan.
3 By 1988 Mujaheddin (resistance fighters), using guerrilla tactics, controlled 75% of the country.
4 In 1989 Soviet forces withdrew.

The American response President Carter said that the invasion had completely changed his view of the USSR. He took several anti-Soviet measures:
1 He suspended ratification of SALT II by the US Senate.
2 He ordered US athletes to boycott the 1980 Olympic Games due to be held in Moscow.
3 He started to rearm.

A 'Second' Cold War, 1979-1985

The Soviet invasion of Afghanistan
1 In December 1979 Soviet troops invaded Afghanistan in order to keep a pro-Soviet government in power there.
2 The invasion was condemned by a large majority in the United Nations General Assembly.
3 It put an end to Superpower detente which was already under strain (page 89).

Afghanistan
1 A country of many tribes, strongly Islamic.
2 Under Soviet influence since 1947.
3 In 1978 a Communist régime took power but met strong opposition from the Afghan people.
4 In 1979 the USSR persuaded the prime minister to 'invite' it to invade.

The USSR
The Soviets wanted to keep control of Afghanistan because:
1 They had rights to gas fields there.
2 American influence was growing in Pakistan.
3 They wanted to ensure that it did not become a fundamentalist Islamic state like Iran in order to
a avoid a ring of Islamic states to the south.
b prevent Islamic minorities within the USSR from being tempted to break away too.

Reagan's policy change
1 In 1980 Ronald Reagan replaced Carter as US President.
2 Reagan believed that detente had caused the USA to lose ground to the USSR.
3 He returned to an aggressive anti-Soviet foreign policy which included
a expanding the USA's armed forces
b basing new modern missiles (eg. Pershing 2 and Cruise) in those European countries which wished to accept them.
c launching the Strategic Defence Initiative (SDI). Nick-named 'Star Wars' this was an expensive programme to develop anti-missile weapons using laser beams. If successful it would mean the USA could not be the victim of a 'first strike'.

Detente again, 1985-1991

New Soviet attitudes

In 1985 Mikhail Gorbachev inherited a serious situation at home when he became leader of the USSR. In response he planned a series of reforms (page 87). In order to carry them out Gorbachev had to change Soviet foreign policy.

Reagan's choices

Gorbachev's aims

- **1** Withdraw Soviet troops from Afghanistan
- **2** Reduce Soviet aid worldwide
- **3** Improve relations with China
- **4** Seek detente with the USA in order to
  a reduce defence spending
  b borrow money from Western banks to pay for imported food, raw materials and equipment
  c persuade Western firms to build factories in the USSR

Action	Possible result
Refuse detente and refuse to help Gorbachev.	This would weaken the USSR and make it cut military spending; but it might also cause Gorbachev to be replaced by a hardline leader hostile to the West.
Return to detente and help Gorbachev.	This ran the risk that the USSR might not cut its arms spending that much. Thus the West would be helping the USSR remain militarily effective.

Reagan's Decision

1 Reagan decided to
a continue to treat the Soviet military threat seriously and to follow a strong defence policy. This might force Gorbachev to make concessions in arms reduction.
b at the same time respond positively to Gorbachev's offer of detente.
2 When Reagan and Gorbachev met they got on very well. This helped detente to develop quickly.

What was achieved?

1 The Intermediate Nuclear Forces (INF) Treaty (1987). The Superpowers agreed to eliminate all intermediate missiles in Europe within three years.
2 Talks made progress on the reduction of NATO and Warsaw Pact conventional forces.
3 a Talks on long range missiles (formerly SALT talks) were renamed Strategic Arms Reduction Talks (START).
b They led to the 1991 START Treaty which agreed significant reductions in weapons.

The end of Soviet control, 1989-1991

1 In 1989
a Soviet control of Eastern Europe collapsed (pages 86-87).
b Gorbachev and US President George Bush, Reagan's successor, announced the end of the Cold War.
2 a In 1991 the USSR itself dissolved when Gorbachev could no longer control the pressure for independence from the nationalist movements in its fifteen member republics.
b It was replaced by a Commonwealth of Independent States (CIS) with the Russian Republic as the dominant member.

1 The years 1979-1985 are often called a 'second Cold War'?
a Why do you think this is?
b Is it an appropriate description?
2 Make a two-column chart to show what
a Reagan **b** Gorbachev did to help to restore detente after 1985?

The United Nations 1: origins, aims and structure

By the end of this spread you should be able to:
1 describe the origins, aims and structure of the
United Nations Organization (UN)
2 describe the similarities and differences between
the UN and the League of Nations

The origins of the UN

The Atlantic Charter, 1941 Produced by Winston Churchill, Prime Minister of Britain, and Franklin Roosevelt, President of the United States, this outlined their hopes for a better world after the war:
1 all countries would have democratic governments
2 they would trade freely with each other and share economic prosperity
3 there would be an international security system to maintain peace.
In 1942 the countries fighting the Axis Powers agreed to call themselves The United Nations. They signed a United Nations Declaration saying they agreed to:
1 support the ideals of the Atlantic Charter
2 continue their co-operation after the war.

The San Francisco Conference, 1945
1 The four most powerful members of the United Nations, the USA, Britain, the USSR, and China, planned the UN in a series of wartime conferences.
2 In 1945, delegates from all the United Nations met in San Francisco to discuss the proposed United Nations Charter. Fifty-one countries signed the Charter and became founder members.

The United Nations system

The United Nations Charter describes the UN's structure (fig. 1) and aims. These are to:
1 maintain international peace and security
2 develop friendly relations among nations
3 co-operate internationally in solving world problems and in promoting respect for human rights and fundamental freedoms.

Membership
1 All countries at war with the Axis Powers in 1945 became founder members. Other countries wishing to join had to prove themselves willing and able to carry out their duties under the Charter.
2 The UN grew as newly independent states joined (page 96). Ex-Axis countries also joined: Italy (1955); Japan (1956); the Federal Republic of Germany and the German Democratic Republic (both 1973).
3 China was represented by the Nationalist government even after 1949 when the Communists drove it into Taiwan. The USA refused to allow the Communist government to join until 1971 when it replaced the nationalists.

Peacekeeping
1 The Security Council may investigate any international dispute.
2 The Charter allows it to deal with an offending country by:
a imposing economic sanctions (ie, telling other countries to cut off trade and financial relations)
b taking military action. Unlike the Council of the League of Nations it has the power to raise a UN army.
3 Each of the permanent members of the Security Council has the power to veto (block) a decision by voting against it (fig. 1).

Specialized agencies (fig. 1 and pages 100-101)
These were set up to enable the UN to help people worldwide
1 to become healthier and more prosperous
2 to become better educated
3 to enjoy fundamental freedoms and human rights.

Money Countries contribute money to the UN according to their national wealth. Although the UN has financial problems, it has always been better funded than the League of Nations and, therefore, able to do more work. Its budget rose from about 20 million dollars in 1946 to about 846 million by 1990.

Fig.1 The structure of the UN

The Security Council
1 Responsible for international peace and security.
2 Consisted of 11 (now 15) members:
a five **permanent members:** China, France, USSR, UK, and USA.
b six (now 10) **non-permanent members,** elected by General Assembly.
3 Each member has one vote.
4 Decisions needed a 'yes' vote from seven (now nine) members including ALL FIVE permanent members.

The Trusteeship Council
1 Supervises the progress of certain colonies, known as 'trust territories', towards independence.
2 Each member of the Council has one vote.
3 Decisions made by majority vote.

The Secretariat
The staff of the UN. Responsible for its administration. All staff have to promise not to take orders from outside the UN.

The Secretary-General is the head of the Secretariat.
1 *Appointment* Recommended to the General Assembly by the Security Council and appointed by a majority vote. Elected for five years and can be re-elected for a further five.
2 *Tasks*
a manage the whole UN organisation
b draw the attention of the Security Council to any problem affecting the peace of the world
c use his or her good offices (position, influence and personal diplomatic skills) to help to resolve international disputes
d lead UN missions to any area to take over UN activities there.

The General Assembly
1 Meets regularly once a year and in special sessions as required.
2 Consists of all members of the UN.
3 Each country has one vote regardless of size.
4 Decisions
a must have a two-thirds majority
b are not binding on member states which may choose whether or not to act on them.

The Economic and Social Council
1 Co-ordinates
a the social and economic work of the UN
b the activities of the specialized agencies
2 Consists of 54 Members of the UN elected by the General Assembly.
3 Day to day work carried out by commissions and committees.
Regional Commissions: Africa; Asia and the Pacific; Europe; Latin America; and Western Asia
Functional Commissions: social development; human rights; drugs; the status of women; population; and statistics

Non-members may use these organizations

The International Court of Justice
1 Consists of 15 judges, representing the world's different legal systems, elected by Security Council and General Assembly to serve for nine years.
2 Can only settle cases where states involved agree in advance to accept its judgements.
3 Advises the General Assembly and Security Council if asked.
4 Based in The Hague.

The Specialized Agencies
Main areas of work are:
1 Refugees
2 International Communications
3 Trade, Industry and Finance (page 101)
4 Education and Training (page 101)
5 The Environment
6 Labour and Working Conditions (page 101)
7 Health and Nutrition (page 101)
8 Atomic Energy

---

1 a Draw a table with three columns. In the left-hand column list the main bodies of the UN.
b In the next two columns make notes on each body's
i membership ii function.
2 Using the information on pages 24-27 and in this section make notes to show what was a similar b different about the following aspects of the League of Nations and the UN:
i aims   iv peacekeeping powers
ii main bodies   v agencies
iii membership   vi budget

The United Nations 2:
The Korean War, 1950-1953

By the end of this spread you should be able to:
1 describe the work of the UN in Korea, 1950-1953
2 explain how successful you think it was

Korea, 1945-1950

1 1945. Japan surrenders to the Allies. Korea a Japanese colony: Soviet troops occupy the north, American troops the south. The 38th Parallel (line of latitude 38° North) divides the two areas of occupation.

2 1947. UN General Assembly decides on elections throughout Korea to choose a national government. USSR refuses to co-operate.

3 1948. In the south voters elect a parliament which sets up the government of the Republic of Korea (capital: Seoul). In the north, the USSR sets up the People's Democratic Republic of Korea (capital; Pyongyang). Each government claims to rule the whole of Korea. USA and USSR withdraw troops but continue to support the two sides with money and weapons

Background

The Cold War and the UN

1 The UN Charter set up a Military Staff Committee representing each of the 'Big Five' on the Security Council. This gave them joint control of any UN force.

2 The Cold War meant

a the Military Staff Committee failed to agree about how to set up a UN force

b the Big Five could not act together as the world's police force

c the USA and the USSR used their Security Council vetos to block any peace-keeping decisions they did not like.

4 1949. Civil war in China ends with Communist victory. Communists set up People's Republic of China (capital: Beijing). Nationalists flee to Taiwan and set up Republic of China.

5 June 1950. North Korean troops invade South Korea.

The UN response

The Security Council

1 decided that the North Koreans had breached world peace and called on them to withdraw to the 38th Parallel which the North Koreans ignored
2 met again and called on UN members to help South Korea repel the North Korean attack
3 asked the USA to take command of the UN operation.

The USSR was absent from the Security Council in protest against China being represented at the UN by the Chinese Nationalist government (page 92). Had it been present it would have used its veto.

The Secretary-General, Trygve Lie, believed North Korea was guilty of calculated aggression against a state which the UN had helped to create. He advised the Security Council to take a strong stand.

The UN in Korea: The course of the War

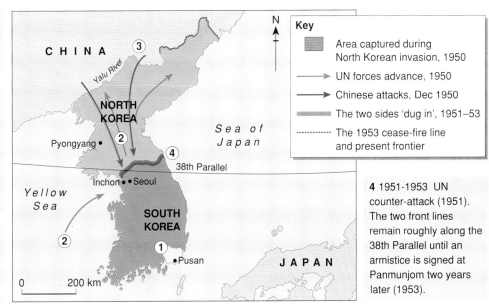

1 June-Sept 1950. North Korean invasion. South Koreans swept back into area around Pusan.

2 Sept-Nov 1950. UN and South Korean troops drive back the North Koreans. Despite warnings from China not to cross the 38th Parallel, they advance almost to the Chinese border.

3 Nov-Jan 1951. The Chinese enter the war. Drive UN forces back again and advance into South Korea.

Key

Area captured during North Korean invasion, 1950

UN forces advance, 1950

Chinese attacks, Dec 1950

The two sides 'dug in', 1951–53

The 1953 cease-fire line and present frontier

4 1951-1953 UN counter-attack (1951). The two front lines remain roughly along the 38th Parallel until an armistice is signed at Panmunjom two years later (1953).

The USA's war?

1 Of the sixteen countries contributing forces, the USA provided the most: 50% of land forces, 93% of air forces and 86% of naval forces.
2 The UN gave the USA unlimited authority to direct military operations.
3 The US President, Truman, not the UN, appointed General MacArthur as Commander-in Chief of UN forces. MacArthur reported to the US President and took orders from him.
4 The war threatened to become one between the USA and China. The USA even considered using nuclear weapons against China.

The superpowers at war Behind the scenes the USSR provided pilots and planes for the Chinese airforce. The USA knew about this but kept it a secret to avoid demands for a war against the USSR.

Results

Korea

1 The war killed 1.5 million South Koreans; 3.5 million North Koreans. Millions more were left homeless and starving.
2 The UN's policy was that Korea should become one country with free elections supervised by the UN. The war did not achieve this. It stopped North Korean aggression and restored the position before the attack.

The UN's reputation The UN gained respect because, unlike the League of Nations, it had taken firm action in the face of aggression.

UN forces Many members felt that
a the USA had used the UN in its battle against Communism
b the forces of the major powers should not be directly involved in future UN operations.

'Uniting for Peace'
1 In 1950 the General Assembly agreed this procedure when the USSR returned to the Security Council and used its veto to prevent further action.
2 It gave the Assembly the power to take over peace-keeping responsibilities if a veto blocked Council action.
3 The USSR claimed this was illegal and refused to accept decisions made in this way.

The Secretary-General In 1953 Trygve Lie resigned because the USSR
1 accused him of supporting the Americans during the crisis and of acting beyond the limits of his office.
2 refused to work with him any more.

1 How did superpower rivalry affect the UN's work in Korea?
2 In what ways was the UN **a** strengthened **b** weakened by its work in Korea?
3 To what extent was the UN's work in Korea a success?

The United Nations 3: expanding membership; the Suez crisis

By the end of this spread you should be able to:
1 explain the impact of its expanding membership on the work of the UN
2 a describe the role of the UN in the Suez crisis
b explain its significance

Expanding membership

The UN soon began to grow (fig. 1). In the 1950s and 1960s most new members were newly independent African and Asian states.

Fig. 1 UN membership

1945: 51
1955: 75
1965: 118
1975: 144
1985: 159

The balance of power

1 Because of the Cold War (page 66) the new nations found the world divided into two camps.
2 Many, especially in Asia and Africa, took up a non-aligned, or neutral, position between the two superpowers. They also took up an independent position in the UN.
3 From about 1960, therefore, Western countries began to lose the automatic majority in the General Assembly that they had held since 1945. They had to take account of new members' views.

New issues Increasingly the General Assembly found itself discussing issues of importance to its Afro-Asian members. For example: human rights, decolonization and the North-South divide (page 100).

How expanding membership affected the UN

Peacekeeping

1 The UN's founders had hoped that the Big Five would work together to provide military forces to overwhelm an aggressor. But the Cold War meant this could not happen (page 66).
2 A larger UN membership made possible a different type of operation known as 'peacekeeping'. Forces provided by smaller nations were used to keep the peace between warring parties (pages 97 and 98).

Western criticism Western countries strongly objected to some of the directions taken by the UN as a result of the voting power of the developing nations.
1 They argued that Afro-Asian countries were willing to condemn the West's human rights record but ignored their own failings.
2 They opposed demands for a 'New International Economic Order' (page 100).
3 They claimed that some specialized agencies such as ILO, WHO and UNESCO were becoming 'politicised' (page 100). Some countries withdrew from them.
4 They pointed out that the 'one nation one vote' system in the General Assembly and other UN bodies meant that the majority of poorer nations which contributed very little to the UN budget could outvote the minority of richer nations which contributed the most. They argued that countries which paid the most should have the greater say in UN affairs.
5 In the 1980s, because of its dissatisfaction, the USA cut its contributions causing a major financial crisis and cutbacks in the UN's work.

1 In what ways did the expansion of the UN make it **a** more **b** less effective?
2 What were the differences between the UN's operations in Korea and Suez? Use pages 94-95 and 97 to compare:
a the forces: **i** their composition **ii** their task **iii** how they were commanded
b the role of **i** the Secretary-General **ii** members of the Security Council **iii** smaller nations.
3 In what ways did the UN prove to **a** ineffective **b** effective in the Suez crisis?

The Suez crisis, 1956

Egypt
The USA and Britain had refused to lend money to help pay for the building of the important Aswan Dam because Egypt had recently bought arms from the USSR. President Nasser, therefore, took over the Suez Canal planning to use the valuable tolls paid by ships passing through it.

Israel
After the Arab-Israeli War (1948) thousands of Palestinian Arabs had left Israel and lived in refugee camps across the border. From there commando groups were making repeated raids. Israel planned to attack Egypt to
1 stop the commando attacks
2 open up the seaport of Eilat by ending the Arab blockade of the Straits of Tiran.

Britain and France
Angered by the Egyptian take-over of the Suez Canal because the Suez Canal Company was largely owned by French and British shareholders. They plotted with Israel to use its attack on Egypt as an excuse to occupy the Suez Canal zone. They hoped it would appear that they were separating the warring parties.

Key
→ Israeli invasion of Egypt
→ British and French attacks on Egypt

26 July Egypt takes over the Suez Canal Company.

29 Oct Israel attacks Egypt.

30 Oct Britain and France order Egypt and Israel to withdraw their forces to a distance of 10 miles on either side of the Suez Canal. Egypt refuses.

31 Oct Britain and France launch air attacks on Egypt.

1 Nov UN General Assembly calls for a cease-fire and the withdrawal of troops.

4 Nov General Assembly agrees to set up UNEF

5 Nov British and French troops land in Port Said area of Egypt.

6 Nov Britain asks the USA for an urgent loan of money. The USA refuses unless the fighting is called off. Fighting stops.

15 Nov United Nations Emergency Force (UNEF) starts to arrive in Egypt.

22 Dec Final withdrawal of British and French troops.

The role of the UN

1 *Uniting for Peace* When Britain and France vetoed a resolution demanding Israel's withdrawal, the Security Council used the 'Uniting for Peace' procedure (page 95) to transfer responsibility for handling the crisis to the General Assembly.

2 *Condemnation* In the General Assembly the actions of Britain and France were condemned by the USA (their main ally), most Commonwealth countries (on which Britain relied) and all the non-aligned nations. Although it took action by the USA to stop them fighting, Britain and France were shocked by this almost unanimous hostility.

3 *UNEF* The United Nations Emergency Force was a new idea suggested by the Canadians: a peacekeeping force provided entirely by smaller countries.

1 It was to act as a buffer between the two sides, not to fight either of them. Its soldiers were to use their weapons only in self-defence.

2 Its commander was responsible directly to the Security Council.

3 Its troops came only from states which were not permanent members of the Security Council.

4 *The Secretary-General*, Dag Hammarskjöld, was given overall responsibility for planning and running the operation.

The United Nations 4: the Congo, 1960-1963

Background to the crisis

1960

30 June Independence Day. Joseph Kasavubu becomes President of the Republic of the Congo. Patrice Lumumba becomes Prime Minister.

July 1 Congolese soldiers mutiny against their Belgian officers.
2 Belgium illegally sends paratroops to protect Belgians still working in the Congo.
3 Moise Tshombe, President of Katanga province, asks for Belgian assistance, and declares Katanga an independent state.
4 Kasavubu appeals for help to the UN.

Stage 1   Taking over, 1960

1960

July 1 UN Security Council decides to
a send a UN force (ONUC) to the Congo
b provide training and technical help
c order Belgian troops to leave.
2 ONUC arrives in Congo. Troops take over from the Belgians except in Katanga. UN experts begin to help Congolese government.

Aug 1 UN refuses Lumumba's demand for ONUC attack on Katanga to force it to reunite with the rest of the country.
2 UN troops enter Katanga peacefully.
3 Lumumba's own forces attack Katanga using Soviet transport planes. Attack fails.

Sept Lumumba dismissed by Kasavubu.

Aims of the UN operation

1 Restore and maintain law and order
2 Help the Congo remain united and prevent civil war
3 Prevent other countries from becoming involved in the Congo's affairs
4 Provide the Congolese with training and technical help to run their public services.

1 For each aim of the UN's Congo operation say
a What difficulties the UN faced in carrying it out
b What it managed to achieve.

By the end of this spread you should be able to:
1 describe the work of the UN in the Congo, 1960-1963
2 explain how successful you think it was

The Congo (now Zaire) was a Belgian colony. In 1960, the Belgians announced that it was to become independent in five months time. But there were no Congolese doctors, engineers or senior government administrators, and no Congolese army officers. **Katanga** was the Congo's richest province. Most of its wealth came from its European-owned mines.

ONUC

Composition Troops from non-aligned states in Africa, Asia and Europe

Rules
1 Force to be used only in self-defence
2 No interference in the Congo's internal affairs. Take no action which might support one group of Congolese against another.

The Secretary-General Dag Hammarskjöld
1 believed that the UN should
a protect new nations
b prevent countries from falling victim to Cold War rivalry.
2 used his powers under the UN Charter to call the first Security Council meeting about the Congo.
3 suggested the creation of a UN force.
4 set up ONUC rapidly and efficiently.

The superpowers
The USA
Strongly backed the UN action. It wanted
1 to prevent Soviet interference in the Congo
2 a government in the Congo friendly to the West.
The USSR
1 wanted to be seen to back UN action to protect a new nation against its 'imperialist' ex-ruler
2 aimed to use the crisis to gain control of the Congo government.

2 a What criticisms were made of the UN's Congo operation?
b What justification, if any, was there for each one?

Stage 2 Preventing civil war, 1961

At the beginning of 1961 the Congo was split between three main rival groups, two of them backed by foreign powers, each claiming to be the government of the Congo:

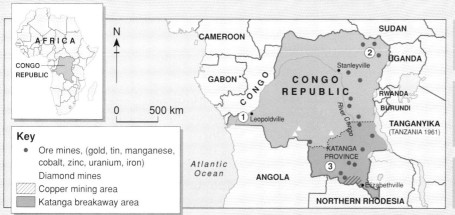

1 The Government of the Congolese Republic
Backed by the UN.

2 Ex-Prime Minister Lumumba,
then, after his death (Jan 1961), Lumumba's supporters.
Backed by the USSR.

3 Moise Tshombe.
President of Katanga.
Backed by Belgium.

Key
- Ore mines, (gold, tin, manganese, cobalt, zinc, uranium, iron)
- Diamond mines
- Copper mining area
- Katanga breakaway area

1961 Feb   UN Security Council authorizes ONUC to use force to prevent civil war.

July   UN arranges for meeting of a new Congolese parliament.

Aug   All rival groups, except Katanga, come together and elect a new central government.

ONUC troops
1 re-established order despite being attacked by different warring groups
2 persuaded Soviet troops and advisers to leave Eastern Province.

UN officials
1 set up a civil service to run the country
2 re-opened public services, eg. hospitals
3 trained Congolese teachers, engineeers, doctors etc.
4 prevented a famine in Kasai Province.

Stage 3 Katanga, 1961-1963

1961 Sept   1 While trying to round up Belgian mercenaries ONUC fights Katangan troops.
2 Death of Hammarskjöld in plane crash. U Thant appointed UN Secretary-General.

Nov   Security Council authorizes ONUC to use force to remove foreign soldiers and advisers from Katanga.

Dec   UN attack followed by ceasefire and talks.

1962   Final UN attack. Tshombe goes abroad.

1963 Jan   Katanga reunited with the Congo.

1964   ONUC leaves the Congo.

ONUC's problems
1 Tshombe could resist the Congo government because
a Belgians ran the mines and made payments to him instead of the national government, so
b he could afford to pay Belgian mercenaries.
2 To reunite the Congo ONUC had to remove the mercenaries; but they refused to leave voluntarily.
3 The Security Council was reluctant to authorize the use of force partly because Britain and France sympathised with Katanga.

Criticisms of the UN

The USSR, Belgium and France all refused to pay their share of the costs of the UN operations in the Congo because they disagreed with its actions. The USSR said it was biased towards the West.

Katanga Some countries said ONUC should not have interfered because this was an internal quarrel.
Bloodshed Others complained when ONUC first fought Katangan troops, arguing that a peacekeeping force should never cause bloodshed.
The Secretary-General Some Western states accused Hammarskjöld of
a exceeding his powers by taking a leading role.
b favouring new and non-aligned nations.

The United Nations 5: the specialized agencies

By the end of this spread you should be able to:
1 describe the aims and work of some major UN agencies

2 suggest how successful they have been in moving the world towards closer co-operation

Achievements

UN agencies have frequently managed to bring about co-operation on global issues which governments could not have achieved on their own (fig. 1).

Problems

As colonies of the European empires gained their independence and joined the UN as new, developing, nations (page 96), they did not always see eye to eye with the older, established, nations which had founded the UN. A number of disputes arose about the role and effectiveness of the specialized agencies.

The North-South divide
1 The new nations criticised UN agencies such as the IMF and the World Bank saying they were good at developing the trade and financial position of rich, developed, countries (mainly in the North) but did very little to help poor, developing, ones (mainly in the South).
2 In 1974 they used their voting power in the General Assembly to pass a declaration calling for a 'New International Economic Order' (NIEO) to give developing nations a larger share of the world's wealth.
3 In 1980 an IMF enquiry produced a report, 'North-South: A Programme for Survival', saying how this could be done. To succeed it needed the support of Northern countries; but they did not give it.

ILO
1 The majority of African and Asian states were hostile to the new state of Israel. In 1975 the General Assembly denounced Israel's policy towards the Arabs in occupied territories as 'racist'.
2 The ILO said that any occupation of territory was a violation of human and trade union rights and condemned Israel's actions.
3 The USA withdrew from the ILO saying that the agency had acted beyond the purposes for which it had been set up.

'Politicisation' In the 1980s UN members accused some of the specialized agencies of becoming involved in political matters which were none of their concern.

IMF
1 Developing countries complained that the USA blocked loans from the IMF and the World Bank to countries such as Cuba and Vietnam because they had Communist governments or were friendly with the USSR.
2 They argued that these important UN agencies were really controlled by the Western nations.

UNESCO
1 In 1977 Western nations opposed a UNESCO plan to set up a 'New World Information and Communications Order' aiming to move control of radio and television services and newspaper networks away from the developed to the developing countries.
2 In the 1980s Britain and the USA withdrew from UNESCO saying it was involved in political issues and wasted its money, a quarter of which was contributed by the USA itself.

1 a Take in turn the WHO, UNESCO, FAO, ILO and the IMF. List
i that agency's main achievements
ii ways in which its work has led to criticism or dispute.
b How successful have these agencies been in moving the world towards closer co-operation?

Fig. 1 The work of some major UN specialized agencies

	Purpose	Examples of projects
WHO The World Health Organization	1 To co-ordinate the fight against disease and medical research. 2 To set drug and vaccine standards. 3 To provide its members with technical help, advice and information. 4 To achieve basic health services for all by the year 2000.	• Attacks on major diseases such as malaria, tuberculosis and smallpox (eradicated by 1980). • Helping governments to set up health services in developing countries. Training staff to work in them. • Programmes to immunize all the world's children against measles, diphtheria, whooping cough, tetanus, polio and TB. Approximately one million lives saved each year.
UNESCO The United Nations Education, Scientific and Cultural Organization	To contribute to world peace by using education, science and culture to promote co-operation among nations and to increase respect for justice, the rule of law and human rights.	• Programmes to promote international understanding after the divisions of the Second World War. • Programmes to teach adults to read and write. • Finding ways to make scientific and technological advances useful to poorer, developing countries. • Research into the currents and make-up of the Indian and Atlantic Oceans. • The rescue of the Nile temples (1964-68) when the Aswan High Dam was built.
FAO The Food and Agriculture Organization	1 To raise levels of nutrition. 2 To improve food production and distribution. 3 To improve the lives of people living in the countryside. 4 To increase the effectiveness of agriculture, forestry and fisheries.	• Freedom From Hunger Campaign to raise money for projects in developing countries. • World Food Programme (1963). A long-term plan to tackle world food needs. Still in progress. • Co-ordination (since 1960) of the attack on locusts in Africa and the Middle East. • Research projects: eg., on soils, irrigation, fertilizers, new types of wheat, barley, rice. • Programmes to help poorer countries to increase their food production.
ILO The International Labour Organization	1 To improve living and working conditions and promote employment worldwide. 2 Set international standards for the protection of workers and the improvement of their conditions.	• Codes of practice to improve working conditions throughout the world. • Andes Indian Project (from 1954) to improve the living and working conditions of very poor Indian people in South America. • Training refugees in Burundi (central southern Africa) in agriculture and rural crafts so that they could earn their own living (1964). • World Employment Programme (from 1969) to increase the number of useful jobs in the world and help to meet people's basic needs. • Danger symbols. A series of warning signs that could be understood throughout the world even by people unable to read.
IMF The International Monetary Fund	1 To help the growth of international trade. 2 To keep stable the rates at which the currencies of different countries can be exchanged for one another.	• Until the 1970s lent money on a short-term basis mainly to the developed nations. • In 1982 took the lead in trying to help developing nations which could not repay their debts to commercial banks. • Since the mid-1970s has become more involved in helping developing countries to expand their trade.

Russia in the early 1900s

By the end of this spread you should be able to describe:
1 the main a economic b social c political features of
Russia in the early 1900s
2 the nature of the opposition to Tsarist rule

Agriculture

1 About 85% of the population lived in the country.
2 Extensive tundra, forest, and desert meant only about 5% of the land (mainly in the south-west) was used for farming.
3 Old fashioned farming methods caused low food production and famines.

Industry

1 Russia was rich in oil and minerals.
2 In 1900 it had only recently begun to industrialize.
3 By 1913, with the help of foreign investment in, eg. factories and railways, it was the world's fifth largest industrial nation.
4 Considering Russia's size and resources, its manufacturing output was still low.

Peoples

1 The total population of about 125 million was made up of more than 20 different peoples.
2 Among the largest groups were;
Russians 55.6 million
Ukrainians 22.4 million
Poles 7.9 million
Byelorussians 5.9 million
Jews 5 million
3 For six people out of every ten, Russian was a foreign language.

Religions

1 About 70% of the population belonged to the Empire's official Orthodox Christian Church.
2 Large minorities belonged to other Churches and religions:
Roman Catholic 9%
Muslim 11%
Jewish 4%

The Russian Empire and its resources

Communications

1 Long distances and poor roads made communication slow.
2 In the Arctic circle, frozen coasts and rivers prevented movement by ship for most of the year.
3 In 1900 the Trans-Siberian Railway was half-complete.

Russian society

Ruling class
The royal family and nobility.
Very wealthy indeed. Owned about 25% of the land. Lived in luxury.

Upper class
Lesser nobles, Church leaders, military officers, top civil servants. Very wealthy.

Commercial class
Bankers, merchants, factory owners, shop-keepers.
Known as Capitalists. Becoming very wealthy with the help of Government loans and contracts.

Working class
Factory workers, street traders.
Very poor indeed. Low wages, long hours, bad housing, food shortages. Resented their treatment by employers. Not allowed to form trade unions.

Peasants
Country people making their living by farming.
Very poor indeed. Since Emancipation (1861) had had to pay for their freedom in 49 yearly instalments. Many in debt. Population increase meant land had to support more people. Many were hungry. Many leaving to try to find work in cities.

ruling class 1%

upper class 11.5%

commercial class 1.5%

working class 4%

peasants 82%

The Tsarist regime

The Tsar
1 An autocrat (a ruler with absolute power).
2 Made laws himself, and appointed and dismissed ministers.
3 Tsar Nicholas II refused to consider any form of national parliament.

The civil service
1 Each department run by a minister.
2 Made sure the Tsar's commands were carried out.
3 Collected taxes.

The secret police
(The Okhrana)
1 Run by the Minister of the Interior.
2 Responsible for preventing criticism of the Tsar.
3 Arrested suspects and had them tried in special courts.

The army
1 The largest peacetime army in the world (2.6 million men).
2 Helped the police maintain law and order.

The Russian Orthodox Church
1 Its version of Christianity was the official religion of the Empire.
2 Priests taught that it was a sin to oppose the will of the Tsar.
3 Tsar Nicholas II's old tutor and chief adviser was both Head of the Church and a Government minister.

Opposition to Tsarist rule

Social Democrats
Followed the ideas of Karl Marx:
1 Throughout history there has been a struggle for power between different classes.
2 Angered by their treatment by the Capitalists (those who owned the wealth of the country) the workers will rise up against them.
3 The workers will take away
a the means of production (e.g. factories)
b the means of distribution (e.g. railways)
c the methods of exchange (e.g. banks).
4 They will then share them out equally. Marx called this 'Socialism'.
5 Eventually a Socialist society will adopt a system of 'Communism', an unselfish system in which people would
a work according to their abilities
b be paid according to their needs.

In 1903 the Social Democratic Party split into two groups:

The Bolsheviks, led by Lenin, wanted the Party to
1 consist of a small, well-disciplined group of skilled revolutionaries who would seize power on behalf of the workers
2 avoid alliances and mass membership.

The Mensheviks wanted the Party to
1 be a mass party to ensure that, when it came, the revolution was as fully supported as possible
2 ally with
a other Socialist parties
b middle class people who wanted constitutional reforms.

Liberals
Wanted a democratic system of government with an elected parliament and the Tsar as a constitutional monarch (as in Britain). Opposed revolution.

Social Revolutionaries
Wanted peasants to have a greater share of the land by confiscating it from the Tsar, the nobles and the Church and giving it to village communes. Used terrorist tactics. Aimed for violent revolution by the peasants. Did not follow Marxist theories.

1 What were the main **a** strengths **b** weaknesses of the Russian Empire?
2 Describe the difficulties which faced Russian peasants and workers.
3 Describe how the Tsar ruled his empire.
4 Make a chart to show the **a** similarities
b differences between the groups which opposed the Tsar's absolute rule.

The 1905 Revolution; Tsar and people, 1906-1914

By the end of this spread you should be able to:
*1 describe and explain the **a** causes **b** events*
c consequences of the 1905 Revolution
2 describe the relationship between the Tsar and

his people, 1906-1914
3 assess the strengths and weaknesses of the Tsarist regime in 1914

Towards revolution

What happened?
1 In 1904-5 Russia fought Japan for control of Korea and Manchuria.
2 The Tsar expected a quick victory that would silence his critics.
3 Russia suffered a series of defeats on land and sea. Japan destroyed both its Pacific and Baltic fleets.

The war with Japan

The results
1 The Tsar became more unpopular because
a the defeats humiliated Russia
b his government was shown to be weak and incompetent.
2 Conditions for working people became worse because of
a increased prices and food shortages
b shortages of materials which led to factory closures and unemployment.

What happened?
1 In January 1905 about 200,000 unarmed workers marched to the Tsar's Winter Palace in St Petersburg to petition the Tsar for
a better working and living conditions
b an end to the war
c a parliament.
2 Soldiers fired on the crowd killing 500.

Bloody Sunday

The results
The massacre
1 undermined the Tsar in the eyes of many who had trusted him to help them
2 increased support for revolutionaries
3 sparked off a wave of riots, strikes, and murders.

The 1905 Revolution

1905

January Strikes in St Petersburg. Many Government officials killed.

February Assassination of Governor-General of Moscow, the Tsar's uncle.

March Start of peasant uprisings. Landlords murdered.

Many non-Russian areas start to demand independence.

May Professional workers (e.g. doctors, lawyers, teachers) support demands for changes in government.

News of Japanese destruction of the Baltic Fleet fuels unrest.

June Mutiny by crew of the battleship *Potemkin*.

July-August Strikes and peasant uprisings continue.

September Treaty of Portsmouth ends war with Japan.

October General strike brings country to a standstill.
The Tsar issues the October Manifesto.
Many strikers return to work.
Liberals welcome the Manifesto and end their opposition.
Revolutionary groups form Soviets (workers councils) in major cities.

December Police and army break up the St Petersburg and Moscow Soviets

1906

January-March The Tsar's forces crush remaining opposition in town and countryside.

The October Manifesto The Tsar promised
1 freedom of speech and the right to form political parties
2 a Duma, or national parliament, elected by all adults
3 to make no new laws without the Duma's approval.

Why did the Revolution fail?

1 The end of the war with Japan released troops to help the Tsar deal with the disturbances.
2 despite some mutinies the armed forces stayed loyal to the Tsar.
3 The October Manifesto divided the opposition. It pleased
a many workers who ended their strikes
b the Liberal's who ended their support for the Soviets.
4 The workers' strikes and peasants' uprisings were not co-ordinated.

Tsar and people, 1906-1914

Broken promises

1 The voting system for the Duma was rigged to give landowners and property owners more influence than peasants and workers. Despite this the first two Dumas were left-wing.
2 The Fundamental Laws (May 1906) showed that little had changed. They announced that
a the Tsar remained an autocratic ruler
b the Duma had no say in most areas of government
c it had limited power to introduce new laws.
3 When the first two Dumas (1906 and 1907) demanded reforms, the Tsar dismissed them.
4 Further changes to the electoral laws excluded Socialists. The next two Dumas were loyal to the Tsar.

Repression
Thousands of terrorists and revolutionaries are executed, exiled or imprisoned.

Results
1 Reduction in terrorism and revolutionary activity.
2 Richer peasants (kulaks) run profitable farms. This
a restores their loyalty to the Tsar.
b provides more food for the cities.
3 Some improvements for city workers but many remain discontented. 1912-1914, frequent strikes.

The rule of Stolypin
1906, the Tsar appoints Peter Stolypin as Prime Minister. Stolypin aims to achieve stability by
1 repressing revolutionaries
2 introducing reforms to improve people's lives.
1911, Stolypin assassinated by a revolutionary terrorist.

Reform
1 The countryside.
a Abolition of peasants' annual payments for their freedom (page 102).
b Peasants helped to leave their village communes, buy their own land and set up farms.
2 The cities. Health insurance scheme set up for workers.

The impact of Rasputin

1 Rasputin was a peasant who
a claimed to be a Starets, or holy man
b appeared able to stop the bleeding of the Tsar and Tsarina's haemophiliac son, Alexi
c became a trusted member of their court and a confidant of the Tsarina, Alexandra.
2 Dislike for him grew because
a he was known to be a drinker and womaniser
b after Stolypin's death his influence over the Tsar's political decisions increased.
3 Rasputin's activities

a brought scandal to the court
b caused hostility which reduced people's loyalty towards the Tsar.

1 What do the events of the 1905 Revolution tell you about the **a** weaknesses **b** strengths of the Tsarist regime?
2 What were the **a** immediate **b** long-term results of the 1905 Revolution?
3 Use pages 102-105. What **a** economic **b** social **c** political problems faced the Tsar between 1900 and 1914? How successfully did he deal with them?

The impact of the First World War; the February Revolution, 1917

By the end of this spread you should be able to describe:
1 the impact of the First World War on Russia
2 a the causes b the events of the February Revolution, 1917

Economic problems
1 Over 15 million men had to join the army. This left fields and factories without enough workers, causing severe shortages of food and materials.
2 The railway system failed to cope with the additional demands of war, causing
a inadequate supplies to the Front
b food shortages in towns
c coal shortages leading to power failures.
3 Food prices rose so that families could afford less food.

Military defeats
1 Russian armies were very large but badly led and poorly equipped.
2 In 1914 they lost two major battles with 250,000 killed, wounded or captured.
3 This caused civilian anger and loss of morale.

Hunger and discontent
Food shortages and price rises caused widespread hunger and discontent. especially among town workers.

The impact of the First World War

Criticism of the Tsar
The Tsar was blamed for
1 military defeats after personally taking command of the army (August 1915).
2 the weak government of the Tsarina, whom he left in charge while he was at army headquarters.
3 his refusal to choose new ministers from the Duma.

Social changes
1 The war created new jobs in armaments factories and on the railways.
2 The number of town workers increased rapidly as peasants left the countryside to take up the new jobs.

Criticism of the Tsarina
The Tsarina
1 was inexperienced and incompetent as a ruler. The Government ceased to function effectively.
2 relied on the advice of the unpopular Rasputin until his murder (December 1916).
3 was personally unpopular because she was a German. Rumours circulated that she and Rasputin were working to ensure a German victory in the war.

The February Revolution, 1917

Winter, 1917

Exceptionally cold weather between January and March made bad conditions worse:

1 Trains could not run, causing acute shortages of food and fuel.
2 The Russian people were gripped by extreme hunger and cold.

1917

(* Dates given in brackets are those according to the Russian calendar which, until 1918, was 13 days behind that of Western Europe.)

March 7 (February 22) 20,000 steelworkers locked out after breakdown of pay talks. Other workers strike in their support.

March 8 (February 23) International Women's Day. Thousands of women demonstrate in Petrograd calling for bread. More workers come out on strike.

March 9 (February 24) Large crowds repeatedly dispersed by police and soldiers.

March 10 (February 25) 250,000 workers, over half the workforce, are on strike. Petrograd paralysed. Tsar orders army to end the disturbances.

March 11 (February 26) Troops fire on crowds killing 40. President of Duma advises Tsar to form a new government urgently. Tsar orders Duma to stop meeting.

March 12 (February 27) Soldiers mutiny. They refuse to fire on the crowds and join the strikers. Duma sets up a Provisional Government. Soldiers, sailors and workers form the Petrograd Soviet.

March 13 (February 28) Tsar sets out to return to Petrograd.

March 14 (March 1) Generals tell Tsar the army no longer supports him.

March 15 (March 2) Tsar Nicholas abdicates in favour of his brother, Grand Duke Michael.

March 16 (March 3) Grand Duke Michael refuses to become Tsar. End of the Romanov dynasty.

The Provisional Government

1 Consisted of twelve members of the Duma.
2 Planned to rule until the people elected a Constituent Assembly to work out a new system of government.

Rival claims to power

The Petrograd Soviet

1 A council of 2,500 deputies elected by workers and soldiers whose interests it aimed to protect.
2 Dominated by Mensheviks who aimed for a workers' revolution but believed the time was not yet ripe for it.
3 Recognized the Provisional Government but was determined to influence it and eventually share power.

---

1 a How did the First World War weaken the Tsar's control of Russia?
b How did the actions of each of the following contribute to the revolution of February 1917

i the strikers ii the soldiers iii the Duma
iv the generals v Grand Duke Michael?
2 Using pages 104-107 make a list of, and write notes on, the a long-term b short-term causes of the overthrow of the Tsarist regime.

The Provisional Government and the October Revolution, 1917

By the end of this spread you should be able to:
1 describe the problems facing the Provisional Government

2 explain the reasons for its failure
3 explain how the Bolsheviks were able to seize power in October 1917

1917

(*Dates given in brackets are according to the Russian calendar)

March	Petrograd Soviet issues Order No. 1.
April	Return of Lenin from Switzerland.
	Lenin's 'April Theses'.
June	Failure of 'June offensive' against Austria.
July	The 'July Days'.
	Lenin flees to Finland.
	Kerensky becomes Prime Minister.

August	Failure of the Kornilov Revolt.
September	Bolsheviks win majority in Petrograd Soviet.
October	Trotsky becomes chairman of Petrograd Soviet.
	Lenin returns from Finland.
	Bolsheviks plan armed uprising.
November 6-7	(October 24-25) Bolshevik Revolution.

The Provisional Government and its problems

	Land	Hunger	The war	Socialist Revolutionaries	The army
Problem	The peasants were demanding their own land.	The workers were demanding food and would riot if they did not get it.	Fight on or make peace?	The government needed to prevent the spread of support for Socialists aiming to overthrow it (e.g. Revolutionary Socialists, Bolsheviks).	The Government needed to control the armed forces.
Response	The Government promised to bring in reforms later.	The Government's powers limited as Petrograd Soviet controlled food supply system.	The Government decided to fight on in order to honour Russia's commitments to her allies, Britain and France.	1 To create a more democratic society the Government: a allowed free speech b allowed a free press c released political prisoners. 2 The Government used the July Days to arrest Bolshevik leaders but did not suppress the movement.	Troops obeyed Petrograd Soviet's Order No 1. Refused Government orders which contradicted those of Soviet.
Result	Peasants angry at delay. Eventually seized land for themselves.	Problem got worse.	Failure of 'June offensive'. Further Russian defeats. Collapse of discipline and morale in army. Rising anger at home. Increased popularity for Bolsheviks who demanded peace.	Socialist Revolutionaries were free to criticize the Government and spread their ideas.	The Petrograd Soviet, not the Provisional Government, controlled the armed forces.

How the Bolsheviks built up their strength and support

The Kornilov Revolt

What happened?

1 In August General Kornilov, the right-wing army Commander-in-Chief, tried to seize power.
2 Prime Minister Kerensky turned to the Bolsheviks to defend Petrograd against Kornilov's troops. He released their leaders and gave weapons to the Red Guards.
3 Bolshevik activists persuaded Kornilov's troops to desert.

Results

The Bolsheviks
1 emerged as heroes
2 gained popularity and won a majority in the Petrograd Soviet
3 became a well-armed fighting force.

The 'July Days'

What happened?

1 Angry at the failure of the 'June offensive', workers, soldiers and sailors rioted, demanding government by the Soviets.
2 The Bolsheviks supported, but did not lead, the riots.

Results

1 The Government
a quelled the riots
b accused the Bolsheviks of working for the Germans
c arrested Bolshevik leaders. Lenin fled to Finland.
2 Although Bolshevik fortunes were at a very low point, the Party was now seen as the leading revolutionary group.

Popular slogans

1 Lenin's ideas were turned into simple, memorable slogans such as
a 'Peace, bread and land'
b 'All power to the Soviets'.
2 As the war went on and conditions worsened, these became increasingly popular.

Lenin and the April theses

1 On his return to Petrograd from exile in Switzerland, Lenin persuaded the Bolsheviks to work for
a the overthrow of the Provisional Government
b the establishment of a Communist regime.
2 In his 'April theses' he called for
a an end to the war
b the Soviets to form a new government
c the land to be given to the peasants
d factories and banks to be owned by the State
e the Bolsheviks to change their name to 'Communists'.

Party organization

Guided by Lenin, an efficient Party organization helped membership to grow from 26,000 to 2,000,000 between April and August:

1 The German government gave money to the Bolsheviks because they argued for peace and might overthrow the Provisional Government.
2 The Party ran numerous newspapers including 'Pravda' (truth).
3 A central committee ran the Party with local committees in the factories and the army.
4 A private army, the Red Guards, was set up in the Petrograd factories.

The Bolsheviks take power

Crisis in Russia, September-October 1917
1 Peasants were killing landlords and taking over land.
2 In the army **a** peasant soldiers deserted to go home to claim land
b angry soldiers, disillusioned with the war and influenced by Bolshevik agents, refused to fight and killed their officers.
3 High prices and food shortages caused more hunger in the cities.

The role of Lenin
1 From Finland Lenin urged the Bolsheviks to take advantage of the chaos and take power by force.
2 In October, he secretly returned and persuaded the Central Committee to act.
3 Because he had to remain in hiding he could not supervise the details of the operation.

The role of Trotsky Trotsky (formerly a Menshevik) who had joined the Bolsheviks after the July Days, masterminded the coup. He
1 arranged for it to begin the night before the Second Congress of Soviets met. He wanted to claim that it was done on behalf of the Petrograd Soviet
2 persuaded soldiers in the Petrograd garrison and the sailors at Kronstadt naval base to support the uprising and provide weapons
3 made detailed plans for the military operation.

The Government Kerensky knew of Trotsky's plans but could not take decisive action against them. He
1 had lost the support of many troops in Petrograd
2 sent inadequate forces to guard the Provisional Government in the Winter Palace
3 left Petrograd to try to raise support but found few generals willing to help.

1 **a** What were the main weaknesses of the Provisional Government?
b How did each one help to cause the Bolshevik Revolution?
2 What part did Lenin play in bringing about the Bolshevik Revolution?
3 What factors contributed to the success of the Bolshevik Revolution?

The October Revolution

(* Dates given in brackets are according to the Russian calendar)

November 6 (October 24)
night Red Guards start to take over key positions: bridges and telephone exchanges.

November 7 (October 25)
Morning Red Guards take over banks, Government buildings, railway stations.
Evening Cruiser *Aurora* bombards the Winter Palace. Red Guards' assault meets no resistance from defenders (army cadets and the Women's Battalion). Government ministers arrested.

November 8 (October 26)
Lenin announces formation of a new government

The establishment of Bolshevik rule, 1917-1924

By the end of this spread you should be able to describe:
1 how Lenin established Bolshevik control in Russia

2 the nature of Bolshevik rule
3 social changes under the Bolsheviks

How the Bolsheviks took control

A new government
1 The Mensheviks and many Social Revolutionaries walked out of the Second Congress of Soviets.
2 The Bolsheviks and their allies now had a majority.
3 Lenin set up a Council of People's Commissars as the new temporary government. He was its Chairman and chose its members.

Government by decree
Lenin's new government ruled by decree aiming to
1 carry out popular reforms
2 show that it was in charge
3 control opposition.

Factories
All factories were put under the control of elected committees of workers.

The press
All non-Bolshevik newpapers were banned.

Land
1 Land was taken from the Tsar, nobles, Church and other landlords and handed over to the peasants.
2 Because the peasants expected to have the land, Lenin decided not to follow Bolshevik policy and take it into State ownership.

The first decrees

Peace
Negotiations to end the war with Germany were to begin at once.

The secret police
A new secret police force (the CHEKA) was set up to deal with the Bolsheviks' opponents.

The Constituent Assembly
1 The Provisional Government had arranged for elections to be held for a Constituent Assembly to set up a new democratic government.
2 In November 1917 these returned 370 Socialist Revolutionary (SR) deputies, 175 Bolsheviks and 162 others.
3 In January 1918, when the Assembly met, Lenin refused to hand over power to the SR majority and ordered it to close.
4 Red Guards enforced his order, killing or wounding over 100 pro-Assembly demonstrators.

Peace with Germany
1 Trotsky, Commissar (Minister) for Foreign Affairs, spun out negotiations hoping for a Socialist revolution in Germany.
2 By 1918 the Germans threatened Petrograd itself. Lenin decided peace had to be made at any price in order to
a keep the army's support
b end the hardship at home
c give the Bolshevik government a 'breathing space'.
3 At the Treaty of Brest-Litovsk (Fig. 1 page 112) Russia had to accept very harsh terms.

Russia lost its richest areas. They contained over 25% of its population, farmland and railways, and about 75% of its coal and iron ore.

Fig. 1 The Treaty of Brest-Litovsk, March 1918

— Russian frontier in 1914

— Russian frontier after the Treaty of Brest Litovsk

Russian lands lost at the Treaty of Brest Litovsk

0   500 km

Victory in the Civil War (page 114)
1 The Bolsheviks survived the military threat from their enemies at home and abroad.
2 They gained firm control
a over much wider territories
b over nationalist groups that had declared independence.

The Red Terror
The CHEKA
1 tortured and killed Bolshevik opponents
2 killed the Tsar and his family during the Civil War to prevent them becoming the focus of opposition
3 used terror tactics to frighten the population into obedience to the Government.

The Communist state
1 In 1918
a the Bolsheviks changed their name to the Communist Party
b the Congress of Soviets approved a new constitution (Fig. 2).
2 By 1922
a the Communist Party was the only legal political party
b Lenin had banned opposition groups within the Party itself
c Soviet Russia had become a one-party state ruled by a dictator.

Religion
The Government
1 suppressed religious worship
2 persecuted priests and monks
3 banned religious education in schools.

Work
A Labour Law (1922) gave workers
1 an eight hour day
2 two weeks paid holiday a year
3 social insurance benefits such as sick and unemployment pay and old-age pensions.

Social changes

Education
1 Literacy campaigns enabled more people to be able to read and write.
2 The sciences were encouraged and subjects thought to be 'useless', such as history and ancient languages, were banned.

Marriage
1 Couples were allowed non-religious weddings.
2 Divorce was made easier.
3 Free love was encouraged.
4 Abortion became available on demand.

Fig. 2 The Communist Party and the Government

The Government appeared to represent the will of the people as expressed through their Soviets (councils of workers, peasants etc.). In reality it was controlled by the Communist Party. Every level of government was controlled by its Party equivalent.

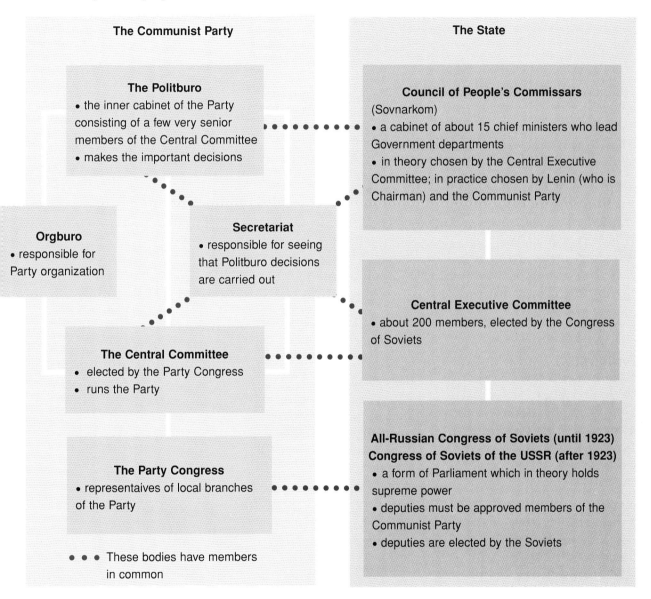

The Communist Party

The Politburo
- the inner cabinet of the Party consisting of a few very senior members of the Central Committee
- makes the important decisions

Orgburo
- responsible for Party organization

Secretariat
- responsible for seeing that Politburo decisions are carried out

The Central Committee
- elected by the Party Congress
- runs the Party

The Party Congress
- representaives of local branches of the Party

● ● ● These bodies have members in common

The State

Council of People's Commissars (Sovnarkom)
- a cabinet of about 15 chief ministers who lead Government departments
- in theory chosen by the Central Executive Committee; in practice chosen by Lenin (who is Chairman) and the Communist Party

Central Executive Committee
- about 200 members, elected by the Congress of Soviets

All-Russian Congress of Soviets (until 1923) Congress of Soviets of the USSR (after 1923)
- a form of Parliament which in theory holds supreme power
- deputies must be approved members of the Communist Party
- deputies are elected by the Soviets

The 1923 constitution

1 Russia became the Union of Soviet Socialist Republics (USSR).
2 Each of the six Republics in the Union ran its own internal affairs such as education and health.
3 The central government in Moscow dealt with important national affairs such as foreign policy and defence.

1 a Make a timeline showing all the actions and events which helped the Bolsheviks take control over the Russian people.
b Explain what each one contributed.
2 a What benefits did Bolshevik rule bring to the Russians?
b What was the cost of those benefits?

The Civil War, 1918-1921; economic developments, 1918-1924

By the end of this spread you should be able to:
1 explain the a causes b consequences of the Civil War

2 explain the reasons for the Bolsheviks' victory
3 describe a War Communism b the New Economic Policy
4 explain their effects

Reasons for the Civil War, 1918-1921

Enemies at home
The Bolsheviks had many different enemies, all anxious to dislodge them:

1 Social Revolutionaries who had won the election and been denied power.
2 Landlords who had lost their lands.
3 Supporters of the Tsar.
4 National groups which wanted independence.
5 Generals who opposed the humiliating terms of the Treaty of Brest-Litovsk.

Enemies abroad
The Allies sent forces to support the Whites because they
1 were angry that Russia had made peace with Germany
2 wanted to destroy the Bolshevik government in case it spread revolution to the rest of Europe.

The Czech Legion
1 Bolshevik officials quarelled with Czech ex-prisoners of war on their way to Vladivostok and the sea route home.
2 Angry Czechs
a took over the Trans-Siberian Railway
b gave protection to 'White' (anti-Bolshevik) groups
c formed the Czech Legion and marched on Moscow.

Popularity
1 The Bolsheviks gained popularity because of their reforms.
2 The Whites were less popular because
a they could be associated with i the Tsar ii landlords iii foreign intervention
b of their harsh treatment of people in the lands they captured.

Unity versus disunity
1 The Bolsheviks
a shared a singleness of purpose
b were fighting for survival.
2 The Whites
a were made up of many different groups with only their opposition to the Bolsheviks in common
b lacked a single leader
c failed to work together. They fought in separate armies, far apart. Trotsky was able to defeat them one by one
d in 1919 lost outside support when the Allies withdrew their forces.

Trotsky
1 created the 'Red Army' with the help of professional officers
2 enforced strict discipline
3 used both encouragement and terror to make his soldiers fight
4 proved an outstanding military strategist.

Why did the Bolsheviks win the Civil War?

Terror
The CHEKA
1 hunted down people who helped the Whites
2 forced the peasants to hand over food to the Government (page 115).

Resources
The Bolsheviks controlled
1 the main cities of Moscow and Petrograd with their factories
2 the railways which allowed them to send supplies and troops where they wished.

War Communism
kept the Red Army supplied with food and weapons.

The results of the Bolshevik victory

1 The survival of Bolshevik rule.
2 The extension of Bolshevik control over a wider area.
3 Famine, industrial collapse, and the New Economic Policy.

War Communism

Aims

1 To ensure that the Red Army was fed and equipped during the Civil War.
2 To introduce a system of Communism.

How it worked	
★ **Nationalisation** **1** Factories with more than ten workers were taken over by the State. **2** A Supreme Council of National Economy decided what each factory should produce. ★ **Workers** **1** Military discipline introduced into the factories. **2** Strikes made illegal. Strikers could be shot. ★ **Peasants** **1** Forced to give all surplus produce to the Government. **2** No longer allowed to	sell it for profit. ★ **Rationing** Food rationed in the cities. ★ **Money** **1** To meet its expenses the Government printed masses of paper money. This caused inflation. The Government allowed money to lose its value. **2** Many money payments abolished, e.g. rents, fares. **3** In place of money, people told to barter goods.

Results

1 The Government managed to feed and equip an army eventually numbering five million.
2 Peasants stopped producing surplus food since they were no longer allowed to sell it for profit. This caused
a 1919-1920, food shortages
b 1921, full scale famine made worse by bad weather and disease. Seven million died.
3 Hunger, low wages and discontent among workers. Fall in industrial output.
4 1921, the Kronstadt mutiny.
a Sailors previously loyal to the Bolsheviks revolted against War Communism.
b Although the Red Army crushed the revolt, Lenin realized he had to make changes if the Bolsheviks were to stay in control.

The New Economic Policy

Aims

1 To keep the Russian people happy by improving their living conditions.
2 To improve industrial output.

How it worked	
★ **Peasants** **1** To give the Government a fixed amount of produce as tax. **2** Allowed to sell any surplus for profit. ★ **Money** People could use money again to make payments.	★ **Factories and business** **1** Small factories given back to their owners. **2** New small businesses such as shops could be privately owned. **3** The State continued to run the large factories and the banks.

Results

1 Many Bolsheviks criticized the NEP because it abandoned Socialist principles.
2 By 1925
a food production had returned to pre-war levels
b industrial production had risen greatly
c in both areas Russia remained backward compared to other industrial nations.

1 a Draw up and complete two columns for the Civil War headed 'Bolshevik strengths' and 'White weaknesses'.
b Explain why the Bolsheviks won the Civil War.
2 How successful was War Communism?
3 What was the significance for the Bolsheviks of **a** victory in the Civil War **b** the New Economic Policy?

The struggle to succeed Lenin, 1924-1929

By the end of this spread you should be able to:
1 describe the struggle to succeed Lenin
2 explain why Stalin rather than Trotsky emerged as leader

A divided Politburo

Before Lenin died in 1924 six of the seven members of the Politburo (page 113) had split into two groups. They were divided about the best way of improving the USSR's economy. The seventh member, Joseph Stalin, was not a passionate believer in either of the two points of view:

The Left Opposition

Leon Trotsky
Grigori Zinoviev
Leon Kamenev

1 Opposed continuation of the NEP because it favoured profit-making peasants
2 Wanted the Government to
a take over the land and force peasants to produce enough food for the towns
b turn the USSR into an industrial country immediately
c return to full Socialist principles.

The Rightists

Nikolai Bukharin
Andrei Rykov
Mikhail Tomsky

1 Wanted to continue Lenin's New Economic Policy (NEP) for at least twenty more years.
2 Hoped to return to Socialist principles once the USSR was strong again.

Fig. 1 Rivals for the succession

Leon Trotsky
Commissar for War

Advantages
1 The most obvious choice to follow Lenin because of his
a strong personality
b intelligence
c powerful leadership qualities shown during the October Revolution and Civil War
2 Popular with the army

Disadvantages
Unpopular in Politburo

Joseph Stalin
General Secretary of the Communist Party
Commissar of Nationalities
Member of the Orgburo (committee reponsible for Party organization)

Advantages
1 As General Secretary held the key post in the Party
2 Could command support because many Party officials owed their position to him

Disadvantages
Thought of as a dull, hardworking administrator

Fig. 2 How Stalin achieved power

**Step 1
Lenin's man, 1924**

After Lenin's death
Stalin
1 encouraged the
cult of Lenin, e.g.
the embalming and
permanent display
of his body
2 presented himself
as Lenin's close
follower, e.g. he
was chief mourner
at his funeral.

**Step 2
Surviving Lenin's
Testament, 1924**

1 Lenin's Testament was
a letter he wrote to the
Party Congress to be
read out after his death.
2 In it Lenin
recommended Stalin
should be replaced as
Party Secretary.
3 Stalin was saved when
the Central Committee
decided to keep the letter
secret because
a it did not want to
provoke disunity
b Kamenev and Zinoviev
defended Stalin. They
wanted his help to
prevent Trotsky becoming
leader.

**Step 3 The dismissal of
Trotsky, 1925**

1 In the debate about
future policy Trotsky
argued for 'Permanent
Revolution'. He wanted
to protect Communism in
the USSR by promoting
Communist revolutions
abroad.
2 Stalin argued for
'Socialism in one
Country'. He wanted
Communists to
concentrate on building
up the USSR's strength.
3 Trotsky's ideas proved
unpopular with the Party.
4 Kamenev and Zinoviev
allied with Stalin and the
Rightists in the Politburo
to dismiss Trotsky as
Commissar of War.

**Step 4 Attacking
the Left, 1926-27**

1 With three of his
allies elected to the
Politburo, and
Rightist support,
Stalin had Trotsky,
Kamenev and
Zinoviev dismissed
from the Politburo.
2 Trotsky and
Zinoviev were then
expelled from the
Party.

**Step 5
Attacking the
Right, 1928-29**

1 In the Politburo,
Stalin now argued
against the NEP
and in favour of
expanding
industry.
2 When the
Rightists opposed
this, Stalin used
his majority to
vote them down.
3 In 1929,
Bukharin, Rykov,
and Tomsky
resigned.

Why did Stalin and not Trotsky emerge as leader?

Stalin
1 successfully presented himself as Lenin's loyal
disciple (Fig. 2)
2 exploited his strong powerbase within the Party
(Fig. 1)
3 supported the popular idea of 'Socialism in one
country' (Fig. 2)
4 successfully played off Left and Right in the
Politburo (Fig. 2).

Trotsky
1 was unpopular in the Politburo
2 suffered from the rivalry of Kamenev and
Zinoviev who agreed with him politically, but
disliked him personally and so allied with Stalin to
block his succession
3 supported the unpopular idea of 'Permanent
Revolution' (Fig. 2)
4 failed to use his popularity in the army to help his
cause.

1 Why was Trotsky not Stalin the favourite to
succeed Lenin?
2 List the factors which caused Stalin rather than

Trotsky to become leader. Use the headings:
a Stalin **i** his qualities **ii** his actions
b Trotsky **i** his qualities **ii** his actions

Stalin's dictatorship

By the end of this spread you should be able to describe the methods Stalin used to control the Soviet Union:

1 terror and the Purges
2 racial and religious persecution
3 propaganda and official culture

Rule by terror

The secret police
1 a In 1922 the CHEKA became the OGPU.
b In 1934 the OGPU became the NKVD.
2 Stalin increased the size of the secret police force and used it to
a hunt down and destroy his opponents
b terrorize ordinary people into obedience.
3 People found guilty of opposition or disobedience were sentenced to death, exile or hard labour.

The labour camps
1 Set up in Siberia and the Arctic north.
2 Run by the secret police.
3 Millions of people were imprisoned and
a forced to do hard manual work on construction and mining projects.
b about 13 million died from cold, hunger and ill-treatment.

Fig. 1 The Great Purge, 1934-38

Ordinary citizens

Neighbours encouraged to inform on one another's crimes or disloyalty to Stalin.
Children encouraged to inform on parents.
Those denounced are arrested, lose their jobs, and are forced to make confessions.

The armed forces	1937	1938-39
Stalin wanted to prevent any possibility of a military coup against him.	The Red Army Commander-in-Chief, Marshal Tukhachevsky, and seven other generals (all heroes for their part in the Civil War) were arrested and shot.	All admirals, many naval officers and half the Red Army's officers executed or imprisoned.

Party leaders	1935	1936	1938
1934 Stalin decides that his popular Politburo colleague, Kirov, is a possible rival. Kirov is murdered, probably on Stalin's orders. Stalin claims the murder is part of a Leftist plot against him and the Party. NKVD arrests thousands of Kirov's supporters and leaders of the old Left Opposition.	Senior Communists arrested: 1108 out of the 1966 delegates to the 17th Congress; 98 out of 139 members of Central Committee. Party branches told to root out anyone who had supported Trotsky. Thousands denounced and expelled.	Zinoviev, Kamenev and other old Left Opposition leaders confess to plotting after NKVD torture and brainwashing. Executed after show trials.	Bukharin, Rykov, Tomsky and other old Rightist leaders executed after similar treatment.

The first purges, 1930-33 Stalin purged (cleared out) anyone who held up, criticized or opposed his plans for industrialization and collectivization. Most of the accused were deported or imprisoned. Some were shot. The first victims were:
1 managers and workers accused of wrecking the Five Year Plans (page 120)
2 Kulaks accused of opposition to collectivization (page 122)
3 ordinary Party members accused of ill-discipline or incorrect attitudes.

The Great Purge, 1934-38
1 In 1934 Stalin turned on the most senior members of the Party.
2 The Purge quickly expanded to enclose the whole population in a grip of terror (Fig 1).
3 One estimate is that one million people were executed and eight million sent to labour camps.

Propaganda and official culture

The cult of Stalin Stalin was worshipped as a leader:
1 pictures and statues of him were everywhere
2 places were named after him
3 people at meetings had to clap when his name was mentioned.

Culture and censorship
1 Writers, artists, film-makers, even composers, had to support the Government by following the policy of 'Socialist Realism'. This meant their work had to:
a deal with the lives of ordinary working people
b show how Communism was developing
c give simple, clear, optimistic messages.
2 Writers had to be members of the Party-controlled Union of Soviet Writers.
3 Books already published which did not follow the correct Party line were adapted or destroyed.

Education
1 Children were taught that Stalin was the 'Great Leader'.
2 They learnt Stalin's version of history.
3 Education became stricter. Stalin wanted schools to produce useful citizens. He
a insisted on uniforms, tests, and examinations
b prescribed the subjects and information that children should learn.
4 By 1939 the majority of people could read.

Religion and nationalities

Religious persecution Stalin continued the attack on religions started after the Bolshevik Revolution:
1 Christian leaders were imprisoned and churches closed down.
2 Muslim mosques and schools were closed and pilgrimages to Mecca banned.

National identities Lenin's policy of encouraging national identities produced demands for greater autonomy rather than the hoped-for conversion to Socialism. Under Stalin national groups increasingly came under attack:
1 the persecution of Muslims was also an attack on the way of life of national groups
2 the campaign against the kulaks (page 123) removed millions of people from national minorities living in rural areas
3 in the 1930s a policy of 'Russification' attempted to impose the Russian culture on the USSR:
a Russian became compulsory in schools
b key jobs went to Russians
c army recruits were sent away from their homelands and placed in ethnically mixed units.

A new constitution, 1936

1 This made some alterations to the 1923 constitution (page 113):
a the USSR now consisted of eleven republics.
b the Congress of Soviets of the USSR became the Supreme Soviet of the USSR with two chambers instead of one.
c elections were to be by secret ballot.
2 The Communist Party kept its close control of both the central government and the government of each republic.
3 Stalin held the posts of
a First (or General) Secretary of the Party
b Chairman of the Politburo
c Chairman of the Council of People's Commissars, or Prime Minister.

1 Make a chart showing
a in column one, the methods Stalin used to control the Soviet Union
b in column two, the people most affected by each method.
2 To what extent did Stalin set up a personal dictatorship in the USSR?

Stalin's economic policies 1

By the end of the next two spreads you should be able to:
1 describe the modernization of industry
2 describe the collectivization of agriculture

*3 explain their **a** causes **b** consequences*
4 describe their impact on the lives of different groups of Soviet people

Industrialization

Stalin wanted to transform the USSR from a backward agricultural country to a modern industrial one. His main reasons were:
1 Security. He believed the USSR was
a likely to be attacked by Western Capitalist states
b would be defeated by them unless it modernized.
2 Successful Communism. By creating and sharing wealth among the Soviet people he hoped to create a strong state based on Communist principles.

The Five Year Plans

To achieve industrialization, Stalin ordered the State Planning Commission (Gosplan) to draw up a series of Five Year Plans. Each Plan set targets which the workers in various industries had to achieve.

Plan 1, 1928-1932/3

1 To enable the USSR to increase its armaments quickly, the Plan emphasised heavy industry, especially coal, iron and steel.
2 All private businesses which had been allowed under Lenin's NEP were closed or taken over by the State.
3 In 1929 Stalin decided the Plan should be achieved in four years rather than five.

Plan 2, 1933-37

1 This Plan promised to concentrate on consumer goods and better housing for the Soviet people.
2 From 1934 the increased threat from Hitler's Germany caused the planners to change their targets in favour of armaments again.

Fig. 1 The first two Five Year Plans

Item	1927/8 Actual	1933 Target	1933 Actual	1937 Target	1937 Actual
Electricity Thousand million kilowatt hours	5.05	17.0	13.4	38.0	36.2
Coal Million tonnes	35.4	68	64.3	152.5	128
Oil Million tonnes	11.7	19	21.4	46.8	28.5
Iron Million tonnes	3.3	8.0	6.2	16.0	14.5
Steel Million tonnes	4.0	8.3	5.9	17.0	17.7

The power and wealth of the USSR

1 Although the Plan targets were not met, all Soviet industries made spectacular advances (Fig. 1).
2 By 1940 the USSR was the world's second largest industrial power (behind the USA).

New industrial centres

Huge towns and industrial centres, like the Magnitogorsk metalworks, were built from scratch deep inside the USSR where they would be safe from invasion.

Urban population

Between 1929 and 1939 the population of the USSR's cities rose by 29 million.

Power and transport

Vast construction projects were completed such as the Dneiper Dam hydro-electric power station and the Belomor Canal.

Skills

1 In 1929 Soviet workers lacked many of the skills needed to implement the first Plan.
2 Between 1929 and 1937 investment in education and training schemes created a skilled workforce.

The economic results of the Five Year Plans

Women were encouraged

1 to work to help to achieve the Plans
2 to have children because of the falling population:
a facilities such as creches were provided in factories to help them both have children and work
b In 1936 the divorce laws (page 112) were tightened up again .

Forced labour

1 Some of the biggest tasks in the Plans were carried out in appalling conditions by prisoners in labour camps.
2 Prisoners built the Belomor Canal and the Moscow Metro.

The workplace To persuade workers to raise their output, the Government used:

1 *Encouragement.*
a It urged workers to match the achievements of model workers such as the miner Stakhanov who was said to have surpassed his targets tenfold.
b Awarded medals. The highest was the Order of Lenin.
2 *Discipline.*
a Fines were imposed for lateness and bad workmanship.
b Workers absent for more than a day were sacked.
3 *Terror.*
a Failures were always blamed on saboteurs rather than on the system.
b the secret police encouraged workers to inform on one another.
c Anyone blamed for obstructing work could be sent to a labour camp or shot.

A new elite

1 Teachers, scientists, engineers, factory managers, and skilled workers were paid far higher wages than ordinary workers.
2 Like many officials, they also received extra benefits such as better housing or the right to buy scarce goods.
3 This group enjoyed a higher standard of living than everybody else. Communist principles of equality were abandoned.

The impact of the Five Year Plans on the lives of the Soviet people

Living conditions

1 *Housing.*
a It was impossible to build enough new houses for the millions of peasants who flooded into the cities.
b Most families had to live in overcrowded, rundown buildings.
2 *Food.*
a At first, shortages led to rationing.
b In the mid-1930s conditions improved. Food remained dull but there were no more famines.
3 *Education.* All workers' children received free primary education.
4 *Health.* Free health care schemes were extended.
5 *Wages.* Workers were poorly paid. Between 1928 and 1933 the value of their wages fell by 50%.
6 *Goods.* There was an acute shortage of all consumer goods including clothes and shoes.
7 *Crime.* Alcoholism, juvenile delinquency, and crime increased.

Stalin's economic policies 2

Collectivization

The problem

1 Soviet peasants used old-fashioned, inefficient farming methods. Even under the NEP they were producing insufficient food for the workers in the cities.

2 If the USSR was to industrialize successfully, its farming had to be improved because:

a even more workers would have to be fed.

b peasants were needed as industrial workers. Fewer peasants, therefore, had to produce the food.

c the Government aimed to sell surplus food abroad in order to make the money it needed to spend on developing industry. There had to be a surplus to sell.

The solution Stalin decided to collectivize the farms. This meant

1 the peasants had to

a give up their small plots of land and animals

b pool them with those of other families to make farms large enough to use machinery and modern farming methods.

2 the State provided each collective farm with machinery (e.g. tractors), other tools and seeds.

3 the Government bought the produce of each farm at a low fixed price.

4 the peasants received a small wage.

Fig. 1 Stages in the collectivization of farming

Stage 1

1927-28

1 The Government encourages peasants to join collectives voluntarily. Very few respond.

2 Faced by a food shortage in the cities, Stalin sends police squads into the countryside to seize food from the peasants.

Stage 2

1929

1 Stalin announces compulsory collectivization. There is widespread resistance.

2 The army, police and secret police are used to enforce the policy.

3 The resistance is strongest among the kulaks, the richest peasants. On Stalin's orders they are eliminated as a class (Fig. 3).

4 Hostile peasants destroy their livestock rather than hand them over to collectives (Fig. 2).

Stage 3

1930 onwards

1 Stalin allows peasants on collectives to own their own small private plots and a few animals. The peasants make these more productive than the collectives.

2 The policy of compulsory collectivization continues.

The economic results of collectivization

1 By 1932 about 62% of the land was collectivized; by 1941 it was almost all collectivized.
2 About 17 million peasants left the land to work in towns and industrial centres.
3 Collectivization failed to increase Soviet agricultural production (Fig. 2). It led to a decline in
a harvest yields
b the numbers of livestock.

Fig. 2 Food production in the USSR, 1928-1933

Item	1928	1933
Grain (Millions of tonnes)	73	69
Cattle (Millions)	70	38
Pigs (Millions)	26	12
Sheep and goats (Millions)	147	50

Fig. 3 The impact of collectivization on the lives of the Soviet people

Famine
Between 1932 and 1934 seven million people in the countryside died from famine caused by
1 harvest failures
2 the amount of food taken by the Government.

How collectivization affected the lives of the Soviet people

Peasants
Their traditional way of life was ended.
1 By 1940 nearly all had given up their own land to work on collective farms.
2 Most of their churches were closed.
3 Including the kulaks, about 10 million peasants were sent to labour camps or deported.
4 About 17 million left the land and went to work in the cities.

The kulaks
As Stalin intended, the kulaks were destroyed as a class. At least five million people in kulak families were made to leave their farms:
1 The kulaks believed to be the most hostile to the Government were handed over to the secret police and sent to labour camps. Their families were deported to inhospitable parts of the country such as Siberia.
2 Of the rest, a few may have been allowed to farm poor land in their own region, but most were deported. Many died of cold and starvation.

1 Make a table to show the a aims b methods c successes d failures e human costs of
i The Five Year Plans
ii Collectivization.
2 Use pages 118-123. What was the impact of Stalin's rule on the lives of
a peasants and their families
b workers and their families
c members of minority nationalities
d members of the armed forces
e writers and artists
f managers and professional people?

The USSR 1941-1964

By the end of this spread you should be able to describe:
1 the impact of the Second World War on Soviet society
2 the policy of De-Stalinization
3 the modernizing reforms of Khrushchev

The impact of the Second World War

Destruction
As a result of German action and the Soviet Union's scorched earth policy (page 45):
1 industrial sites such as factories, dams and mines were wrecked
2 about 70,000 villages, 98,000 farms and 4.7 million homes were destroyed
3 about 65,000 kms of railway track was torn up.

How the Second World War affected the USSR

Industry
1 The Third Five Year Plan had been interrupted by the war. In 1946 Stalin launched a Fourth.
2 Although the Soviet people were desperate for household goods, the Plan emphasized the building up of heavy industry.
3 Because of the Cold War (page 66) large amounts of industrial production were set aside for armaments.
4 The Plan was a success. In 1950 a Fifth Plan was begun.

Food and farming
1 There were serious food shortages.
2 Agricultural recovery was held back by shortages of
a people to work the farms
b machinery.
3 By 1953 agricultural production had begun to reach pre-war figures.

Families
1 About 20 million Soviet citizens were killed.
2 About 25 million people were left homeless. Houses had to be shared.
3 Everyone faced shortages of food and consumer goods.

Religion
1 To help him unify the country during the war, Stalin
a allowed religious worship and teaching again
b restored the Church to its former position: some churches were reopened and some bishops restored to office.
2 After the war the Church held on to these freedoms.

Dictatorship
During the war Stalin had presented himself as 'father' of a patriot people defending their homeland. Afterwards he returned to his harsh dictatorial style:
1 Thousands of prisoners returning from the West were sent to labour camps because they had been 'contaminated' by Capitalist values.
2 People who disobeyed his orders were purged.
3 He launched a campaign against Jews:
a thousands of Jewish intellectuals were arrested and accused of 'anti-Soviet' activities
b Jewish theatres and newpapers were banned
c a group of Jewish doctors was accused of plotting against him.
4 Ethnic populations whom Stalin believed to be disloyal were moved from their homelands.

Isolation and restrictions
After the war Stalin did not want the Soviet people to compare life in the USSR with life in Western Europe. To prevent this he
1 forbade them to
a travel abroad
b marry foreigners
2 made the newspapers print stories about poor conditions in the West.

1 What was the impact of the Second World War on Soviet society?
2 What aspects of political and social life in the USSR did the policy of De-Stalinization
a change b keep the same?
3 Make a table using the headings Agriculture, Industry, and Social Policies to show a the successes b the failures of Khrushchev's attempts at modernization.

▶ Khrushchev and De-Stalinization

New leaders; new attitudes

1 In 1953 Stalin died. He was succeeded by a collective of several leaders who wanted to put an end to the tyranny of Stalin's regime. This process became known as De-Stalinization.

2 Nikita Khrushchev was a leading member of the group:

a From 1955 he was mainly responsible for making Soviet policy

b From 1958 to 1964 he was the USSR's undisputed leader.

Speech to the Twentieth Party Congress, 1956

In a secret speech to senior Party members, Khrushchev attacked Stalin for

1 his dictatorial methods

2 the purges of the 1930s

3 his mistakes during the Second World War.

Immediate changes

1 The Government ended the cult of Stalin by

a destroying statues and pictures of him

b renaming the many places named after him, e.g. Stalingrad became Volgograd.

2 Thousands of political prisoners were released from the labour camps; but the camps themselves were not closed.

Limited freedoms

1 Although the secret police force lost some of its power, the Government continued to use it.

2 Freedom of expression was increased a little:

a Some banned writers were permitted, especially if they criticized Stalin.

b Although writers and poets could deal with a wider range of subjects, the Party continued to control what was published.

3 Some performers were allowed to travel abroad to give shows.

4 National languages were allowed to develop again; but every citizen had to become fluent in Russian as well.

5 The religious freedoms granted by Stalin came under attack:

a churches and monasteries were closed

b the Government refused to register new priests

c believers who met to worship in each other's homes were arrested and imprisoned.

▶ Khrushchev and modernization

Abroad Khrushchev followed a foreign policy based on the idea of 'peaceful co-existence' (page 67).

At home he aimed to:

1 increase food production

2 improve the living standards.

Food production

1 Khrushchev introduced new schemes:

a Collective farms were merged into vast units.

b Previously uncultivated 'virgin lands' were ploughed up and sown; but incorrect farming methods caused soil erosion allowing windstorms to destroy over half the new lands.

c Peasants were forced to grow maize to feed animals; but most of it was sown in areas with an unsuitable climate.

2 The schemes failed to increase food production sufficiently:

a food rationing had to be introduced

b in 1963 the USSR had to buy grain from the USA.

Industry

1 Khrushchev's Seven Year Plan (1958-1965)

a aimed to expand the chemical industry, oil and natural gas, and the space industry

b failed to meet its overambitious targets.

2 Although the Soviet economy grew less rapidly under Khrushchev, the output of heavy industries expanded steadily: e.g. between 1955 and 1965 the output of oil and electricity increased by nearly 300%.

3 Consumer goods such as radios, cars and refrigerators became more available, but were still scarce by the standards of Western Europe.

Social policies

1 Educational opportunities improved, especially in science and technology which were encouraged because of the space programme.

2 Pensions and welfare benefits were increased, including maternity leave.

3 By 1960 the number of houses being built each year had nearly doubled compared to 1955.

The 1920s boom in the USA

By the end of this spread you should be able to describe and explain:
1 the USA's return to isolationist policies after the First World War

2 the expansion of the US economy during the 1920s
3 the factors on which this was based

Background to the 1920s

Wealth and resources The USA was a powerful industrial country:
1 It possessed vast resources (e.g. wood, coal, oil, iron).
2 It had a large population.
3 Its railway, mining, and manufacturing industries were all strong.
4 The First World War had strengthened its position because
a the Allies bought munitions and armaments which expanded the coal, steel, and engineering industries
b during the fighting the exports of Britain, France and Germany fell, and American firms were able to take over the business.

Isolation When the First World War ended, the majority of Americans wanted to return to the USA's old policy of isolation, keeping out of foreign disputes:
1 Although President Wilson (a Democrat) had played a big part in setting up the League of Nations, both Houses of Congress (dominated by Republicans) voted that the USA should not join.
2 Congress also decided that the USA should not sign the Treaty of Versailles.

Republican policies In the 1920s the USA had Republican presidents (Harding 1920-23; Coolidge 1923-28). They aimed
1 to follow a policy of isolation
2 to concentrate on internal developments, especially the growth of prosperity through industry and trade. This involved:
a Low taxes. These i encouraged business owners to invest ii gave consumers more money to spend.
b Tariffs. *The Fordney-McCumber Act* (1922) increased tariffs on foreign goods entering the USA. This made them more expensive and encouraged Americans to buy home-produced goods instead.

The expansion of the US economy

Between 1922 and 1929 the USA experienced a business boom. The total annual wealth produced by the country increased by 40%. The average income per head of the population increased by 27%.

Consumer industries led the boom

Films and entertainment	Motor vehicles	Electrical goods
1 Cinemas and dance halls were built across the USA. 2 The Hollywood film industry grew rapidly.	Between 1920 and 1929 1 the number of Americans owning cars rose from 8 million to 23 million 2 annual car production rose from 1.6 million to 5.6 million.	1 The increased availability of electricity supplies created a demand for electrical goods such as radios, refrigerators, vacuum cleaners and washing machines. 2 Between 1920 and 1929 the number of radios in American homes increased from 60,000 to 10 million.

New technology

1 The start of radio broadcasting in 1921 created a demand for radios.
2 The widespread availability of electricity supplies created a demand for electrical goods.
3 The chemical industry created new cheap materals such as rayon, bakelite and cellophane.
4 In 1928 the invention of 'talking pictures' boosted the film industry.

Mass production

1 Techniques of mass production enabled household goods and cars to be produced more cheaply. Between 1914 and 1926 the purchase price of a Ford Model T fell from $850 to $295.
2 This encouraged demand which in turn created more jobs.

Advertising

Improved advertising techniques helped to create demand.

Shares

1 As companies made profits, their share prices rose.
2 The system of buying 'on the margin' allowed ordinary people to buy company shares on a hire purchase basis. They hoped that a rise in the share price would mean they could
a pay for their purchase
b also make profit.
3 Millions of Americans became share owners. This
a boosted investment in industry
b increased many people's sense of prosperity and willingness to spend on goods.
4 The weaknesses in the system were revealed when confidence fell (page 134).

The impact of the motor industry

The expansion of the motor industry stimulated other industries:
1 The building of vehicles created a demand for products such as steel, rubber, and glass.
2 Roads had to be built. This created jobs in the construction industry.
3 Cars ran on petrol. This boosted the oil industry.

Government policy

1 Tariffs (page 126)
2 Low taxes (page 126)

The USA's resources

(page 126)

Hire purchase

1 Finance companies fuelled demand for consumer goods by enabling people to buy them on the 'never-never'.
2 In weekly instalments the purchaser repaid
a the cost price of the goods
b the interest on the loan.

What factors helped to create the boom?

Wage rises

1 During the 1920s the average wage of industrial workers doubled.
2 This helped to boost demand.

1 Which industries expanded during the 1920s boom?
2 Make a table to show
a the factors which contributed to the 1920s boom
b what each factor contributed.

Economic weaknesses in the 1920s

By the end of this spread you should be able to describe and explain:
1 how a some American industries

b agriculture did not prosper in the 1920s
2 the continuation of poverty
3 weaknesses in the economy in the late 1920s

Areas of decline

The older industries

Some major industries, such as coal and textiles, did not expand during the 1920s.
1 Coal lost ground to the newer forms of energy, oil, gas, and electricity. Many coal mines were closed.
2 Textiles depended on the demand for clothes. The industry was hit by
a the new women's fashion for shorter skirts and dresses. These required less material than before.
b the popularity of new synthetic materials such as rayon.

Agriculture

1 After 1920 the wartime prosperity of American farmers ended because
a the demand from Europe fell as European farmers started to produce again after the war
b American farmers, often using modern machinery, overproduced causing a fall in food prices at home.
2 With lower incomes many farmers could not afford to make repayments on the money they had borrowed to buy their land. The banks which had lent the money started to evict them. In 1924 about 600,000 farmers lost their land.
3 By 1929 millions of farmworkers were out of work.

The continuation of poverty

In 1929 a survey showed that 60% of American families earned less than the $2,000 regarded as the minimum needed for basic necessities. The poorest groups were
1 farmers and farmworkers
2 black people
3 unskilled 'new' immigrants in the big cities (page 132).

Trade problems

1 In reply to the USA's tariffs against goods from abroad, foreign countries imposed tariffs on American goods.
2 This made it hard for American businesses to sell their goods abroad.
3 The USA could not export its surpluses when demand at home began to fall.

Unequal distribution of wealth

The richest 5% of the population earned 33% of all the money earned in the USA. This inequality of wealth meant that
1 only a relatively small number of Americans could really afford the cars and household goods being manufactured
2 some of the rest bought using hire purchase (page 127)
3 even so, by the late 1920s there were not enough people willing to buy the volume of goods being produced.

Weaknesses in the economy

The old industries

These failed to expand (page 128).

Over-production

By the late 1920s more goods were being made than there were people who could afford to buy them. As a result, companies
1 lowered their prices
2 made smaller profits
3 started to lay off workers.

Agriculture

The crisis in agriculture (page 00) had a knock-on effect on industry:
1 farmers and farmworkers could not afford to buy goods
2 shops in farming areas bought less from the manufacturers
3 the manufacturers
a made less profit
b had to lay off workers
4 with factory workers unemployed, the demand for goods fell yet again.

Trusts

1 Trusts were giant firms which dominated the business world.
2 Taking advantage of the freedoms given to businesses by the Republican governments, they worked together to maximize profits by:
a keeping wages low
b keeping prices high.
3 In the long-term this depressed demand because it meant that many people could not afford to buy their goods.

---

1 Use pages 126-129. In the 1920s which Americans **a** prospered **b** continued to be poor?
2 What factors caused a reduction in the demand for goods in the late 1920s?
3 Use pages 126-129. How did Government policy contribute to

a the boom of the 1920s
b weakness in the economy in the late 1920s?
4 Use pages 126-129. To what extent were the 1920s a time of economic prosperity

American society in the 1920s: 1

By the end of this spread you should be able to describe and explain:

1 the 'Roaring Twenties'
2 changes in the role of women

Films

1 By 1930 about 100 million Americans went to the cinema each week.
2 Stars such as Mary Pickford, Charlie Chaplin and Buster Keaton became household names.
3 Films promoted the new fashions and taught people new ways to behave.
4 Girls wanted to copy the on-screen behaviour of stars like Joan Crawford who perfectly portrayed the flapper.

Dancing

1 Dancing became a popular pastime and dance halls were opened up across the country.
2 The Charleston and the Black Bottom were popular new jazz dances.
3 The older generation, brought up on the Waltz, were appalled by the dancers' sensuous movements and by partners embracing

Jazz

1 Popular music flourished in the 1920s helped by radio programmes and gramophone records.
2 Jazz, with its black African-American origins, became the most popular of all.
3 Famous players included Louis Armstrong, Benny Goodman and Fats Waller.
4 Many parents and older people objected to the openly sexual nature of some of its songs and dances.

The 'Roaring Twenties'

For many prosperous Americans, the 1920s were a time of entertainment, excitement, new fashions and freer behaviour.
1 Young people in particular wanted to relax and have fun after the horrors of the First World War.
2 Young women led changes in fashion and social behaviour.
3 Cheap cars, radios, and gramophones changed the way people lived.
4 The music and film industries expanded and helped to shape new attitudes.

Behaviour

1 Young people's sexual behaviour became freer, especially among college students.
2 Sales of cigarettes doubled.

Flappers

1 The well-off middle and upper-class young women who led the new fashions in women's clothes and behaviour were known as 'flappers' because of their short skirts.
2 Their behaviour shocked the older generation. They
a wore make-up and smoked in public
b drove cars
c went out with men unchaperoned
d wore short hair, short shirts, backless gowns and silk stockings rolled just above the knee.
3 Others admired them as 'new women' leading the way to a freer life-style.

1 What did Americans mean when they talked about the 'Roaring Twenties'?
2 What were the social effects of
a prosperity b the availability of consumer goods?
3 a Which aspects of women's lives
i changed ii stayed the same?
b For which social classes of women did life change the most?

Work

Before the First World War
1 Women were employed in traditionally 'female' areas of work such as domestic service, textiles, clerical and secretarial work, and teaching.
2 Upper and middle class women were expected not to work but to wait for a suitable husband.

In the 1920s
1 During the war, to release men for the armed forces, many women took over jobs in traditionally 'male' areas of work, such as manufacturing and heavy industry.
2 After the war most women were forced back into 'womens' jobs to make way for returning servicemen.

3 The number of working women increased by 25% to 10.5 million in 1929.
4 The number of upper and middle class women in jobs increased, especially in teaching and secretarial work.
5 Most women continued the unpaid work that they had always done in the home and on the land.

The Vote

Before the First World War
1 Campaigners made the right of women to vote an important political issue.
2 By 1920 women in only four states had the right to vote.

In the 1920s
In 1920 all women were given the right to vote.

The changing roles of women

Note: changes in fashion and behaviour started among the younger and wealthier women in the cities. They then spread to rural areas and to other social groups.

Fashion

Before the First World War
Women were expected
1 to have long hair (often worn up)
2 to wear
a tight under-garments including corsets
b full-length dresses revealing very little flesh.

In the 1920s
1 many women stopped wearing corsets
2 hem-lines went up
3 hair was cut short in bobs.

Behaviour

Before the First World War
Women were expected
1 not to smoke in public
2 not to drive cars
3 not to play vigorous games
4 if they were unmarried, to be accompanied by a chaperone when they went out in the company of a man.

In the 1920s
Women
1 smoked in public
2 drove cars
3 began to take part in strenuous sport
4 went out with men unaccompanied by chaperones.

American society in the 1920s: 2

By the end of this spread you should be able to describe and explain:
1 the Red Scare
2 race relations and the role of the Ku Klux Klan
3 the introduction and repeal of Prohibition
4 gangsterism and organized crime

The Red Scare

'Reds' were people suspected of Communist, Socialist, or Anarchist sympathies, particularly in the trade unions.

The Scare. In the 1920s the authorities hounded 'Reds'. Two Italian Anarchists, Sacco and Vanzetti, were executed for a murder they almost certainly did not commit.

Reasons for the scare

1 Many Americans, especially leading industrialists, feared
a the activities of trade unions
b Socialist ideas.
They thought they were contrary to the American belief in free enterprise and democracy.
2 They were frightened by
a the Bolshevik Revolution (page 110)
b a series of union-led strikes in 1919.

Lynchings

In the southern states, mobs of white people regularly took the law into their own hands and hanged black people for their alleged offences. The authorities did not prevent this.

Segregation

The 'Jim Crow' laws of the southern states meant that black people were segregated from white. For example, they were forced to go to separate schools, use separate buses and trains, and live in separate neighbourhoods

Education and jobs

Black people had the lowest standards of education and the poorest paid jobs.

Race relations

'New' immigrants

1 Before the First World War huge numbers of so-called 'new' immigrants entered the USA from southern and eastern Europe.
2 In the 1920s a series of *Immigration Laws*
a cut down the total number of immigrants per year from 850,000 (pre-war) to 150,000 (in 1929)
b ensured that the majority were White Anglo-Saxon Protestants (WASPS) from Germany, Scandinavia, and Britain, rather than 'new' immigrants.
4 Members of 'new' immigrant communities were frequently accused of being 'Reds' and arrested.

Why was there hostility to 'new' immigrants?

1 Racial prejudice. White English-speaking Americans looked down on ethnic groups speaking different languages and with different cultures.
2 Religious prejudice. The majority of Americans were Protestants. 'New' immigrants were often Catholic or Jewish.
3 'New' immigrants tended to be poor and unskilled. Those that became involved in fighting for better conditions were branded as 'Reds'.

The Federal Government

1 In the 1920s black organizations such as the National Association for the Advancement of Coloured People (NAACP) campaigned for the Government to
a bring in a law against lynching
b to give black people the vote.
2 The Government did not act. It wanted to avoid a confrontation with southern politicians over 'states' rights' (page 140).

Migration to the North

1 The post-war industrial boom encouraged thousands of black people to leave the agricultural South for better paid work in the cities of the North.
2 Although legal segregation did not apply in the North, black Americans still encountered racism:
a they were given the lowest paid jobs
b in hard times they were usually the first to be laid off.

Discrimination against black people

The vote

The laws of many southern states meant that few black people could vote.

The Ku Klux Klan

Membership
1 Open only to WASPS.
2 Increased after the war reaching an all time high of about 5 million in 1923.
3 Included some police officers, judges, and politicians.
4 Especially strong in the South and West of the USA.
5 In 1926, following the conviction of a Klan leader for rape and murder, membership fell to 300,000.

Aims
1 To defend white superiority against black people and other ethnic minorities.
2 To defend Protestant superiority against Catholics and Jews.
3 To 'clean up' American society by attacking anyone, such as drunks and gamblers, who threatened moral standards.

Activities
1 Secret ceremonies wearing costume of white mask and cloak.
2 Used coded language.
3 Lynchings of black people.
4 Violence and terror, such as beating-up or whipping victims, and burning property.

Prohibition and organized crime

1918 Law passed to prohibit the sale or manufacture of alcohol
1920 Prohibition law comes into force
1933 End of prohibition

Reasons for prohibition
1 The Anti-Saloon League campaigned effectively for many years:
a It had strong support from Protestant Churches in rural areas whose members were critical of standards of behaviour in the cities.
b It helped to get supporters of prohibition elected to Congress.
c By 1917 alcohol was banned in 18 states.
2 Organizations like the League persuaded many Americans that drink caused
a drunkenness, violence, and crime
b poverty and hunger in families because men spent their wages on it
c absence from work.

Organized crime
1 The alcohol trade was driven underground and became a hugely profitable business.
a Bootleggers (dealers in illegal alcohol) supplied the drink.
b Speakeasies (illegal bars) served it.
2 The business attracted big gangs which
a ran protection rackets
b bribed and intimidated judges and politicians
c fought each other for control of the trade.

Al Capone, in Chicago, led the most powerful and notorious gang.

1 He was involved in gambling and brothels as well as bootlegging and speakeasies.
2 He used bribery to control the mayor and the police.
3 His position depended on the use of violence.
a He is thought to have ordered the murders of 227 rival gangsters in four years.
b In 1929 seven members of Moran's gang were gunned down in the St Valentine's Day Massacre.
4 In 1931 federal officers managed to have him convicted for tax evasion.

Why was prohibition abolished?
1 Prohibition was a failure.
a Drinking continued. In 1933 there were 200,000 speakeasies in the USA.
b Enforcement proved impossible.
2 The flouting of prohibition brought the law in general into disrepute.
3 Americans were disturbed by
a the growth and violence of organized crime
b the widespread corruption.

Use pages 130-133.
1 a Make a three-column chart to show i the changes that took place in US society in the 1920s ii the groups affected by each change iii whether the change was for better or worse.
b In what respects did US society not change in the 1920s?
2 a Make a two-column chart to show i the ways in which life was free for Americans in the 1920s ii the ways in which it was unfree.
b For which groups was life least free? Give your reasons.

The Wall Street Crash and the Depression, 1929-1932

By the end of this spread you should be able to describe and explain:
1 the causes of the Wall Street Crash

2 its consequences
3 the a economic b social effects of the Depression

The long-term causes of the Crash

Economic weaknesses By the late 1920s the American economy suffered from several major weaknesses (page 129).

Over-valued shares
1 For companies falling demand and falling prices meant lower profits.
2 Lower profits eventually had to mean a lower share price.

3 In 1929 share prices were higher than they should have been. Once investors realized this they would start to sell.

The cycle of decline Historians argue about whether the main problem with the economy was over-production or under-consumption (a lack of demand). By 1928 these two factors had pushed the USA into the start of an economic depression:

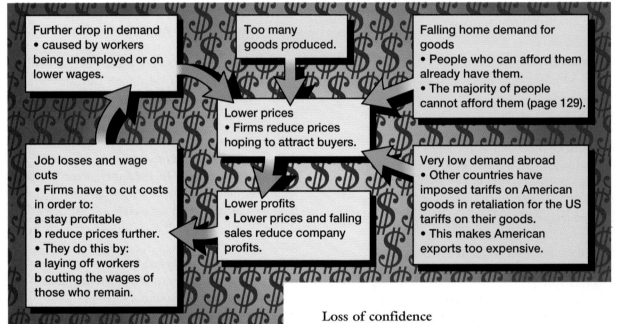

Further drop in demand
• caused by workers being unemployed or on lower wages.

Too many goods produced.

Falling home demand for goods
• People who can afford them already have them.
• The majority of people cannot afford them (page 129).

Lower prices
• Firms reduce prices hoping to attract buyers.

Job losses and wage cuts
• Firms have to cut costs in order to:
a stay profitable
b reduce prices further.
• They do this by:
a laying off workers
b cutting the wages of those who remain.

Lower profits
• Lower prices and falling sales reduce company profits.

Very low demand abroad
• Other countries have imposed tariffs on American goods in retaliation for the US tariffs on their goods.
• This makes American exports too expensive.

The short-term causes of the Crash

Speculation
1 Between 1924 and 1929 the value of shares rose by five times.
2 Share prices were driven up by the number of people wishing to invest in order to make what appeared to be a guaranteed profit. About a million Americans became shareholders.
3 Many people who did not have the cash to buy shares bought them 'on the margin' (page 127).

Loss of confidence
1 In September 1929 some investors realized that
a there were problems with the US economy
b their shares were over-valued
c they should sell while the going was still good.
2 As they sold, share prices began to fall slowly.
3 Investors who had bought 'on the margin' realized their shares could become worth less than the loan they had taken out to pay for them.
4 This triggered off a rush to sell. Between 24 and 29 October share prices tumbled as people sold at any price rather than be left with nothing. Shareholders lost a total of $8,000 million.

The consequences of the Crash

Financial Many individuals and businesses were ruined.

1 Many people who had borrowed money to buy their shares went bankrupt because they could not pay back the loan.

2 Some people lost their homes because they could no longer afford the mortgage.

3 Banks which had given people loans to buy shares could not get their money back:

a Some banks ran out of money and had to close down.

b People with savings in those banks lost their money.

4 Farmers were evicted when banks, short of cash, tried to get back their loans.

5 Thousands of companies went out of business because their shares were worth so little.

Economic

1 Demand fell again because

a so many people lost money

b many people lost their jobs when companies closed

c those who had money lost confidence and spent as little as possible.

2 Companies cut back production and started to lay off more workers.

The Depression

1 From 1929 to 1941 the USA experienced an economic slump, the Depression.

2 The Crash did not cause the Depression.

a Unemployment had been on the increase since 1926. Prices and profits had begun to fall significantly several months before the Crash.

b The main causes were the weaknesses in the American economy (page 129).

3 The Crash did make the Depression much worse than it might otherwise have been.

The effects of the Depression

Economic

Between 1929 and 1933

1 The value of goods sold in shops fell by 50%.

2 The total wealth produced by the country (Gross National Product or GNP) fell by just under 50%.

3 About 10,000 banks stopped trading.

4 Thousands of companies went out of business. Some 20,000 went bankrupt in 1932 alone.

5 The number of unemployed workers rose from 1.5 million to 12.8 million.

6 Farm income and the wages of farm workers fell by 50%.

7 Thousands of farmers were evicted from their land for failing to make mortgage repayments.

Social

1 Unemployment plunged millions of families into hunger and misery.

a There was no system of unemployment benefit.

b Many people relied on hand-outs of bread and soup from soup kitchens run by charities.

c Many had to give up their homes because they could not pay the rent or mortgage. They built houses out of rubbish in shanty towns named 'Hoovervilles' after the President who was blamed for their plight.

2 The number of Americans committing suicide rose during the Depression to a peak of 23,000 people in 1932. By 1940 the suicide rate had returned to the level of 1926.

---

1 a Use pages 129 and 134 to make a list of

i the long-term

ii the short-term causes of the Wall Street Crash.

b Write a short note about each cause.

2 What were the immediate consequences of the Crash?

3 How did the Depression affect

a the American economy

b the lives of the American people?

From Hoover to Roosevelt: Government responses to the Depression, 1929-1933

By the end of this spread you should be able to describe:
1 the reactions of President Hoover to the Depression
2 the Presidential election of 1932
3 Roosevelt's inauguration and the Hundred Days
4 the introduction of the New Deal

President Hoover and the Depression

Hoover's attitudes
1 Hoover believed
a that the Government should not interfere in people's lives
b in what he called 'rugged individualism', the idea that people should work hard for themselves and not expect the Government to help them.
2 He thought that the American economy was fundamentally strong and would soon recover from the Depression on its own.

Government action Because of his attitudes it was some time before Hoover took action to combat the Depression and its effects.

Government action under Hoover

1930 Taxes cut by $130 million to try to give people more money to spend.
1931 Money given to help build river dams such as the Hoover Dam. This was to create jobs.
1932 Reconstruction Finance Corporation set up to lend money to help struggling businesses to survive. *Emergency Relief and Reconstruction Act* gave money to the states to help unemployed people.

Protest
1 In the state of Iowa farmers
a organized a strike to try to create food shortages and so drive prices up.
b attacked trucks being driven to market
c banded together to resist officials carrying out evictions.
2 The Bonus Army, 1932:
a Veteran soldiers of the First World War wanted bonuses due in 1945 to be paid now.
b Over 20,000 marched on Washington and set up a Hooverville outside the White House.
c Hoover ordered the army to clear them out.

The 1932 Presidential election

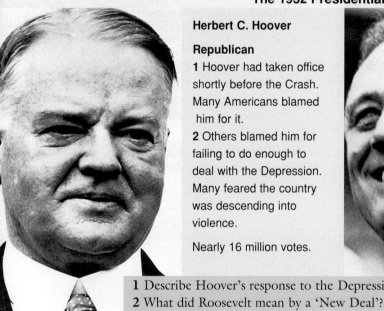

Herbert C. Hoover

Republican
1 Hoover had taken office shortly before the Crash. Many Americans blamed him for it.
2 Others blamed him for failing to do enough to deal with the Depression. Many feared the country was descending into violence.

Nearly 16 million votes.

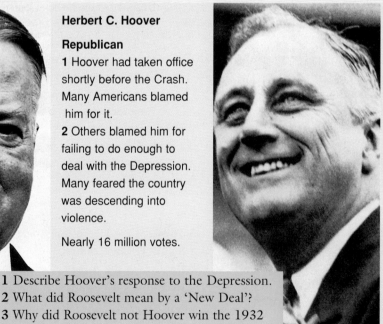

Franklin D. Roosevelt

Democrat
1 He had battled successfully against polio. Many saw him as a fighter.
2 As Governor of New York State he had tried to help ordinary people with old age pensions and some unemployment relief.
3 He believed the power of government should be used to create a fairer society.
4 He promised 'a new deal for the American people'.

Nearly 23 million votes.

1 Describe Hoover's response to the Depression.
2 What did Roosevelt mean by a 'New Deal'?
3 Why did Roosevelt not Hoover win the 1932 Presidential election?
4 How did Roosevelt try to restore confidence during the Hundred Days?

The Hundred Days

Roosevelt's inauguration

1 Under the American Constitution, Roosevelt had to wait four months before he could take over from Hoover. During this time the economic situation worsened:

a unemployment rose to 15 million

b thousands of banks went out of business.

2 In March 1933, at his inauguration, Roosevelt

a promised 'action and action now'

b said that his first priority was to put people back to work.

The banking crisis In panic people were withdrawing their money causing banks to collapse.

1 Roosevelt ordered all banks to close while officials inspected their accounts.

2 Only well-run banks with plenty of money were allowed to re-open. These were given Government backing.

3 Roosevelt used a radio broadcast to tell Americans about these measures and to reassure them.

4 The run on the banks stopped.

Fireside chats Roosevelt's radio broadcast about the banks was the first of series. They became known as 'fireside chats' because people felt the President was chatting directly to them at home.

1 Roosevelt was the first president to use radio in this way. He talked in a very effective informal style.

2 By making direct contact with Americans in this way, Roosevelt

a kept people informed about his actions

b gave individuals hope and restored public confidence in the Government.

The New Deal

Roosevelt summoned Congress into emergency session from March to June 1933 (the Hundred Days). During this time legislation was passed which laid the foundation for his promised New Deal.

Aims of the New Deal

1 Relief. Help the unemployed.

2 Recovery. Rebuild the economy.

3 Reform. Create a fairer and more just society.

The First New Deal programme, 1933

Item	Purpose
Emergency Banking Act	To restore confidence in the banking system by supporting strong banks and closing weak ones.
Securities and Exchange Commission	To control share dealing in order to prevent the speculation which caused the 1929 Crash from happening again.
Economy Act	To cut Government expenditure by reducing the pay of Government employees by 15%.
Abolition of Prohibition	To end the ban on alcohol.
Home Owners Loan Corporation (HOLC)	To help home owners who had difficulty paying their mortgage.
Civilian Conservation Corps (CCC)	To provide conservation work for unemployed young men.
Federal Emergency Relief Administration (FERA)	To give money to the states to help unemployed and homeless people.
Civil Works Administration (CWA) In 1935 became the Works Progress Administration (WPA)	To provide work for unemployed people.
The Tennessee Valley Authority (TVA)	To develop the poverty-stricken Tennessee Valley area.
Agricultural Adjustment Administration (AAA)	To help farmers to increase their profits.
National Recovery Administration (NRA)	To encourage employers to a improve industrial workers' pay and working conditions b charge fair prices for goods.

The New Deal 1

By the end of this spread you should be able to describe:
1 the work of the Alphabet Agencies
2 their successes and failures.

The Alphabet Agencies

Much of the legislation of the Hundred Days set up new organizations to deal with the USA's problems. These soon became known as the Alphabet Agencies because people referred to them by their initials.

The work of the Alphabet Agencies

Agency	Purpose	Action	Successes	Failures/Criticisms
Civilian Conservation Corps (CCC)	To provide conservation work for unemployed young men.	• Camps jointly organized by the US Army and US Forestry Service. • 18-25 year-old men given six months work in return for food, shelter, and pocket money.	• 300,000 people joined in 1933. By 1941 2.5 million people had taken part. • The scheme was popular with participants and many found work afterwards. • Employers respected the programme. • Millions of trees planted; reservoirs, forest roads, fire look-outs and canals built.	
Federal Emergency Relief Administration (FERA)	To give money to the states to help unemployed and homeless people.	The Government gave each state one dollar for every three the state spent on the relief of poverty.	Gave help to people in desperate need.	The Government wanted to shift the emphasis as soon as possible onto the provision of paid work rather than of handouts (see CWA and WPA).
Agricultural Adjustment Administration (AAA)	To help farmers to increase their profits.	• Schemes were introduced to help farmers reduce their production and so drive up the price of their produce. • Government money was used to pay farmers to destroy crops and slaughter animals.	Over-production ended and prices rose.	• The Government was criticized for paying farmers to produce less. • The schemes made life worse for farm-workers, many of them black, because reduced production left them without work. Many had to look for work in other parts of the country.

Agency	Aims	What it did	Problems
Authority (TVA)	...stricken Tennessee Valley area.	...years in an area covering six states. • problems of flood control in winter and irrigation in summer. • They enabled cheap electricity to be made for the region. • Lakes behind the dams and a system of locks made much of the river navigable. • Farming and manufacturing started to flourish.	• Many people were put to work on projects of little value. • A lot of Government (i.e. taxpayers') money went into the scheme.
Civil Works Administration (CWA), 1933-34 Works Progress Administration (WPA), from 1935	To provide work for unemployed people.	Unemployed people were found work and paid wages for doing it. • About two million people a year given work. • Schools, roads, and airports built. • Thousands of writers, actors, and artists employed on creative projects. • Millions of people earned a small wage rather than nothing. They became purchasers again which helped towards economic recovery.	
National Recovery Administration (NRA)	To encourage employers to a improve industrial workers' pay and working conditions b charge fair prices for goods.	• Codes of practice for employers drawn up on minimum wages, hours and conditions of work, and prices. • Companies signing up to the scheme were allowed to display the Blue Eagle symbol of Government approval. • 2.5 million firms, employing 22 million workers, joined the scheme. • Child labour was abolished in the USA.	• The scheme was voluntary. Many employers refused to join. • Members began to violate the codes. • Workers went on strike in protest.

1 a Make lists of the programmes run by the Alphabet Agencies which aimed to helped i unemployed people ii agriculture iii industry.
b Say whether you think each programme was successful or unsuccessful. Give your reasons.
2 What a social b economic changes did the Alphabet Agencies bring about?

The New Deal 2

By the end of this spread you should be able to:
1 explain a who opposed the New Deal b why they did so
2 describe the features of the second New Deal
3 describe the impact of the New Deal on unemployment
4 explain the a strengths b weaknesses of the New Deal

The Supreme Court

1 Its nine, mainly Republican, judges ruled that several New Deal measures were unconstitutional and, therefore, illegal.
2 The judges argued that organizations such as the NRA and AAA cut across the right of states to run their own affairs.
3 After his 1937 election victory Roosevelt proposed a new law to allow him to retire some of the judges and appoint new ones:
a Faced with this threat the judges declared the New Deal legislation to be constitutional after all.
b Roosevelt's threat made him unpopular. The Supreme Court was the guardian of the constitution. People accused him of seeking to rule as a dictator.

Radicals

1 Until his death in 1935, Huey Long, Senator for Louisiana,
a argued that Roosevelt was not doing enough to help the poor
b started the 'Share Our Wealth' campaign to confiscate private fortunes of over $3 million and use the money to help the poor.
2 Dr Frances Townsend campaigned for pensioners to receive $200 per month.

The second New Deal

In 1935 Roosevelt introduced a second wave of New Deal legislation (Fig. 1). The emphasis was on protecting workers' rights and social security benefits. He aimed to:
1 extend and improve upon the first New Deal
2 replace the work of those agencies said to be unconstitutional by the Supreme Court.

Republican politicians argued that
1 relief was a waste of taxpayers' money
2 the Government was interfering in people's lives
3 the New Deal made people too dependent on the Government
4 the Government was interfering with the freedoms of business.

Businessmen objected to the way the New Deal
1 interfered with their freedom to run their businesses as they wished
2 supported worker's rights, especially their right to join a trade union.

States' rights campaigners
1 They argued that some of the Federal (central) Government's New Deal legislation clashed with the right of individual states to make their own laws.
2 They objected to schemes, like the TVA, which forced states to co-operate.

Who opposed the New Deal?

Fig. 1 The second New Deal programme, 1935-37

Item	Purpose
National Labour Relations (Wagner) Act (1935)	To replace NRA codes declared illegal by the Supreme Court by 1 giving workers the right to join trade unions 2 preventing employers from victimising union members.
Social Security Act (1935)	To provide the USA's first system of social welfare by 1 setting up a national system of old-age pensions 2 providing help for **a** people with physical disabilities **b** children in need 3 setting up a national system of unemployment insurance.
Soil Conservation Act (1935)	To replace the AAA programme declared illegal by the Supreme Court. It enabled the Government to continue to subsidize farmers who cut their production.
National Housing Act (1937)	To provide money for home loans and to cut down high rents.
Fair Labour Standards Act (1938)	To regulate hours and conditions of work and to fix minimum wages.

Fig. 2 How did the New Deal affect unemployment?

1 The New Deal reduced unemployment from the very high level of 1933.

2 In 1938 unemployment rose again because

a Roosevelt cut back Government expenditure for fear of the USA going into debt

b world trade declined again.

3 In 1938, elections to Congress returned a Republican majority. This meant Roosevelt could not have any new laws passed to combat unemployment.

4 The problem was eventually solved, not by the New Deal, but by

a the rearmament programme

b entry into the Second World War (page 48).

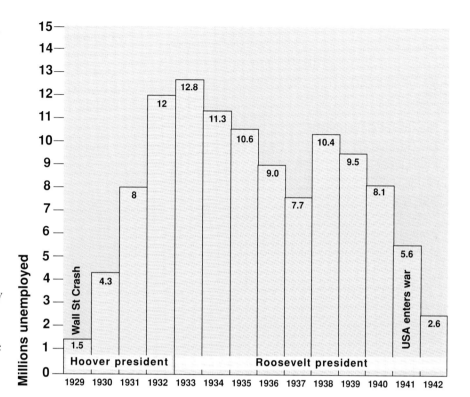

The strengths and weaknesses of the New Deal

Strengths

1 Millions of poor people received relief (food, shelter, clothing).

2 Millions of jobs were created.

3 Extreme political movements, such as Communism and Fascism, did not take hold in the USA.

4 Construction work on projects such as roads and dams helped the future development of agriculture and industry.

5 Government social security and welfare schemes

a helped many ordinary people

b continued into the future.

6 Workers rights and conditions were improved.

7 Many Americans began to believe in themselves again.

Weaknesses

1 Unemployment was reduced but not ended.

a In 1938 it rose again (Fig. 2)

b It was the rearmament programme and entry into the Second World War that eventually solved the problem (Fig. 2).

2 The programme lacked total support. It was hampered by opposition (page 140).

3 The programmes were least helpful to unskilled workers. This group included many black people.

4 The programme did nothing to improve the civil rights of black people.

5 Most women continued to be paid less than men for the same work.

1 a Who were the main opponents of the New Deal?

b What were their objections?

2 In what respects was the second New Deal different from the first?

3 a Make a chart to show Roosevelt's i successes ii failures for each of the three aims of the New Deal (page 137).

b To what extent was the New Deal a success?

The impact of the Second World War

By the end of this spread you should be able to describe the impact of the Second World War on:
1 the US economy
2 US society

Employment
1 Government spending on the armed forces ended the Depression.
2 Unemployment fell from 9.5 million in 1939, to 670,000 in 1944.

The role of Government
The Government
1 took powers to control the economy centrally through organizations such as the War Production Board
2 ran up large debts in order to pay for the war.

Agriculture
Farmers prospered again as a result of
1 the guaranteed market provided by the armed forces
2 several years of good weather.

National and personal wealth
Between 1941 and 1945
1 the USA's Gross National Product doubled
2 the income of the average person doubled
3 standards of living rose.

How the war affected the US economy

Big business
The large corporations
1 won large Government contracts for military supplies
2 increased **a** their profits **b** their power.

Consumer industries
1 Many continued to flourish as unemployment fell and demand picked up.
2 On Government orders some factories went into the lucrative business of weapons manufacture.

Old industries
The traditional industries such as coal, iron, steel, oil, and ship-building were boosted by the demands of the war.

War production

 Aircraft: 296,000

 Tanks: 102,000

 Artillery guns: 372,000

 Small guns and rifles: 20 million

 Trucks: 2.5 million

1 In what respects did the US economy gain from the Second World War?
2 a How did the role and status of i women ii black people change during the Second World War?
b To what extent were these changes permanent?

The impact of the war on US society

Women

Before the war	During the war	After the war
In 1940, 12 million women formed 27% of the total labour force.	In 1945, 18.5 million women formed 33% of the total labour force.	Most women gave up their jobs to provide work for the returning men.
Most women worked in the home, unpaid.	Most of their jobs were in shipyards, aircraft factories and armaments factories where they replaced the men who were called up.	In 1950 women formed 29% of the total labour force.
In 1940, about 17% of married women did paid work outside the home.	About 300,000 women joined women's sections of the forces.	In 1950 about 25% of married women did paid work outside the home.
Women worked mainly as domestic and clerical workers, secretaries, teachers, and nurses.	In a few states women were given equal pay to men. In most they were paid less for doing the same job.	Attitudes towards women had changed and their confidence had increased.
Women were generally paid less than men, even for doing the same job.		

Black people

	Before the war	During the war	After the war
In the forces	There were only two black officers in the US army. None in the navy. There were less than 4,000 black soldiers, mainly in support, rather than fighting, units. Blacks had to serve in segregated units.	1941-42, the forces opened all positions to qualified black people. Over 1 million blacks joined the forces. Blacks continued to serve in segregated units. The pilots of the black 332nd Fighter Group won a Distinguished Unit Citation.	In 1948 President Truman ended segregation in the US forces.
At home	Segregation and the 'Jim Crow' laws operated in the South (page 132).	Thousands of black people migrated to the industrial cities of the North. By 1944 about 2 million blacks were working in war factories. President Roosevelt was forced to ban discrimination against black people in industrial and Government jobs. Black Americans expected that after the war they would be given equal rights. Membership of the National Association for the Advancement of Coloured People (NAACP) rose from 50,000 in 1941 to 450,000 in 1945.	Segregation continued in the Southern states.

Economic growth; McCarthyism

By the end of this spread you should be able to describe:
1 the growth of the US economy, 1945-1970
2 its social impact in the 1950s
3 a the nature b the impact of McCarthyism and the
'red scare' in the 1950s

Economic growth

Between 1945 and 1970 the economy of the USA expanded rapidly bringing prosperity to millions of middle class Americans.
1 Between 1945 and 1960 the Gross National Product (GNP) nearly doubled.
2 In the 1950s the USA produced half the world's goods.

3 The numbers out of work remained reasonably low:

Unemployment in the USA as a percentage of the population
1948: 3.4%
1955: 4.4%
1963: 5.6%

4 The ownership of consumer goods increased:

Percentage of families owning:		
	1948	**1960**
Cars	54	75
TVs	3	90
Refrigerators	77	99

The social impact of economic growth

Teenagers

1 Teenagers had money to spend. Entertainment and fashion changed to meet their demands.
2 Their search for excitement and a freer style of life brought them into conflict with the older generation.
3 Many adults disapproved of the new Rock 'n' Roll music with its heavy beat and sexually explicit words and movements.
4 Juvenile crime increased in the 1950s.

Women

1 After the war women were expected to work at home as wives and mothers. In 1950 the average age at which women married was 20.
2 In many families the mother went out to work anyway in order to help pay for the consumer goods the family wanted.
3 In 1960 forty per cent of women went out to work, mostly in low paid jobs.
4 In the 1960s many women began to question assumptions about motherhood and homemaking (page 148).

The suburbs

1 Middle-class families moved out of city centres into newly-built suburbs.
2 Suburbs were self-contained areas with their own shopping and leisure facilities.
3 In the suburbs ownership of the latest consumer product became a status symbol.
4 Many women felt isolated and bored there.
5 Churches provided a focus for community life. In 1960 church attendance was 15% higher than in 1940.

Inequalities

1 In the 1950s, despite general prosperity, 22% of all Americans lived below the poverty line.
2 Black people and the elderly were most likely to be poor. Fifty six per cent of the black population lived below the poverty line.
3 There was no national health service. Poor people could not afford the costs of private health insurance.

McCarthyism

What was it?

1 A campaign against Communists led by Senator Joe McCarthy between 1950 and 1954.

2 Without offering proof, McCarthy accused hundreds of people, ranging from scientists to entertainers, of secretly working for the USSR.

3 During the campaign, over two thousand people were summoned to appear before the Senate's House Un-American Activities Committee (HUAC).

4 In 1953 McCarthy became chairman of the Senate's Permanent Committee of Investigation. Televised hearings exposed him as a bully and a liar.

5 In 1954 McCarthy's methods were condemned by the Senate. He was forced out of public life.

The consequences of McCarthyism

1 For a time McCarthy's 'witch-hunt' was supported by the press and public opinion. No politician could afford to criticize him.

2 The thousands of innocent people who appeared before Senate hearings lost their jobs and had their lives ruined. About 400 were tried and sent to jail.

3 The 'witch-hunt' came to include those with liberal or left-wing opinions which were branded 'un-American'.

4 The USA's reputation for justice and freedom of expression was severely damaged.

Events inside the USA

These built up American fears of widespread infiltration by Soviet spies.

The Hiss trial, 1948

1 Hiss, a former State Department official, was accused of handing State secrets to the USSR.

2 He was convicted of perjury, but not of spying.

The Rosenberg trial, 1950

1 Julius and Ethel Rosenberg were convicted of selling nuclear weapons secrets to the USSR during the Second World War.

2 In 1953 they were executed.

Why was fear of Communism so strong?

Events outside the USA

These built up American fears of a worldwide Communist threat.

The Berlin blockade, 1948
The Western powers successfully resisted a Soviet attempt to drive them out of Berlin (page 65).

The first Soviet A-bomb test, 1949
Until then Americans had felt secure because only the USA possessed this weapon.

Victory for the Chinese Communists, 1949
The USA had been backing the defeated Nationalist Government (page 67).

The invasion of South Korea, 1950
The invasion of pro-American South Korea by Communist North Korea led to the Korean War (page 94).

1 What effect did the growth of the US economy have on American society in the 1950s?

2 Why were so many Americans ready to believe Senator McCarthy's allegations in the 1950s?

The Civil Rights movements

By the end of this spread you should be able to describe:
1 the Civil Rights movements
2 their achievements

Segregation

In the South, the position of black people had changed little since the 1920s (page 132).
1 Under the 'Jim Crow' laws blacks were segregated from whites. They had to go to separate schools and use separate buses, shops, restaurants, and cinemas.
2 Black people had the lowest standards of education and the poorest paid jobs.
3 State laws meant that few black people could vote.
4 The Ku Klux Klan (page 133) continued to be active.

From segregation to civil rights

Schools, 1954-1960
1 Twenty states, as well as Washington DC, ran segregated school systems.
2 In 1954, in the case of Brown v Topeka, the Supreme Court ruled that segregated schools were illegal under the constitution.
3 Arguing 'states rights' (page 140) southern states continued to resist integration.
4 The Ku Klux Klan organized violence and murders to intimidate black people.
5 In 1957 President Eisenhower sent US troops to enable nine black teenagers to join the previously all-white High School at Little Rock, Arkansas.
6 In 1960, out of 2 million black school children in the South, only 2,600 went to integrated schools.

The Montgomery Bus Boycott, 1955
1 In Montgomery, Alabama, black people boycotted the bus service in protest against segregation.
2 The Ku Klux Klan led attacks on the homes of black leaders.
3 In 1956 the Supreme Court ruled that segregation on buses was illegal.
4 After thirteen months the bus company gave in.

1954	The Supreme Court rules against segregated schools
1955	The Montgomery bus boycott
1956	The Supreme Court rules against segregated buses
1957	President Eisenhower sends Federal troops to enable nine black pupils to join Little Rock High School, Arkansas *Civil Rights Act* passed
1960	Start of 'direct action' protests
1962	President Kennedy sends Federal troops to enable a black student to attend the University of Mississippi
1963	Police attack demonstrators in Birmingham, Alabama. Major civil rights demonstration in Washington DC.
1964-1968	Anti-Discrimination Laws passed (Fig. 1)
1965	Emergence of the Black Power movement. The Watts riot.
1966-1967	Further inner city riots. Carl Stokes elected Mayor of Cleveland
1968	Murder of Martin Luther King

The Civil Rights Act, 1957
1 Eisenhower's Act
a made discrimination illegal
b guaranteed all Americans the right to vote
c created a Federal Civil Rights Commission to prosecute those who denied people their rights.
2 It indicated the Federal Government's concern to end segregation. But in the face of opposition in the South it changed little.

Dr Martin Luther King, a Baptist pastor, led the Montgomery Bus Boycott. He believed
1 since the governments of the southern states continued to act illegally, they would have to be forced to abandon segregation
2 the use of violence was morally wrong
3 civil rights campaigners should use non-violent direct action.

Direct action, 1960-1963

1 Thousands of campaigners took part in sit-in protests against segregated services in the South.

2 In 1963 American and world opinion was

a shocked by a violent attack by police on peaceful demonstrators in Birmingham, Alabama

b impressed by i the march of 250,000 campaigners (including 60,000 whites) on Washington DC ii Martin Luther King's 'I have a dream' speech.

Fig. 1 The Anti-Discrimination Laws of the 1960s

1964
Civil Rights Act   ~ Lyndon Johnson ~ .

1 Gave black people equal rights to enter restaurants, hotels, shops, and places of entertainment.

2 Outlawed racial discrimination in employment.

3 Set up Equal Employment Opportunity Commission to investigate complaints.

1965
Voting Rights Act
Outlawed racial discrimination over the right to vote.

1967
Inter-racial marriages
The Supreme Court ruled that to forbid these was unconstitutional.

1968
Civil Rights Act (Fair Housing Act)
Made racial discrimination in housing illegal.

Kennedy and Johnson

1 Although cautious in his approach to civil rights because he needed the support in Congress of Democrats from the South who opposed change, President Kennedy

a appointed the first black i federal judge

ii ambassador iii commander of a US warship

b in 1962 sent Federal troops to enable a black student to attend the University of Mississippi

c proposed major civil rights legislation.

2 Following Kennedy's death, President Johnson ensured that his anti-discrimination proposals became law (Fig. 1).

Black Power

Racial discrimination Despite the success of civil rights campaigners in the South, black people continued to live under serious disadvantages.

1 In the 1960s the average income of a black family was only just over half that of a white family.

2 In 1967 one third of all black families were living below the poverty line.

3 In the North, where 50% of black people now lived, they experienced the worst housing, high unemployment and poor schools.

The militant response

1 In the mid-1960s Malcolm X, leader of the Black Muslims, called for a separate black state.

2 The Black Power movement

a believed the only way for black people to achieve equality was to fight for it

b called for militant action to replace non-violent methods of protest.

3 In 1968 the murder of Martin Luther King by a white sniper caused many black people to join the Black Power movement.

Riots The anger of black people turned to violence.

1 In 1965 riots in Watts, a black ghetto in Los Angeles, killed 34 people and injured over 1,000.

2 In 1967 there were riots in several other major cities. In Detroit they left 40 people dead and 2,000 injured.

The 1970s and 1980s

1 The enforcement of civil rights laws meant that schools were more integrated.

2 Racial discrimination and violence continued.

3 Most black Americans used their votes to try to improve their position. They aimed to vote black people into power wherever possible

a In 1967 Carl Stokes had become the first black Mayor of a major city - Cleveland

b By 1985 over 10% of elected officials in the USA were black.

1 a Make a time-line to show the most significant events in the struggle for the civil rights of black Americans in the South.

b Make notes to say what each event contributed.

2 In what respects had the lives of black Americans

a improved b not improved by the 1980s?

Protest movements

By the end of this spread you should be able to describe:
1 the protest movements of the 1960s and 1970s
2 their results

A divided society

Despite the prosperity of many Americans in the 1960s and 1970s, and despite the hopes for social reform placed in Presidents Kennedy and Johnson (page 150), the USA remained a deeply divided society. Protest movements reflected many of the divisions. For the Civil Rights Movement see pages 146-147.

The Women's Movement

The growth of feminism

1 In the 1960s many women began to react against the 1950s emphasis on their role only as wife and mother.
2 In 1963 Betty Friedan published an influential book, *The Feminine Mystique*. It argued that
a men and women should raise their families in equal partnership
b women should work outside the home.
3 In 1966 Friedan and others founded the National Organization for Women.

Feminist demands

Feminists used demonstrations, petitions and legal action to campaign
1 for better wages for women and equal wages with men for doing the same work
2 for opportunities to compete for top level jobs
3 for child care for working parents
4 against male sexism.

Results

1 An awareness of discrimination against women and a shift in public opinion against it.
2 An end to discrimination in Government jobs.
3 Equal educational opportunities for women.

The growth of opposition

1 In 1964 most Americans approved of President Johnson's decision to increase US involvement in Vietnam (page 79).
2 Within a few years opposition developed because of
a the number of American casualties
b televised reports of the suffering and devastation.

Opposition to the Vietnam War

Results

1 The combination of international pressure, the cost of the war and protest at home caused President Nixon to withdraw from Vietnam (page 81).
2 The violence and anger generated by opposition to the war, and the fact that it was the USA's first ever military defeat, left its mark on American society for the rest of the century.

The protests

1 Anti-war demonstrations became common
a on college campuses where students often burnt the American flag
b on the streets. In 1969 more than 250,000 people marched in protest.
2 Black leaders criticized a war in which black soldiers with no civil rights were being sent to fight a war supposedly in support of freedom.
3 Thousands of young Americans chosen to fight in the war tore up their draft cards or went into hiding.
4 In 1970 troops shot dead four students during an anti-war protest at Kent State University, Ohio. This hardened public opinion against the war still further.

Take each of the protest groups shown on this spread and make a chart to show
1 its aims
2 what actions it took
3 the results.

Hippies

1 generally came from middle-class homes.
2 wore distinctive clothes and long hair.
3 took drugs and followed mystical religions.
4 engaged in permissive sexual behaviour and urged people to 'Make love not war'.
5 symbolized their belief in non-violence with flowers: 'Flower power'.
6 often lived in communes.
7 influenced many college students with their attitudes and behaviour.

Student protests

In the late 1960s students staged sit-ins and strikes on campuses across the USA. They wanted
1 more say in how their courses were run and what they were taught
2 an end to restrictive college rules.

Music

1 Music was at the heart of the youth rebellion from the political protest songs of Bob Dylan to the rock festival at Woodstock in 1969.
2 Rock music became a symbol of youth rebellion and new attitudes to sex and personal freedoms.

The Youth Revolt

Causes

Many young people rejected their parents' values and lifestyles. They were angry about
1 the Vietnam War
2 racism
3 the idea that the only important thing in life was to get a good job
4 the contrast between prosperity and poverty in the USA
5 what they saw as the hypocrisy of politicians.

Results

1 The older generation of parents and teachers condemned young people's behaviour and attitudes.
2 Social attitudes in general and especially towards sex and drugs became freer.
3 Regulations in colleges were relaxed.
4 Student protest played a large part in the successful opposition to the Vietnam War.
5 The majority of the 'rebellious youths' went on to have conventional careers.

Native American Indians

Disadvantages

They were the most disadvantaged minority group in the USA.
1 Many lived in reservations cut off from economic developments.
2 Compared to other Americans
a their unemployment rate was ten times higher
b their average life-span was twenty years less.
3 Their suicide rate was 100 times greater than that of white Americans.

Protest

1 In 1968 Native Americans founded the American Indian Movement (AIM) to try to regain lands which they claimed the Government had taken illegally in the nineteenth century.
2 In 1973 the occupation of Wounded Knee, and the subsequent police siege, publicized the Native American cause throughout the USA and the world.

Results

1 AIM won several legal claims against the government and Native American Indians were awarded large sums of money.
2 Sometimes they rejected the money saying they wanted back their lands.
3 Natives Americans remained disadvantaged but had publicized the cause for which they continued to fight.

Social reform; the Watergate scandal

By the end of this spread you should be able to describe:
1 a the social reform ideas of i Kennedy ii Johnson
b what they achieved
2 a the Watergate scandal b its impact

Social reform

In 1960 the new, 43 year-old, Democratic President, John F. Kennedy,
1 recognized that serious social problems existed alongside the USA's overall prosperity
2 inspired faith in the idea that governments could improve people's lives.

The 'New Frontier' and the 'Great Society'

Kennedy offered Americans a 'New Frontier'. After Kennedy's assassination in 1963, his successor, Lyndon Johnson, spoke of the 'Great Society'. The social problems which both Presidents aimed to solve were
1 civil rights
2 poverty, poor housing, and unemployment, especially in the inner cities
3 inadequate medical care.

What did Kennedy achieve?
Kennedy was hampered by the Republican majority in Congress.

- **Unemployment**
  The period for which unemployment benefit could be paid was increased.

- **Health**
  Congress rejected a scheme to provide healthcare for the elderly.

- **Civil rights** See page 147.

- **Poverty** The minimum wage was increased.

- **Education**
  Congress rejected plans to give federal money to State schools.

- **Housing**
  1 Some money was spent to improve housing in poor areas.
  2 Congress rejected a housing bill aimed at slum clearance.

What did Johnson achieve?
Johnson used the sympathy following Kennedy's assassination to push through social legislation that Kennedy had begun. The cost of the Vietnam War forced him to abandon many of his plans for social reform.

- **Health**
  1 'Medicare' provided medical insurance for the over 65s.
  2 'Medicaid' provided hospital care for the poor.

- **Poverty and unemployment**
  1 Minimum wages were increased and applied to more industries.
  2 *The Economic Opportunity Act* (1964) provided money to
  a train disadvantaged youths aged 16-21
  b provide low-income students with jobs to help them work their way through college
  c recruit people to work and teach in slum areas.

- **Civil rights** See page 147.

- **Education**
  Federal money was provided to expand education.

- **Housing**
  The Development Act (1964) provided money to replace inner city slums with new houses.

- **Environment**
  New laws set standards for
  1 clean water
  2 air quality.

Continuing problems
1 The new programmes were insufficient to solve the problems of unemployment, poor housing, and poverty in the inner cities.
2 The middle-class 'urban flight' to the suburbs increased. Inner cities became more run down.
3 Nationally between 1960 and 1968
a crime increased by 120%
b violent crime increased by 107%.

From Johnson to Nixon

1 In 1968 the USA was engulfed by riots and protests against the Vietnam War, poverty, and continuing racial discrimination.
2 Many blamed President Johnson whose decision to send troops to Vietnam (page 79)
a embroiled the USA in a costly war
b prevented him from spending money on reforms at home.

3 Dismayed by his unpopularity, Johnson decided not to run for a second term of office. His successor was Richard Nixon, a Republican.
4 Nixon
a withdrew US ground troops from Vietnam (page 81)
b brought about détente with the USSR (page 88)
c made an historic visit to China (1972) to improve relations.
5 In 1972 Nixon was re-elected for a second term.

The Watergate Scandal

The events of Watergate

1972
1 During the Presidential election campaign, police arrest burglars inside the Democratic Party's headquarters in the Watergate building in Washington.
2 Investigations by journalists on the *Washington Post* newspaper reveal that the burglars were paid to steal information to discredit Nixon's democratic opponent.
3 Nixon and his White House staff deny any involvement with the break-in.

1973
1 The Senate sets up a Special Committee to investigate the affair.
2 Under questioning, James Dean, Nixon's lawyer, changes sides and accuses Nixon of obstructing justice.
3 On national television Nixon assures Americans he is innocent of wrongdoing.

4 It is revealed that Nixon has tape-recordings of all conversations in the Oval Office.
5 After much resistance Nixon is forced to hand the tapes over to the Committee.
6 The tapes reveal that
a when Nixon found out that his senior staff had been behind the Watergate burglary, he i ordered a cover-up ii used his Presidential powers to block investigations.
b Nixon considered himself above the law.

1974
1 Demands for Nixon to be impeached (put on trial) increase.
2 President Nixon resigns.
3 Nixon's successor, Gerald Ford, grants him a pardon so that he cannot be prosecuted.

The impact of Watergate
1 Americans' respect for their political system was severely damaged. For years to come they distrusted politicians.
2 There were moves to restrict the growing power of the President. A strengthened *Freedom of Information Act* made it easier for citizens to obtain official documents and find out about Government activities.
3 Americans took some comfort from the fact that the President's wrongdoings had been exposed by other elements in the political system which had functioned well: the newspapers, the law courts and Congress itself.
4 In 1976 the relatively unknown Democratic candidate, Jimmy Carter, was elected President.

Americans hoped that a newcomer to national affairs might 'clean up' politics and restore their faith in the Presidency. He failed because of
a an economic downturn
b misjudgements in foreign affairs
c his failure to secure the release of American hostages held in Iran.

1 What were the 'New Frontier' and the 'Great Society'?
2 How successful was a Kennedy b Johnson in carrying out his ambitions for social reform?
3 a Write a short paragraph to summarize the events of the Watergate affair.
b What effect did the scandal have on the American people?

The origins of the Weimar Republic

By the end of this spread you should be able to describe:
1 the revolution of 1918 and the establishment of a republic

2 the main features of the Weimar constitution
3 the impact of the Treaty of Versailles on attitudes to the Weimar Republic

The 1918 revolution

Demands for change

1 Germany was not a democracy. It had an elected parliament but this could be overruled by the Kaiser (Emperor) and the Chancellor, his chief minister.
2 In 1918 the German people were
a starving because of the Allied blockade (page 11)
b without heating and light because of a coal shortage
c angry at the Kaiser's failure to give them victory in the war.
3 Many Germans demanded
a peace as quickly as possible
b better supplies of food
c improved working conditions
d a free press and the right to express their opinion openly
e the right to vote for all adults
f a parliament with the power to control the Government.

Allied conditions for making peace

The USA's President Wilson added to the pressure for change. When the German Government proposed a truce he refused to negotiate unless Germany became a democracy.

From Empire to Republic, 1918-1919

1918

1 The Kiel Mutiny (Oct.)
a Sailors of the Grand Fleet refuse orders to put to sea to fight the British.
b Workers and soldiers take over Kiel and nearby ports.
c Led by Socialists, workers' and soldiers' councils are set up on the Soviet model (page 107) to run the towns.

2 The revolt spreads
a Cities throughout Germany join the revolt.
b Spartacus League demands a Communist system of government.
c Socialists demand the Kaiser's abdication.

3 Abdication of the Kaiser (9 Nov.)
a Army generals withdraw their support from Kaiser Wilhelm II.
b Chancellor, Prince Max of Baden, persuades him to abdicate in order to avoid a Bolshevik revolution (page 110).

4 Germany declared a Republic (9 Nov.)
Friedrich Ebert, leader of the Social Democratic Party becomes Chancellor.

5 The armistice (11 Nov.)
Ebert's government signs an armistice with Allied powers.

1919

6 Defeat of Spartacist uprising (Jan.)
See page 155.

7 National elections (Jan.)
a No party has overall majority.
b Ebert's Social Democrats are the largest single party.

8 Foundation of the Weimar Republic (Feb).
a New parliament meets at Weimar to draw up a new constitution.
b Ebert elected the first President of the Weimar Republic.

The Weimar constitution

Germany (The Reich)

Central government

The German states
Each state had its own elected government to deal with internal affairs

Representatives sent from each German state

Reich law overrides the law of a state

Elected every four years by all adults over 20

Guaranteed freedoms
1 Freedom of speech
2 Freedom to meet openly and express opinions
3 Freedom of the press
4 Freedom from arrest without reasonable cause

Parliament (Reichstag)

Reichsrat (Upper House)
Could not block legislation which had a two-thirds majority in the Reichstag

Reichstag
Controlled taxation
Elected every four years by all adults over 20 using a proportional representation system

Chosen from the Reichstag and responsible to it.

President
1 The head of state
2 Could dissolve Reichstag and order new elections
3 Chose the Chancellor, usually from the majority party in the Reichstag
4 In an emergency, could
a use the army to put down an attempted revolution
b suspend the constitution and rule by personal decree

Elected every seven years by all adults over 20

Chancellor and ministers
Responsible for day to day government

The Treaty of Versailles

Attitudes to peace When the 1918 armistice was signed:
1 Many Germans wanted peace and hoped
a the Fourteen Points (page 16) would apply
b the Allies would be fair on Germany since they had started to create a democracy.
2 Many others wanted to fight on saying it was humiliating and unnecessary to ask for a truce.

Anger and protest
1 In May 1919, when the Allies announced the terms of the Treaty of Versailles, nearly all Germans were furious (page 20):
a The German Government refused to sign the Treaty. Its ministers resigned.
b Sailors scuttled the High Seas Fleet in Scapa Flow
2 German generals advised that Germany would lose if it went back to war.

3 Ebert's new government signed the Treaty.

The impact of the Treaty
1 Nationalists accused Ebert's government of
a 'stabbing the army in the back' by signing the 1918 armistice, saying it could have won the war.
b betraying the country by signing the Treaty.
2 Because of this many people began to lose faith in
a the Government
b the new Weimar Republic.

1 a Make a time-line to show the main events associated with the revolution of 1918
b What were i the causes ii the consequences of the revolution?
2 Describe the main features of the Weimar constitution.
3 How did the Treaty of Versailles affect German attitudes to the Weimar Republic?

Political divisions and disorders, 1919-1923

By the end of this spread you should be able to describe:
1 the main political divisions in Germany in the 1920s

2 the political weaknesses of the Weimar Republic
3 political disorders, 1919-1923

The main political and military groups in the 1920s

Group	Aims	Additional Information
Communists	1 To improve workers' conditions. 2 To install a government based on soldiers' and workers' councils, or 'soviets' (page 107).	
Socialists	1 Improve workers' conditions. 2 Keep Germany a democratic republic. 3 Uphold the freedoms guaranteed by the Weimar constitution.	Socialists were split between moderates and extremists. The extremists sympathised with the Communists and were prepared to use revolutionary methods to achieve social and political change.
Centre	1 Keep a democratic form of government, but not necessarily a republic. 2 Co-operate with the Allies to return Germany to international favour. 3 Negotiate with the Allies to alter the worst features of the Treaty of Versailles, e.g. reparations, the right to rearm. 4 Avoid aggression.	
Nationalists	1 Govern in the interests of landowners and industrialists. 2 Return to an authoritarian, non-democratic, form of government. 3 Overturn the Treaty of Versailles: rearm, regain lost territory. 4 Unite the German speaking people in a Greater Germany.	
National-Socialists	See page 158.	Although the National-Socialists started out with some Socialist aims, Hitler quickly dropped them.
Army	1 See Nationalists. 2 Restore the influence of the army on the government of Germany.	The army was supposed to be politically neutral, but its senior officers held strongly Nationalist views. They 1 tried to recruit very patriotic Germans 2 tried to find ways to rearm in secret 3 supported the activities of the Free Corps.
Free Corps	1 See Nationalists. 2 Destroy Communism. 3 Replace the democratic Republic with an authoritarian form of government.	1 The Free Corps was a volunteer organisation consisting of ex-soldiers recently returned from the war. They were embittered by Germany's surrender and hostile to Communism. 2 The organization was given money by arms manufacturers whose profits depended on Germany being aggressive and well-armed.

What were the political weaknesses of the Weimar Republic?

1 Germans were unused to a democratic, parliamentary, form of government.

2 There was a wide range of political opinion in Germany. People would find it hard to compromise.

3 The proportional representation system meant no one party was likely to have an overall majority. The strongest party had to form a coalition with others. This might lead to weak government.

4 Army officers and judges were strongly sympathetic to militant nationalists. This
a encouraged disorder
b weakened the Government.

5 The governments of the different states might have opposite political opinions to
a each other
b the central government.
This could undermine national unity.

6 Instead of abolishing private armies, the Government relied on the Free Corps to put down Communist uprisings. This encouraged Nationalist-inspired disorder.

Political disorder

Threats from the Left	Threats from the Right

1919

Spartacist uprising (January)
1 Spartacus League and other left wing groups
a form German Communist Party (30 Dec. 1918)
b decide on armed revolution.
2 Uprising in Berlin crushed by Ebert's government using members of the Free Corps.

Communist riots (March)
1 Communists lead riots and strikes in Berlin.
2 The Government uses the Free Corps to suppress them

1920

Ruhr rising (21 March)
1 German army suppresses Communist-recruited workers who rise up against Kapp's supporters.
2 To restore order the Free Corps shoots over 2000 workers.

Kapp Putsch (13 March)
1 The Free Corps, led by Kapp, takes over Berlin aiming to restore the Kaiser.
2 The German army stays neutral, but civil servants refuse Kapp's orders.
3 Workers call a general strike in support of the Government. Kapp flees.

Assassinations (1920-1922)
Right wing extremists carry out a series of political murders against republican politicians.

1 a Make a diagram to show which of the main German political groupings in the 1920s had aims in common.
b In each case i what were those common aims
ii what divided those groupings?
2 a Make a time-line to show political disorders 1919-1923
b What happened in each case?
c Which actions of i the Government ii the judges might have encouraged right wing extremists?

1923

Munich Putsch (Nov)
1 Failure of Hitler's attempt to launch Government take-over from Bavaria (page 159).
2 Hitler imprisoned for five years. Released after nine months.

Economic crisis, 1923, and the Stresemann years, 1923-1929

By the end of this spread you should be able to:
1 describe and explain the economic crisis of 1923
2 describe
a the recovery of Germany's economy, 1923-1929
b the strengthening of Germany's place in world affairs
c the role of Gustav Stresemann in these achievements
3 describe the cultural achievements of the Weimar period

Economic crises, 1919-1923

Reparations and the invasion of the Ruhr (see page 21)

Hyperinflation
1 In 1923 prices rose so fast that historians call it a year of *hyperinflation*.
2 Workers were paid twice a day so that their families could buy things before prices went up again.
3 Worst hit were
a people who had saved money
b people, such as pensioners, who lived on fixed incomes.

The impact of the crises
1 Hyperinflation hurt the middle classes most of all. They
a lost confidence in the Weimar Republic and the idea of democratic government
b feared the return of inflation
c became more ready to listen to extreme Nationalists.
2 Although Stresemann dealt successfully with the Ruhr crisis, many people agreed with Hitler when he argued that Stresemann
a should have driven the French out of the Ruhr
b should have refused to pay reparations
c was betraying Germany by continuing to work with the Allies.

The Stresemann years, 1923-1929

Gustav Stresemann belonged to the German People's Party. He was a respected politician whose aims were to restore
1 stability and prosperity at home
2 Germany's position in Europe.
To achieve these aims he was prepared to co-operate with the Allies.

1923	France invades the Ruhr
	Huge increase in rate of inflation
	Stresemann becomes Chancellor and Foreign Minister
	Failure of Munich Putsch
	Rentenmark established
	Stresemann ceases to be Chancellor but remains Foreign Minister
1924	Dawes Plan
1925	Hindenburg elected President
	Locarno Treaties
1926	Germany admitted to League of Nations
1928	Kellogg-Briand Pact
1929	Young Plan
	Death of Stresemann
	The Wall Street Crash

Steps to economic recovery

1923
Restore Allied confidence
Stresemann
1 called off the Ruhr strikes
2 agreed to resume reparations payments.

Deal with inflation
Stresemann
1 replaced the old worthless mark with a new currency, the *rentenmark*
2 created a central bank, the *Reichsbank*, to control the new currency.

1924
The Dawes Plan
Under the deal negotiated by Stresemann
1 reparations payments were re-organized so that Germany should pay only what it could afford each year
2 the French agreed to withdraw from the Ruhr
3 the Americans agreed to make loans to Germany.

Foreign loans
With foreign confidence restored, Germany could borrow from abroad:
1 Between 1924 and 1929 foreign loans amounted to 25,000 million gold marks (over three times the amount of reparations payments in the same period).
2 They were used to
a build new factories and machines
b build new houses and public buildings
c help farmers.

1929
The Young Plan
Under pressure from Stresemann the Allies agreed to
1 reduce the total amount of reparations
2 extend the payment period to 60 years.

Germany and the world Stresemann started to restore Germany's status with:
1 The Locarno Treaties (1925) (page 27). Germany signed these as the equal of the other European powers.
2 Germany's admission into the League of Nations (1926).
3 The Kellogg-Briand Pact (1928) (page 27).

The results of Stresemann's policies
1 The mark became a stable currency.
2 Unemployment fell.
3 Living standards improved.
4 Extremist parties became less popular.

Underlying weaknesses
1 Germany's prosperity relied on American loans. It would not last if they were recalled.
2 Many of those people who had opposed the Weimar Republic before the Stresemann years (page 155) still remained hostile.
3 Although they received little support, extreme Nationalists were still active. They attacked Stresemann for agreeing to the Young Plan.
4 In 1929 the Great Depression showed how fragile Germany's new stability really was (page 161).

Cultural achievements

In the 1920s Germany became a world centre for the arts:
1 a The Weimar Arts and Crafts School (the Bauhaus) became a centre for experiment in arts and architecture.
b The Warburg Institute in Hamburg was a leading centre for art studies.
c German museums collected the latest 'modernist' paintings and sculptures.
2 Berlin became a centre for challenging new plays, often politically left-wing, from writers such as Berthold Brecht and Arthur Schnitzler.
3 Music and opera flourished in Berlin and many other cities such as Hamburg, Munich, and Frankfurt.
4 Germany developed a major film industry producing more films in the 1920s than the rest of Europe put together.

1 How did reparations lead to hyperinflation in 1923?
2 What was the effect of hyperinflation on the German people?
3 Describe the achievements of Gustav Stresemann.
4 In what respect did Germany remain weak, 1923-1929?

Hitler and the Nazi Party, 1920-1928

By the end of the next three pages you should be able to describe and explain:
1 the development of the Nazi Party's
a ideas b organization c methods, 1920-1928
2 the role of Hitler
3 the Munich Putsch and its consequences

Adolf Hitler: early career

1 Born into Austrian, middle-class family.
2 Left school without qualifications. Worked in Vienna as a painter, selling his postcards on the streets.
3 Moved to Munich, 1914, joined German army.
4 1914-1918, message carrier in trenches. Won six medals including Iron Cross, First Class. Reached rank of Corporal.
5 Became army spy in Munich checking on extremist political organizations.
6 Joined the small German Workers' Party. Became its leader.
7 1920, renamed it the National Socialist German Workers' Party. Left army.

The Nazi Party, 1920-1923

Organization
1 1921, Hitler made chairman and absolute leader.
2 Party emblem: the swastika
3 The SA (Sturmabteilung or stormtroopers), commanded by Ernst Röhm
a protected Nazi meetings
b broke up rivals' meetings.
4 Based in Bavaria where right wing views were popular. Began to build up branches outside Bavaria.
5 Membership rose from about 50 in 1919 to over 50,000 in 1923. A result of
a Hitler's success as an orator
b Party newspaper founded to spread its views
c the attraction of the Nazi programme.

The Nazi programme ▶

Demand	Appealed to
1 Union of all Germans into a Greater Germany.	Nationalists.
2 Abolition of Treaties of Versailles and St Germain.	Nationalists, ex-soldiers, and many other Germans who detested the Treaties.
3 Only people of the German race to be allowed German citizenship. Jews, therefore, excluded and to be denied the right to hold office.	Nationalists, and the many people looking for someone to blame for Germany's troubles.
4 The State to take over some private businesses.	Socialists.
5 Workers in big industries to share in the profits.	Socialists, and workers.
6 Generous State help for people in their old age.	Pensioners affected by inflation.
7 State help to create a strong and healthy middle class.	Middle classes, and business people.
8 Replace the republican, parliamentary, system of government with an autocratic system to create strong central government.	Nationalists.

The Munich Putsch, 1923

Reasons for the Putsch

1 In 1923 anti-Government feelings were high because of

a anger at Stresemann's decision to end the Ruhr resistance (page 157)

b high prices and food shortages.

2 Hitler believed

a the Nazis were strong enough to lead a take-over of the Weimar government. He planned to march on Berlin at the head of 15,000 men.

b the Bavarian leader, Ritter von Kahr, would support him. In fact, von Kahr wanted to declare Bavaria independent of the Weimar Republic and refused to help. Hitler, therefore, decided to force him to declare his support.

3 Hitler had the support of the war hero, General Ludendorff.

What happened?

8 November Hitler interrupts a meeting in a Munich beerhall to force Von Kahr and two other Bavarian leaders to promise their support. Röhm and the SA take control of Government offices and the military headquarters in Munich.

9 November Bavarian leaders go back on their promise and call in the army. Armed police disperse 2000 SA marching to rescue Röhm. Hitler and Ludendorff arrested.

The consequences

Publicity

National newspaper reports of Hitler's 24-day trial meant that his views were spread throughout Germany for the first time.

Lenient treatment

The judges appeared sympathetic to the Nazis. They

1 acquitted Ludendorff

2 found Hitler guilty of treason but sentenced him to only five years in prison with the chance of early release for good behaviour (he was released after nine months)

3 gave other Nazi leaders light sentences.

A new policy

1 His failure taught Hitler that, as long as the Army supported the Republic, he could not gain power through an armed coup.

2 He decided

a to abandon ideas of seizing power

b to turn the Nazis into a parliamentary party

c if necessary to form coalitions with other parties

d to win over i the Army ii industrialists (to fund the Party).

'Mein Kampf' ('My Struggle')

Written in prison, Hitler's autobiography set out his ideas about the need to:

1 create a Greater Germany (page 34)

2 find *Lebensraum* or 'living space' (page 34)

3 overturn the Treaty of Versailles (page 34)

4 keep the German 'Aryan' race pure so that it could become the 'master race' (page 170)

5 get rid of the Jews (page 171)

6 destroy Communism because it was a dangerous political creed

7 have a strong dictator or 'Fuhrer' as Germany's leader (page 164)

8 use propaganda to win popular support (page 165).

The Nazi Party, 1920-1928

1920 German Workers' Party becomes the National Socialist German Workers' (Nazi) Party Hitler issues a 25-point programme describing the Party's aims	**1924** Hitler in prison for nine months. Writes 'Mein Kampf'
	1925 Hitler re-founds the Nazi Party SS created to be Hitler's personal bodyguard Party branches set up nationally
1921 Hitler becomes Chairman and absolute leader of the Party SA created as a private army to deal with opponents	**1926** Publication of 'Mein Kampf' **1927** Party membership about 40,000 **1928** Party membership over 108,000
1923 Failure of the Munich Putsch Party membership about 50,000	

The Party re-launched

1 In 1925 Hitler was allowed to re-found the Nazi Party which had been banned. In 1927 he was allowed to make public speeches again.
2 He was confirmed as the Party's supreme leader.
3 He began to play down the Party's Socialist ideas.

The growth of the Nazi Party, 1924-1928

Organization

1 In 1925 Hitler created the SS (Schutzstaffel), a group of personal bodyguards swearing loyalty to him alone. In 1929 Heinrich Himmler became their commander.
2 In 1926 Joseph Goebbels was appointed to build up the Party in Berlin.
3 Party branches were set up all over Germany.
4 Nazi organizations were set up such as the Hitler Youth and the Nazi Teachers' League.
5 In 1927 Party membership was about 40,000.

Elections

1 Germany's revival under Stresemann (page 157) meant that only a small minority of people were interested in the Nazis.
2 In 1924 the Party won 14 seats in the Reichstag; in 1928 it won 12.

---

1 Show how the Nazi Party programme appealed to a wide range of Germans.
2 How did the failure of the Munich Putsch affect the development of the Nazi Party?

3 a Make a chart to show the main developments in the Nazi Party, 1920-1928.
b Do you think the Party was stronger in 1928 than in 1920? Give your reasons.

Hitler's rise to power, 1929-1933

By the end of the next three pages you should be able to describe and explain:
1 the impact of the Depression on Germany

2 political crises, 1929-1933
3 the Nazi rise to power
4 the role of Hitler

Fig. 1 The impact of the Depression on Germany

Collapse of business
1 The Wall Street Crash (page 134) meant that
a American banks
i demanded repayment of the loans they had given to German businesses
ii stopped giving them new loans.
b American demand for German goods fell.
2 This caused many German businesses either to go bankrupt and close down or to lay off workers.

Unemployment
The number of jobless rose:
Mid-1929: just under 1 million
Early 1930: 3 million
Early 1932: 6 million

Lower wages
Those still in work suffered from lower wages and short-time work.

Distress
1 Millions of people found themselves hungry.
2 Thousands of families could not afford the rent and became homeless.

Support for extremists
Many Germans
1 blamed the Government for the distress
2 became frightened that inflation would return
3 lost confidence in the Republic and democracy
4 turned to extremist parties.

How did the Nazis strengthen their support, 1929-1933?

Economic crises

The Depression caused people to turn to extremist parties (Fig. 1). The Nazi vote rose and fell according to the number of people out of work.

Nationalist support

The Nationalists' decision to support the Nazis in 1933 was important because it
1 helped President Hindenburg to overcome his dislike of Hitler. He thought him an upstart and did not like Nazi methods.
2 ensured a Nazi majority in the Reichstag.

Nazi appeal

1 The Nazi programme appealed to many different groups in German society (page 158).
2 By blaming the Jews for Germany's problems, Hitler
a provided people with a scapegoat
b united Germans against an outsider.
3 To a depressed and demoralized people Hitler offered a vision of a confident, powerful Germany able to overcome its enemies at home and abroad.

Reasons for increased support for the Nazis

Industrialists

1 Hitler persuaded powerful industrialists that
a the Nazis were not Socialists
b he would prevent the Communists from taking power
c he would run the country in ways that were good for big business.
2 They provided the Nazi Party with the money needed to run its organization and election campaigns.

Propaganda

Under the guidance of Goebbels, the Nazis spent huge sums to put across their message in highly effective campaigns.
They used
1 posters and pamphlets
2 eight Nazi-owned newspapers
3 mobile units to organize entertainment and speeches in different localities
4 stirring mass rallies using music, lighting and banners as a backdrop for Hitler's speech-making skills.

Violence

By 1932 the SA numbered 600,000. The SA's violent attacks on rival politicians and political meetings helped the Nazis by
1 disrupting their opponents' campaigns
2 attracting many young people, unemployed and disillusioned, who admired the discipline and aggression of the SA.

1 Explain how the Depression helped Hitler and the Nazis.
2 a Make a chart to show how the Nazis increased their seats in the Reichstag between 1930 and 1933.
b What were the reasons for this increase?
3 How did Hitler
a become Chancellor
b secure a Nazi majority in the Reichstag?

Political crises and the rise of the Nazis, 1930-1933

The Nazi Party

The Government

1930

March Brüning becomes Chancellor

Nazis increase seats from 12 to 107.

September Reichstag elections

March 1930
1 The coalition government disagrees about measures to combat the Depression.
2 The Social Democrat majority resigns.
3 President Hindenburg asks Brüning, the Centre Party leader, to become Chancellor.

Chancellor Brüning
1 has no majority in the Reichstag. Hindenburg, therefore, uses article 48 of the Weimar constitution (page 153) to make laws by decree.
2 fails in unpopular attempt to deal with economic crisis by reducing unemployment benefit and wages.
3 fails to gain support at elections causing Hindenburg to continue government by decree.
4 is eventually sacked on the advice of General von Schleicher, an influential senior army officer.

1931
1932

March Presidential elections

Hitler challenges Hindenburg who wins with 19.4 million votes. Hitler's political position strengthened by winning 13.4 million votes.

May Von Papen becomes Chancellor

Nazis become largest party with 230 seats, but have no overall majority. Hindenburg refuses to appoint Hitler as Chancellor.

July Reichstag elections

Nazis lose 34 seats but with 196 remain largest party.

November Reichstag elections

Chancellor Von Papen
1 a Nationalist with little support in the Reichstag.
2 depends on government by decree
3 fails to increase his Reichstag support in two elections.
4 is removed when Von Schleicher warns Hindenburg that there will be Nazi and Communist uprisings if he continues in office.

Von Schleicher becomes Chancellor

Chancellor Von Schleicher
1 fails to gain Reichstag support.
2 resigns when Hindenburg refuses his request for government by decree.

1933

Start of the Nazi terror. Minister of the Interior in Prussia, Hermann Goering, enrolls Nazis in police and breaks up opposition meetings.

SA smashes Communist and Socialist election campaigns by arresting 4,000, shutting down newspapers, and breaking up meetings.

January Hitler becomes Chancellor

February Start of Nazi terror

Nazis accuse Communists of starting the Reichstag fire as part of an anti-Government plot.

Reichstag Fire

With 288 seats the Nazis still lack overall majority. Form alliance with Nationalists.

March Reichstag elections

Chancellor Hitler
1 agrees to lead a cabinet of mainly Nationalist ministers.
2 calls an election to strengthen his position.
3 following the Reichstag fire persuades Hindenburg to suspend people's freedoms under the constitution (page 153) on the grounds of a national emergency.
4 after the election secures a Nazi majority in the Reichstag by
a persuading Nationalists (with 42 seats) to work with him
b excluding Communists.

The Nazi regime 1: the end of democracy, 1933-1934; methods of control

By the end of this spread you should be able to describe:
1 how Hitler changed Germany from a democracy to a Nazi dictatorship, 1933-1934
2 how the Nazis used a the Nazi Party
b the police c propaganda and censorship to control the German people

From democracy to dictatorship

Step 1 Dictator

The Enabling Law, March 1933
Gave Hitler the power to make laws for the next four years without Reichstag approval.

Step 2 Eliminate national opponents

The states
1 State parliaments re-organized to give Nazis a majority.
2 Nazi governors appointed to all states with power to make state laws.

Trade Unions
1 SA arrest all union officials and confiscate funds.
2 Workers made to join new Nazi-controlled 'German Labour Front'.

Political parties
1 Social Democratic Party and Communist Party banned:
a their leaders arrested and imprisoned
b SA occupy their offices and confiscate their funds.
2 Smaller parties forced to disband.
3 July 1933, new law forbids all political parties except the Nazi Party.

Step 3 Eliminate Nazi opponents

The Night of the Long Knives, 30 June 1934
On Hitler's orders, SS men arrest and murder Röhm and other SA leaders and opponents.

Reasons
1 Röhm wanted to
a merge the SA with the Army
b take control of the Army
c put Socialist policies into practice.
2 Hitler no longer needed the SA. He
a was embarrassed by its continuing violence
b feared Röhm as a rival
c needed the support of Army officers who opposed Röhm
d opposed Socialist policies.

Step 4 Führer

Death of Hindenburg, August 1934
Hitler
1 takes over combined role of President and Chancellor with title of 'Führer and Reich Chancellor'.
2 automatically becomes head of the Army.

The Army oath
Every member of the armed forces made to swear 'unconditional obedience' to Hitler.

Methods of control

The Nazi Party was organized to keep an eye on every German citizen:
1 The country was divided into 42 districts coinciding with its Provinces. A District Leader (*Gauleiter*) was in charge of each one.
2 Within each district the chain of command then passed to Area Leaders, Local Group Leaders, Cell Leaders and finally Block Leaders (*Blockleiters*).
3 Block Leaders were in charge of the smallest unit of all, the block, which was a block of flats or group of houses.
4 The job of the 400,000 Block Leaders was to
a keep an eye on, and listen to gossip about, the people in their block
b report anything suspicious to their Party superiors, who in turn told the police.

The SS

1 The SS were an elite group of committed Nazis numbering over 200,000 in 1935. Most belonged to the General SS.

2 Specialist SS units

a looked after Germany's internal security

b guarded concentration camps

c hunted down Nazi enemies.

3 In 1936 Hitler placed both the Gestapo and all Germany's regular police forces under the control of the SS chief, Heinrich Himmler.

The press

1 Non-Nazi newspapers and magazines closed down or taken over.

2 Goebbels told editors what they could print.

Radio

1 All radio stations placed under Nazi control.

2 Cheap mass-produced radios sold. Sets installed in cafes and factories. Loudspeakers placed in the streets.

3 Broadcasts included many speeches by Hitler. Also pro-Nazi plays and stories.

Books, theatre, art, and music

1 Many writers, artists and composers persuaded or forced to create works in praise of Hitler and the Third Reich.

2 Books written by Jews, Communists, and anti-Nazi university professors and journalists banned. Many destroyed in public book-burnings, 1933.

3 Jazz music banned because it was originated by black people.

4 Much modern art declared 'degenerate'. Art galleries forced to get rid of it.

The Gestapo The Secret State Police. Used to suppress hostility to Nazi rule at home and in occupied territories.

Concentration camps

1 Run by the SS to detain 'enemies' of the Nazis.

2 First permanent camp created at Dachau, 1933. Six camps operating by 1939.

3 Main categories of prisoner:

a Jews (page 171).

b 'Politicals': for example, Communists or anyone who criticised Hitler

c Priests (page 167).

d 'Work-shy': people who had turned down two job offers.

e 'Anti-socials': for example, tramps, homosexuals, prostitutes.

f Confirmed criminals.

Films

1 Cinema popular. Over 100 German films made each year.

2 All film plots shown to Goebbels before production.

3 Political films made. Love stories and thrillers given pro-Nazi slants.

Rallies and campaigns

1 Annual mass rally (page 162) at Nuremburg.

2 1936 Olympic Games, in Berlin, used as propaganda opportunity. Spectacular parades held on other special occasions.

3 Local rallies, marches and fundraising campaigns led by SA and Hitler Youth (page 166).

4 Clever use of poster campaigns.

Ministry of Public Propaganda and Enlightenment led by Joseph Goebbels

---

1 a What actions did Hitler take between 1933 and 1934 to change Germany from a democracy to a Nazi dictatorship?

b How did each action contribute to this?

2 How was the Nazi Party organized to help the Nazis to control the German people?

3 How did the SS and the police help the Nazis to control the German people?

4 Make a list of the various methods used by the Nazis to control the German people through propaganda and censorship.

The Nazi regime 2: education and young people; religion; opposition to Nazi rule

By the end of this spread you should be able to describe:
1 a the methods used to control young people
b young people's experience of Nazi rule.

2 a Nazi attitudes to religion b the role of the Churches
3 Opposition to Nazi rule

Education and young people

Schools

1 Teachers had to swear an oath of loyalty to Hitler and join the Nazi Teachers League.
2 Textbooks were re-written to fit the Nazi view of history and racial purity.
3 PE classes were increased; religious education was abandoned.

School leavers

1 Expected to work. Technical and vocational training available for the majority who left school at 16.
2 About 15% went into higher education. Under Nazi rule the number of girls in higher education fell.
3 Overall educational standards dropped.

The Hitler Youth Movement

1 1936, membership of the Hitler Youth Movement (Fig. 1) was made compulsory. Other youth organizations were banned.
2 Membership rose from over 2 million in 1933, to over 7 million by 1939.
3 Aimed to teach Nazi ideas. Emphasis on the importance of the group rather than of the individual.

Teenage rebels

1 Although the Nazis wanted a disciplined population, juvenile crime, smoking, and drinking increased.
2 Although the Hitler Youth was compulsory, about one million young people did not join. Some defied authority by forming their own groups such as the Edelweiss Pirates.

Fig.1 The Hitler Youth Movement

DJV	JM	HJ	BDM
Deutsches Jungvolk German Young People Boys aged 10-14	Jungmädelbund League of Young Girls Girls aged 10-14	Hitler Jugend Hitler Youth Boys aged 14-18	Bund Deutscher Mädel League of German Girls Girls aged 14-18
Typical activities Learning Nazi ideas and songs Athletics Hiking and camping Map reading		**Typical activities** Learning Nazi ideas Athletics Cross country marching Camping Map reading Learning military skills	**Typical activities** Learning Nazi ideas Athletics Cross country marching Camping Learning domestic skills Preparation for motherhood

Religion

Nazi attitudes
1 The Nazi Party claimed to approve of Christianity and to offer freedom of religious belief.
2 In fact the Nazis attacked the Christian Churches and suppressed all religious sects.

The Catholic Church
1 1933, Hitler signed a Concordat with the Pope agreeing to allow the Catholic Church to run its churches, schools and newspapers. In return, bishops took an oath of loyalty to Hitler.
2 1937, the Pope issued an Encyclical (Papal Letter) condemning Hitler and the Nazis because of
a their closure of many Catholic churches and organizations
b their racist ideas and the persecution of the Jews.
3 Catholic priests were arrested and sent to concentration camps.
4 Majority of Catholics accepted Hitler's regime.

The Protestant Churches
1 German Protestants were divided between over 20 different Church groups.
2 1933, Hitler attempted to gain control of them by setting up a single 'Reich Church' under a Nazi bishop.
3 The Reich Church was anti-Christian and promoted Nazi values.
4 Over three-quarters of Protestant pastors, led by Niemöller, formed a rival 'Confessional Church' and opposed the persecution of the Jews.
5 Niemöller and others were sent to concentration camps.

Opposition to Nazi rule

Young people
1 About one million failed to join the Hitler Youth Movement.
2 Some joined forbidden rival groups such as the Edelweiss Pirates.
3 The number of anti-Nazi groups, such as the White Rose student group in Munich (arrested and guillotined in 1944), increased during the war years.

Left wingers
Many Communists and Socialists were imprisoned. During the war some groups acted as spies and saboteurs.

Priests and religious groups
1 Many individual priests spoke out against the regime, such as the Protestant Pastor Niemöller and the Roman Catholic Cardinal Innitzer.
2 Jehovah's Witnesses refused to co-operate.
3 In 1941 the Roman Catholic Archbishop of Munster, von Galen, led opposition to the euthanasia programme (page 170).

University teachers, writers, and artists
Most of those who opposed the Nazis were forced to emigrate and had to express their opposition from abroad.

Who opposed the Nazis?
It was very difficult to oppose the Nazis effectively. Most people who tried to do so were arrested by the Gestapo and sent to concentration camps or executed.

Conservatives
1 Some landowners, diplomats, and lawyers had disliked Nazi methods from the start.
2 Others, including some army officers, had at first supported Hitler's ambition to restore Germany's place in the world, but then came to oppose him because of
a his failures in the war
b dislike of Nazi methods.
3 The most important group of these opponents was known as the Kreisau Circle. Its members planned how to restore a democratic government once Hitler had been overthrown. In 1944 the failure of their 'July plot' led to many arrests and executions.

---

1 How did the lives of the majority of young people change under Nazi rule?
2 a How did Hitler treat the Christian Churches?
b How did the Churches react?
3 Describe the different sorts of people who opposed the Nazis.

The Nazi regime 3: economic policy; work and leisure; women

By the end of this spread you should be able to describe:
1 Nazi economic policy
2 work and leisure under the Nazis
3 the impact of Nazi rule on a the lives of women
b their role and status

Economic policy

The National Labour Service
1 A scheme to provide young men with manual labour jobs.
2 From 1935 compulsory for six months for all men aged 18-25.
3 Workers lived in camps, wore uniform, received very low pay, and did military drill as well as work.

Public works
Unemployed men were used to build Government-funded roads, motorways, houses, hospitals, schools, and military barracks.

Employment
1 After the 1933 election Hitler's first priority was to provide work for Germany's over six million unemployed.
2 By 1939 those out of work numbered only 100,000.

Conscription and rearmament
1 From 1935 all men aged 18-25 were compelled to do military service for two years.
2 Hitler's rearmament programme created more jobs in the armaments industry.

Jews and women
Many Jews and married women were driven out of their jobs, which then became available for other people (neither group was then registered as unemployed).

New jobs
The 'Self Sufficiency' programme provided new jobs in new industries.

Rearmament and self-sufficiency
1 Hitler aimed to rearm; but Germany could not afford the high cost.
2 In 1936 he appointed Hermann Goering to supervise a Four Year Plan to develop the economy.
3 In order to reduce the amount spent on imports Goering planned to make Germany self-sufficient in
a raw materials, especially oil, rubber, and steel
b food.
4 Many artificial substitute goods were produced, eg. rubber and oil from coal, coffee from acorns.
5 The plan had only limited success. Germany still needed substantial imports.

Work and leisure

Working conditions
1 Trade unions were banned (1933) and replaced by the German Labour Front:
a workers needed Government permission to move jobs
b the Government arranged all new jobs
c the right to bargain for higher wages was abolished
d strikes were made illegal
2 Limits on working hours were scrapped. Many Germans worked long hours.
3 Many jobs were poorly paid, but better than the dole.
4 Many jobs (e.g. public work schemes) involved hard manual labour and poor living conditions.

Women

The position of German women in the 1920s
1 Women over 20 had the right to vote.
2 Many worked in the professions, especially the civil service, law, medicine, and teaching.
3 Those employed in the civil service were paid the same as men.

Nazi attitudes
1 Women were inferior to men.
2 Their job was to raise children (preferably males) and run the household.

Jobs
1 Women doctors, civil servants, lawyers, and teachers were forced to leave their jobs.
2 Schoolgirls were
a trained for work at home
b discouraged from going on to higher education.

How did the Nazis treat women?

1933 Law for the Encouragement of Marriage
1 Aimed to increase Germany's falling birth-rate by providing loans to help young couples to marry provided the wife left her job.
2 Couples were allowed to keep one quarter of the loan for each child born up to four.

Appearance
1 Women were encouraged to
a keep healthy
b wear their hair in a bun or plaits.
2 They were discouraged from
a wearing make-up or trousers
b dyeing or styling their hair
c slimming (which was thought bad for childbearing).

The Motherhood Cross
Medals awarded on Hitler's mother's birthday (12 August) to women with large families: bronze for five children; silver for six or seven; gold for eight or more.

Sterilization
Women classed as 'unfit' to bear children because of a physical or mental disability, physical weakness, or having given birth to a weak child were compulsorily sterilized.

Training
A new national organization, the German Women's Enterprise, organized courses, classes and radio talks on household topics and the skills of motherhood.

'Strength Through Joy' A Party organization run by Doctor Robert Ley, Director of the German Labour Front, to keep workers happy and hardworking by providing activities for their leisure hours. Programmes included:
1 cheap walking and skiing holidays. Also cruises (for loyal Party members only)
2 outings to the opera and theatre
3 adult evening classes
4 savings schemes to help people buy a cheap Volkswagen (People's Car).

1 a What methods did Hitler use to create work for unemployed people?
b What new opportunities for work did he create?
2 What changes did the policy of rearmament bring to the German economy?
3 How did Nazi policies change a working conditions b leisure opportunities?
4 a make a list of the changes which Nazi rule made to the lives of women.
b Do you think the Nazis raised or lowered the status of German women? Explain your reasons.

The Nazi regime 4: racialist beliefs; the persecution of minority groups and the Jews

By the end of this spread you should be able to describe:
1 the Nazis' ideas about race and citizenship
2 their treatment of a the Jews b other minority groups

Racialist ideas and citizenship

Citizenship The Nazis believed
1 Only those people who were members of the German race had the right to be citizens of Germany.
2 Jews, in particular, should be denied the rights of citizenship, for example to vote and hold public office.

Nazi beliefs

Racism The Nazis believed
1 The blonde-haired, blue-eyed Nordic Germans (or Aryans) were a Volk, or race.
2 They were the master race. All the other, inferior, races were arranged in a heirarchy beneath them.
3 Near the bottom of this hierarchy came black peoples, and beneath them 'non-people' such as gypsies and Jews.
4 It was their duty to keep the German race 'pure' by
a having children only with fellow Aryans
b restricting what other races could do, especially the Jews.
5 It was their destiny to conquer the lands of inferior races, such as the Slavs to the east, and use them to provide resources and living space for the master race.

The persecution of minority groups

'Undesirables' The Nazis' persecuted minority groups in Germany who refused to conform or who they believed threatened the 'purity' of the German race. As well as the Jews, these so-called 'undesirables' included:
1 homosexuals. Many were sent to concentration camps.
2 gypsies. German gypsies were rounded up and sent to concentration camps where many died. Gypsies living in countries conquered by Germany during the war were hunted down and shot or gassed.
3 the mentally ill. Many were sent to concentration camps.

The euthanasia programme 'Euthansia' means 'a quiet and easy death'. In 1939 Hitler started a programme under this name to kill people with mental and physical disabilities who the Nazis judged to lead worthless lives at the expense of the State:

1 over 5,000 children in clinics were killed by starvation or lethal injections.
2 over 71,000 adults were killed by injections or gassing.
3 In 1941 Hitler stopped the programme in the face of protests started by Catholic priests.

1 Explain what the Nazis believed about
a race b citizenship.
2 a List the different groups of people persecuted by the Nazis.
b In each case say what reasons the Nazis would have given for doing this.
3 a Make a time-line to show how the Nazis took away the rights and freedoms of the German Jews.
b How else did they persecute them?

The persecution of the Jews

Propaganda

1 Hitler blamed the Jews for:
a Germany's defeat in 1918
b the inflation of 1923
c the economic collapse of 1929-1932.
2 In schools
a children were taught in lessons to hate the Jews
b textbooks put across anti-semitic (anti-Jewish) ideas.

3 Nazi-controlled newspapers and magazines bombarded adults with anti-semitic articles and cartoons.

Emigration

1 Between 1933 and 1939 about half the population of Jews in Germany emigrated, mainly to Palestine, the USA, and Britain.
2 About 250,000, mostly the poorest, remained in Germany.

The attack on rights and freedoms, 1933-1939

1933	Hitler orders boycott of Jewish shops and businesses. SA paint *Jude* (Jew) on windows and try to persuade public not to enter. Law to exclude Jews from Government jobs. Thousands of Jewish civil servants, lawyers, and university teachers sacked.
1934	Local councils ban Jews from public spaces such as parks, playing fields, and swimming pools.
1935	The 'Nuremburg Laws' passed, 15 September: 1 *The Reich Law on Citizenship*: only those of German blood can be German citizens; deprives German Jews of citizenship and the right to vote and hold Government office. 2 *Law for the Protection of German Blood and Honour*: forbids marriage or sexual relations between Jews and German citizens.
1936-7	Professional activities of Jews banned or restricted - includes vets, dentists, accountants, surveyors, teachers, and nurses.
1938	Qualifications of Jewish doctors cancelled. Jews with non-Jewish first names must add and use the name 'Israel' (for males) or 'Sarah' (for females). Crystal Night (9 Nov.). Following the murder by a Jew of a German diplomat in Paris, SA start three-day campaign to destroy Jewish shops, homes, and synagogues throughout Germany. About 90 killed and 20,000 arrested and put into concentration camps. Jewish children excluded from German schools and universities.
1939	Jews no longer allowed to run shops and businesses. Jews forbidden to own radios and to buy cakes and chocolate.

The Nazi regime 5: the impact of war; the Final Solution

By the end of this page you should be able to describe:
1 the changes brought about in Germany by the coming of war
2 the Final Solution

The impact of the Second World War

The 'euthanasia' programme (page 170)

How did the war affect life in Germany?

The Final Solution

Poland By 1940 nearly 2 million Polish Jews lived under the German occupation of western Poland:
1 They were forced to live in ghettos (walled-off areas in cities).
2 Those fit to work were used as slave labour.
3 Thousands died of starvation every month.

Special Action Groups
1 Special SS groups were formed in 1941 to follow the German armies into the USSR.
2 They were ordered to execute all resistance fighters, Communist Party officials, and Jews.
3 Over 800,000 people, mostly Jews, were killed by mass shootings or gassing in vans using carbon monoxide.

The Wannsee Conference, January 1942
1 Nazi leaders met to discuss how to kill all European Jews, the 'final solution'.
2 They decided to evacuate them by rail to five secret 'extermination camps' to be built in remote areas of Poland and equipped with gas chambers.

The Holocaust
1 About 4.5 million Jews were killed in the death camps, either by hard labour, starvation, or gassing.
2 Altogether the Nazis killed about 6 million European Jews.

The economy

1 After the easy victories of blitzkrieg (page 44) Germany faced
a tough opposition from the USSR (page 45)
b a long, drawn-out war against the other Allies.
2 Hitler ordered huge increases in arms production. The German economy became even more committed to war production.
3 As Minister of Armaments and Munitions, Speer took control of the armaments industry using a Central Planning Board.
4 As more men were called up, the number of industrial workers fell. To solve the labour problem, the Government used
a prisoners of war
b people from conquered countries who were rounded up and treated as slaves. Thousands died in appalling conditions.
c a very few women. Hitler opposed the conscription of women, so hardly any were recruited.

Civilian life

1 Shortages. At first some shortages of raw materials and food were met by conquered countries, e.g. oil from Romania, wheat from Poland. But as the war continued food and goods were in ever shorter supply. The German people
a were allowed very low rations
b had to save any refuse or materials which could be used for the war effort.
2 Bombing. From 1942 the British launched mass bombing raids on civilian targets (page 50). These left thousands of families homeless. Many became refugees.

---

1 How were each of the following groups of people affected by the outbreak of war:
a industrial workers b civilians c Jews
d those with physical or mental disabilities?
2 What changes did the war bring to the German economy?
3 a What was the Final Solution?
b How was it carried out?

Index

174

175